Bloom's Modern Critical Views

Bloom's Modern Critical Views

Bloom's Modern Critical Views

HONORÉ DE BALZAC

Edited and with an introduction by
Harold Bloom
Sterling Professor of the Humanities
Yale University

CHELSEA HOUSE
PUBLISHERS
A Haights Cross Communications Company
Philadelphia

©2003 by Chelsea House Publishers, a subsidiary of
Haights Cross Communications.

A Haights Cross Communications ⬥ Company

Introduction © 2003 by Harold Bloom.
Printed and bound in the United States of America
10 9 8 7 6 5 4 3 2 1

Library of Congress Cataloging-in-Publication Data

Honoré de Balzac / edited with an introduction by Harold Bloom.
    p. cm. — (Modern ciritical views)
Includes bibliographical references and index.
    ISBN 0-7910-7042-5
    1. Balzac, Honoré de, 1799–1850—Criticism and interpretation. I.
Bloom, Harold. II. Series.
    PQ2181 .H67 2003
    843'.7—dc21

                                    2002009599

Chelsea House Publishers
1974 Sproul Road, Suite 400
Broomall, PA 19008-0914

http://www.chelseahouse.com

Contributing Editor: Pamela Loos

Cover designed by Terry Mallon

Cover: Michael Nicholson/Corbis

Layout by EJB Publishing Services

Contents

Editor's Note

My introduction centers upon Vautrin—master criminal, genius of energy, and Balzac's other self—in *Lost Illusions*, *A Harlot High and Low*, and *Père Goriot*.

Lawrence R. Schehr analyzes the start of *Lost Illusions*, with its complex "fool's gold" that fuses poetry and cash, after which William W. Stowe explores the role of subject-matter in Balzac's "systematic realism."

The "philosophical" story, "El Verdugo," is examined in its linguistic complexities by Janet L. Beizer, while the large issue of Balzacian representation is surveyed by Roland Le Huenen and Paul Perron.

In a superb essay, D.A. Miller meditates upon social conformism in Balzac, demonstrating its power in Vautrin, criminal mastermind and eventual super-cop, who finally symbolizes the condition of money itself.

David F. Bell sees *The Wild Ass's Skin* as an orgy of language, while Jane A. Nicholson contextualizes *Cousin Pons* in Bakhtin's dialectics.

Eugénie Grandet is read by Alexander Fischler as a complex interplay of the heroine as a type of the Virgin Mary and as someone to be feared, though ambiguously.

Scott McCracken attempts to reconcile historical criticism with the modes of "textuality" in considering *Cousin Bette*, after which Leslie Anne Boldt examines metaphorical structures in *Old Goriot*.

We are returned to *Cousin Bette* by James McGuire, who finds an ironic victory of heterosexuality and money over "the sterility of lesbianism," to use the language of the Church and the State.

The fictive universe of *Goriot* is anatomized by Martin Kanes, while Beatrice Guenther studies the stances towards death in Balzac's narrative art.

In this volume's final essay, Christine Raffini confronts what might be called Balzac's *energetics*, which she interprets as allegories of conflict.

Introduction

I love best about Balzac that he renews, for me, the romance of reading, as even Henry James and Flaubert do not. Like every other young reader who first comes to Balzac in adolescence, I was swept away by the marvelous Vautrin, first encountered by me in *Père Goriot*:

> Vautrin, the forty-year-old with dyed side-whiskers, stood somewhere between these two and the rest of the lodgers. He was one of those about whom ordinary people say: "Now that's really *somebody*!" He was broad-shouldered with a well-developed chest and bulging muscles, and thick, square hands, the knuckles decorated with great tufts of flaming red hair. His face, scored by premature wrinkles, showed signs of a toughness that belied his good-natured, easy-going manners. His booming bass voice, which matched his loud cheerfulness, was emphatically pleasant. He was obliging and full of laughter. If a lock stopped working, he'd quickly take it apart, figure out what was wrong, file it down, oil it, then put it back together again, observing, "I know all about such things." There were a lot of other things he knew about—ships, the sea, France, foreign nations, business, psychology, current affairs, the law, hotels, and prisons. When anyone complained too much, he'd immediately offer his services. More than once, he'd lent money both to Madame Vauquer and to some of her lodgers, but his debtors would sooner have died than not repay him, because for all his friendliness he had a look about him, deep, determined, that made people afraid. The very way he spat showed his unshakable composure; put in a difficult position, he'd obviously never hesitate to commit a crime, to get himself out of it. Like a stern judge, his glance seemed to pierce to the bottom of every issue, every conscience, every emotion.

Burton Raffel's translation splendidly conveys Balzac's fascination with Vautrin, the novelist's own daemon or genius. Graham Robb, Balzac's best biographer, tells us that the novelist's friends called him "Vautrin." Like Vautrin, Balzac divided the cosmos between deceivers and the deceived: the grand crimemaster exemplifies Balzac's own cynical egomania. Again like Balzac, Vautrin is a monster of energy: a force of nature who also happens to be a man.

Vautrin is overtly homoerotic; Balzac, sublime womanizer, projected his own barely repressed sexual duality, reminiscent of Byron's who, with Molière, Sir Walter Scott, Victor Hugo, Voltaire, and Rabelais, can be considered Balzac's literary forerunners. There is something of Byron's Manfred and Cain in Vautrin: the line of descent from Milton's Satan is clear, since Vautrin has read *Paradise Lost*. There is a Byronic-Satanic aura surrounding Vautrin, at once sinister, compelling, and strangely genial, intermixed with the savagery.

"Vautrin" is one of the pseudonyms of Jacques Collin, known to all as "Death-Dodger." The powerful scene of his arrest in Part Three of *Père Goriot* justifies his nickname:

> "In the name of the law, and the name of the King," announced one of the officers, though there was such a loud murmur of astonishment that no one could no one could hear him. But silence quickly descended once again, as the lodgers moved aside, making room for three of the men, who came forward, bare hands in their pockets, and loaded pistols in their hands. Two uniformed policemen stepped into the doorway they'd left, and two others appeared in the other doorway, near the stairs. Soldiers' footsteps, and the readying of their rifles, echoed from the pavement outside, in front of the house. Death-Dodger had no hope of escape; everyone stared at him, irresistibly drawn. Vidocq went directly to where he stood, and swiftly punched Collin in the head with such force that his wig flew off, revealing the stark horror of his skull. Brick-red, short-clipped hair gave him a look at once sly and powerful, and both head and face, blending perfectly, now, with his brutish chest, glowed with the fierce, burning light of a hellish mind. It was suddenly obvious to them all just who Vautrin was, what he'd done, what he'd been doing, what he would go on to do; they suddenly understood at a glance his implacable ideas, his religion of self-indulgence, exactly the sort of royal sensibility which

tinted all his thoughts with cynicism, as well as all his actions, and supported both by the strength of an organization prepared for anything. The blood rose into his face, his eyes gleamed like some savage cat's. He seemed to explode into a gesture of such wild energy, and he roared with such ferocity that, one and all, the lodgers cried out in terror. His fierce, feral movement, and the general clamor he'd created, made the policemen draw their weapons. But seeing the gleam of the cocked pistols, Collin immediately understood his peril, and instantly proved himself possessor of the highest of all human powers. It was a horrible, majestic spectacle! His face could only be compared to some apparatus, full of billowing smoke capable of moving mountains, but dissolved in the twinkling of an eye by a single drop of cold water. The drop that doused his rage flickered as rapidly as a flash of light. Then he slowly smiled, and turned to look down at his wig.

"This isn't one of your polite days, is it, old boy?" he said to Vidocq. And then he held out his hands to the policemen, beckoning them with a movement of his head. "Gentlemen, officers, I'm ready for your handcuffs or your chains, as you please. I ask those present to take due note of the fact that I offer no resistance."

That prenatural transition from absolute rage to cunning composure is definitive of Vautrin. Is it not also definitive of the astonishing genius of Balzac? The best critical remark yet made about Balzac is Baudelaire's: "even the janitors have some sort of genius." The genius-of-geniuses, in Balzac, is Vautrin, though the novelist himself might have voted for his idealized visionary, Louis Lambert.

Zola, Balzac's disciple, dared to compare the author of *The Human Comedy* to Shakespeare. Balzac cannot sustain the comparision: if somehow you fused Dante and Cervantes, you would have Shakespeare's equal. Proust, the culmination of the French novel, charmingly said of Balzac: "He hides nothing, he says everything," and yet indicated the "silence" also to be found amidst all that disclosure.

It seems odd to me that Henry James, who condemned the novels of Tolstoy and Dostoevsky as "loose, baggy monsters," asserted that he had learned "the lesson of Balzac." Though James does not say so explicitly, it must have been the lesson of energy, of psychic force. Perhaps Balzac helped teach Henry James the fictive economy of energy, the transformation of instinctive vitality into art.

That returns me to Vautrin, the most vitalistic of all Balzac's creatures. Toward the close of *Lost Illusions*, the young poet Lucien Chardon, determined upon suicide, encounters a supposed Spanish priest, Carlos Herrera, Canon of Toledo, another disguise of Death-Dodger. Herrera-Vautrin restores Lucien to life with a torrent of money, at the expense of a clear enough homoerotic bond between the criminal-priest and the poet.

That bond is the center of the great novel, *A Harlot High and Low* (*Splendors and Miseries of the Courtesans*). Part Four of the novel is the extraordinary *The Last Incarnation of Vautrin*, in which Death Dodger becomes the head of the Sûreté, as titanic a police-chief as he had been King of the Underworld. It is as if Milton's Satan had entered again into God's favor and emerged as the Archangel Michael. Perhaps it is Balzac's ultimate thrust at societal power, and also the expression of the novelist's nostalgia for possession of and union with that power.

LAWRENCE R. SCHEHR

Fool's Gold: The Beginning
of Balzac's Illusions perdues

The first part of *Illusions perdues*, like many if not most of the introductory sequences in Balzac's novels, lays out the fundamental fictional groundwork on which the rest of the text is predicated. It is not only a question of plot, character, presentation, and development; it is also the positing of the work's epistemological and ontological axioms. These are the basic assumptions upon which the fiction is built and which the rest of the text in some way attempts to cover up. *Illusions perdues*, along with its continuation in *Splendeurs et misères des courtisanes*, is Balzac's most sustained text. It is in the first part of the novel that the *mise-en-fiction* of the "illusions" occurs: and illusions of creating characters and of garbing fiction as truth. What follows here is a brief exegesis of the fool's gold of these illusions.

While Lucien spends a rather humiliating evening with Madame de Bargeton and the high society of Angoulême, his sister Ève and David Séchard are enjoying a stroll along the banks of the Charente. Their conversation turns to Lucien and they speak at great length about his projects, goals, and expectations. Later on, their words become more intimate, and during a tender moment, David proposes. But although she is in love with him, Ève hesitates to accept because of the difference in their financial positions. In order to assure her that this is not a problem—"dissiper les scrupules que vous cause ma prétendue fortune"[1]—David tells

From *Symposium* XXXVI, no. 2. ©1982 by the Helen Dwight Reid Educational Foundation.

her of the rather poor state of affairs he is in, due in part to the wily dealings of his father. He also alludes to the fact that he is not really directing his interest toward making money. All his time and energy are spent in experimentation on new processes of paper-making. He proceeds to enlighten Ève, who is quite ignorant in these matters. He tells her all about the nature of paper-making and printing: "David lui donna sur la papeterie des renseignements qui ne seront point déplacés dans une œuvre dont l'existence matérielle est due autant au Papier qu'à la Presse" (p. 116). Yet the reader is not privy to this conversation; it is mediated by the narrator who takes the floor and summarizes David's discourse: "cette longue parenthèse entre cet amant et sa maîtresse gagnera sans doute à être d'abord résumée."

Instead of letting David continue his explanation, the narrator interrupts to silence his character. He gives us his own version of David's words. In a style that could be characterized as that of rather dry expository writing, Balzac offers a brief overview of the history of paper-making. Why does he choose to intervene here, placing himself in the enunciative position, the position of authority, instead of giving his character free rein? By calling the explanation a "parenthesis" in David's conversation, when in fact it fits quite naturally into the flow of David's discourse by transforming the mode of enunciation, the narrator brings undue attention to a seemingly lackluster expository passage: "Lorsque les immortels Faust, Coster, et Guttenberg eurent inventé LE LIVRE, des artisans, inconnus comme tant de grands artistes de cette époque, approprièrent la papeterie aux besoins de la typographie" (p. 117). "LE LIVRE" jumps off the page: the invention of the book was a marvelous ("le papier, produit non moins merveilleux que l'impression à laquelle il sert de base") and revolutionary discovery, one which changed the face of the western world, changing an entire civilization. But after all, this is common knowledge. Why emphasize it by a change in the mode of discourse, and by typography?

Soon after the same evening in Angoulême, during which David was or was not discussing printing, Lucien goes to Paris in order to become known as the great author he is. But his initial idealism turns to disappointment as he begins to understand the mechanisms of the literary world: "Lucien traversa le Pont-Neuf en proie à mille réflexions. Ce qu'il avait compris de cet argot commercial lui fit deviner que, pour ces libraires les livres étaient comme des bonnets de coton pour des bonnetiers, une marchandise à vendre cher, à acheter bon marché" (p. 219). Literature, an isolated form of language, becomes a commodity circulating in a capitalist society.

In Lucien's case, just as in David's, the narrator becomes the enunciator at a crucial moment: "Je me suis trompé, se dit-il frappé néanmoins du brutal et matériel aspect que prenait la littérature" (p. 219). The point of view is shifted in the middle of the sentence from the character to the narrator. Thus at two different points in the novel where there is a question of discovery or illumination, a shift in voice occurs away from the characters back to the narrator. Caught up in their own problems with books, and caught up in a book themselves, they do not appear to be able to attain an adequate distance from the book to explain the situation. Only the narrator is capable of talking of the book or of literature. By replacing the voices of Lucien and David, "the two poets," at critical moments, Balzac reasserts his own position of authority over theirs. At the same time, having lost the relative independence of the speaking subject, Lucien and David are relegated to the position of objects in the narrator's discourse, *just as* the printed word is the object of his narration. David and Lucien are incapable of speaking the truth about the printed word because, from the vantage point of the narrator, the characters and the printed word are of the same logical type.

At the time when the story opens, provincial printers are still using their old methods of printing, employing wooden presses and leather balls rubbed with ink. The new ink rollers and modern presses invented by Charles Stanhope have not yet made any inroads in the French provinces. The difference in printing methods is immediate testimony to a temporal dichotomy determined by the (future) installation of modern methods of production. Thus, the state of printing in Angoulême is evidence of a society that has not developed a totally capitalist economy. It remains bound to a tradition in which the bourgeoisie is not yet all-powerful; in other words, Angoulême retains its pre-revolutionary class structure, replete with an influential aristocracy. The older system of production or, more accurately, the society founded upon that system, is able to maintain the ideological structure of a society that nurtures class illusions, *arrivisme*, and an illusory hierarchy. This ideological structure is the heritage of an idealist tradition in which a certain stability of form and structure is always maintained: there is a grounding of values (signifieds) and they are anchored to a stable signifier, God, king, nobility, or the like. For example, there is a concrete relation between artisan and product, between the time, energy, and materials invested (signified) and the finished product (signifier). Thus M. Séchard maintains "une superstitieuse affection" (p. 4) for his old tools, for they are to him a direct perceivable link between production and product.

Thus the illusions, whether M. Séchard's, David's, or Lucien's, nurtured in this antiquated society are in essence illusions of nonalienated meaning. For M. Séchard, the illusion takes the form of the direct investment of value in an object. For Lucien and for David, it is the various manifestations of the written word that are given meaning. Of course, the illusion remains a viable situation as long as there is a unique frame of reference, for example, the society and class structure of Angoulême. However, as soon as another frame of reference is introduced, the illusion is seen for what it is.

But the temporal dichotomy between old and new already indicates multiple frames of reference. While it allows for the exposition of the state of affairs in Angoulême, it is also a portent of the advent of full-fledged capitalism and of necessary disillusionment. When the bourgeoisie has completely acceded to power, when the temporal threshold is crossed, the disillusionment begins. And even if this division is only intimated on the first page, the rest of Balzac's text shows the fulfilment of capitalist society very neatly, if somewhat grotesquely signified by "les dévorantes presses mécaniques" (p. 4).

The Cointet brothers and David Séchard are marked by the illusion of the written word. Unlike M. Séchard, they are affected by its difference from vocal presence, affected by the absence it contains. Moreover, they are in some measure affected by the mechanizations and alienations of capitalism (even if David would like to ignore it). The former as exploiters and the latter as victim operate the devouring machines of modernity that depend on the floating signifiers of capital and writing. But unlike the Cointets, M. Séchard is representative of the older society and, like M. Sorel in *Le Rouge et le noir*, "il ne sut jamais ni lire ni écrire" (p. 4). He is, in an ironic fashion, untouched by writing: for him, all signifiers remain as the signs of a presence and not of an absence—black spots on a white page, the bearer of power and money.

M. Séchard, who wishes to sell the printing-house to his son, enters into a business proposition with him: "pour le bonhomme il n'y avait ni fils ne père en affaire" (p. 9). Yet if he is a shrewd businessman, he is still not a full-fledged capitalist: M. Séchard is incapable of imagining any abstract investment of value in capital. All that exists for him is the old system in which investment is directly related to production. Characteristically, he wants to retire to his farm, to tend his crops, where investment and returns are directly related. Perhaps though, beyond his myopic viewpoint, despite his stubborn anachronism, he has visceral awareness of the wave of the future: "je ne suis pas instruit comme toi, mais retiens bien ceci: la vie des Stanhope est la mort du caractère. Ces trois presses te feront un bon user, l'ouvrage sera proprement *tirée*, et les Angoumoisins ne te demanderont pas davantage" (p. 14). David, however, quite aware of the new order, understands the mechanisms of capitalism (to a certain extent), if only because he is literate; as his father remarks: "Ah! tu achetais des livres? tu feras de mauvaises affaires. Les gens qui achètent des livres ne sont guère propres à en imprimer" (p. 18). In his father's eyes, David is too, too well-read. To us, David simply shows himself to be aware of the existence of the book or the printed word in general as a commodity in a capitalist system of exchange, but of course he chooses to ignore high awareness most of the time. David invests money in an object with little directly observable value (a book). Instead of being the product of an artisan, as it is for M. Séchard, the book is now a commodity in a system demanding that it have value.

The implications are clear: the realization of the book as commodity is swiftly followed by the alienation of literature and its transformation into exchange-value in the market-place. Literature is now something to be bought and sold, not according to any intrinsic worth but rather according to the laws of supply and demand, according to what the market will bear. As Lukàcs remarks,

> *Lost Illusions* is a tragi-comic epic showing how, within this general process [bourgeois evolution], the spirit of man is drawn into the orbit of capitalism. The theme of the novel is the transformation of literature (and with it of every ideology) into a commodity. The transformation of literature into a commodity is painted by Balzac in great detail. From the writer's ideas, emotions and convictions to the paper on which he writes them down, everything is turned into a commodity that can be bought and sold.[2]

Even if David is aware of the hopelessness of the situation in which his father places him— "Mon père, vous m'égorgez" (p. 17)—he acquiesces out of what might be termed filial duty, but not without a final nod of his head to the capitalist machine of which he is rapidly becoming a victim, thanks to the Cointet brothers and to his shrewd father who offers him bleak alternatives: either nothing or an invocation of the entire societal mechanism of courts. In order to get his mother's legacy, "Il faudrait lui intenter un procès interminable, coûteux et déshonorant. Ce noble cœur accepta le fardeau qui allait peser sur lui, car il savait avec combien de peines il acquitterait les engagements pris envers son père" (pp. 18–19).

One more item remains in this opening section of Balzac's novel, one which completes the propulsion of David and the printing-house into the capitalist society: the sale of the newspaper to the Cointets. David is forced to sell them the paper after having been slandered by them—after having been victimized by words with no grounding in reality—this sale is "le suicide de l'imprimerie Séchard" (p. 22). Fossil and anachronism, David's printing-house is now a mute attestation to the advent of capitalism in Angoulême, to the use of the written word as a commodity, and to the first victimization of the "poet" (David) by the devouring mechanical press. Thus, from the initial pages of the novel, the written word is taken as a commodity, invested in various manners with value. It is testimony as well to an absence—of the old order and of a concrete relation between value and product. Even here, there are already many signs of the illusions to be lost.

Saved from ignominy and suicide by working for David, Lucien is able to build up his illusions of literary glory. From the beginning, he, just like David, is aware of the mechanisms of capitalism: "Tous deux, l'esprit gros de plusieurs fortunes, ils possédaient cette haute intelligence qui met l'homme de plein-pied avec toutes les sommités et se voyaient jetés au fond de la société. Cette injustice du sort fut un nœud puissant" (pp. 25–26). Both however believe in the power of the printed word, a creative force to which all societal obstacles will yield, they categorically refuse to be disillusioned. "Puis tous deux étaient arrivés à poésie par une pente différente. Quoique destiné aux spéculations les plus élevées des sciences naturelles Lucien se portait avec ardeur vers la gloire littéraire; tandis que David, que son génie méditatif prédisposait à la poésie, inclinait par goût vers les sciences exactes" (p. 26). The two poets have an awareness of an ever-present division. As seen initially, this division is represented as a spatio-temporal break between two forms of society. "Également pauvres, mais dévorés par l'amour de l'art et de la science, ils oubliaient la misère présente en s'occupant à jeter les fondements de leur renommée" (p. 32). For both of them, the means of crossing this boundary is poetry, the creation of the written word. Accession to an outdated aristocracy by merit is of course an illusory accession in a society that is fundamentally bourgeois. It is this displaced desire, this faulty *arrivisme* that will prove to be part of Lucien's undoing in Paris. But if Lucien's *arrivisme* were directed toward the bourgeoisie exactly as it is directed toward the aristocracy, it would still be based in the same illusory system of thought.

A belief in the power of the printed word, a power devolving from real value, is shared by Lucien and David and is the most compact form of their illusion. It is the clear evidence of its bases: "Ils lisaient les grandes œuvres qui apparurent depuis la paix sur l'horizon littéraire et scientifique, les ouvrages de Schiller, de Goethe, de lord Byron, de Walter Scott, de Jean Paul, de Berzélius, de Davy, de Cuvier, de Lamartine" (p. 32). It is an illusion of the romantic that perpetuates a belief in the organizability of phenomena by the written word. The belief takes two forms linked together, however, by a common epistemology. Either there is an initial order that can be recuperated and represented by the poet—in which case then the conception is based in, and on, a theological metaphysics. The written word, as representation of this order is the reproduction and revival of the presence; it becomes a *parole pleine*, effectively a *logos* that in sublimating the absence contained in the written word, in refusing to recognize this absence, becomes part of an onto-theological system. Or on the other hand, the written word is the means of organization itself: the act of enunciation by which the writer structures the world is the means for the ego of acceding to a higher epistemological plane. Thus with the concept of the transcendental ego, there is an investment of power in the enunciation, through which the ego is able to overcome obstacles by its organization of these obstacles.

Lucien and David reinforce their illusory investment of the world with the magic or metaphysics and transcendence by their choice of reading. Such, however, believe that the investment of creative power in the written word makes his ego transcendent. After spending hours reading Chénier, "la vie leur était un rêve d'or, ils avaient tous les trésors de la terre à leurs pieds. Ils apercevaient de ce coin d'horizon bleuâtre indiqué du doigt par l'Espérance à ceux dont la vie est orageuse, et auxquels sa voix de Sirène dit: 'Allez, volez, vous échapperez au malheur par cet espace d'or, d'argent ou d'azur'" (33).

It is noteworthy that this conception of Poetry as an equivalent for gold, however illusory it might be, still fits quite well into the pattern established for the pre-capitalist system of exchange. As a tangible presence of value, gold, as opposed to paper money, is a heritage of an older system, one in which M. Séchard continues to operate. Although aware of the structures and functions of capital, Lucien and David remain attached to the older system, in which gold both anchors the system and is also a means of control as well. In the first case, gold is seen to have a metaphysical determination in its role as grounded and grounding signifier. In the second, as a means of control, it is a potential for transcendence. The metaphorization of the written word to a gold standard is the illusory romantic vision captivating the protagonists of the novel. The written word remains the simulacrum of the *logos*, representation of a presence and of a transcendental signifier. Lucien and David remain prisoners in an anti-Platonic cave. Blinded by the brilliance of the golden "shadows" on the wall, they are unwilling to go up into the gray world of capital.

The basic structure of the plot mechanism for the novel as a whole has been set up in Balzac's first section about "Les deux poètes." It can be summarized as the illusory belief in an epistemological and ontological system for which there is an anchoring in a concretely determined (physical or metaphysical) value. To the protagonists bound by such an illusion, the written word is the means of overcoming the obstacles in their paths. They confer upon it a measurable exchange-value, grounding this value both in a direct investment of the word by work, and in the creative power of the word, in its poetics. The exchange-value attributed to the word finds its equivalent in the gold and silver of the aristocracy, a class to which Lucien, especially, aspires. If the various changes and accessions are envisioned in this section, they are only posited, for the exposition remains entirely static. The end of the segment recapitulates the divisions within the illusory system, deferring at least for the moment any consideration of the real division between the Old Régime systems and those of capitalism. The end of this section is just the crystallization of Lucien's illusion:

> Le jeune ambitieux qui venait de s'introduire dans l'hôtel de Bargeton en jetant la gloire comme un pont volant entre la ville et le faubourg, était inquiet de la decision de sa maîtresse comme un favori qui craint une disgrâce après avoir essayé d'étendre son pouvoir. Ces paroles doivent être obscures à ceux qui n'ont pas encore observé les mœurs particulières aux cités divisées en ville haute et villa basse; mais il est d'autant plus nécessaire d'entrer ici dans quelques explications sur Angoulême, qu'elles feront comprendre Madame de Bargeton, un des personnages les plus importants de cette histoire. (p. 36)

With the introduction of Madame de Bargeton, the tensions intimated in the initial pages begin to be activated, as Lucien begins his climb toward acceptance by the aristocracy. Lucien has been presented at her house, an action which is seen as doubly revolutionary. Lucien has trespassed on noble soil, in the eyes of the provincial aristocracy; he has trodden on land that should be forbidden to him. His trespass is all the more unforgivable since the action occurs during the Restoration, which, by its reactionary measures, "étendit la distance morale qui séparait, encore plus fortement que la distance locale Angoulême de l'Houmeau. La société noble, unie alors au gouvernement, devint là plus exclusive qu'en tout autre endroit de la France" (p. 39). Introduction of Lucien by Madame de Bargeton is even more revolutionary than simple ignorance of formalized class barriers because its authors were men such as Lamartine, Victor Hugo, Delavigne, Constant, Canalis and Cousin, "les libéraux comme les Royalistes" (p. 39).[3] The act of writing itself, whether performed by a conservative or a liberal, is a challenge to societal systems. On a superficial plane, even a reactionary philosophy written in a book necessitates, through the act of reading, a reexamination of the topic. At the same time, there is recognition of the status of literature as an institution. In their attempts to maintain literature as a sovereign domain, authors necessarily struggle against that which is external to their work.[4] Madame de Bargeton however is a patroness of the arts with a "goût extravagant, manie hautement déplorée dans Angoulême." In her artistic fervor "elle commençait à tout typiser, individualiser, synthétiser, dramatiser, supérioriser, analyser, poétiser, prosaïser, colossifier, angéliser, néologiser et tragiquer" (p. 45). Here ironic assault on the language parallels the assault on society operated by the poets and their followers. It is an attack on an established order, it is a rape of society and of its systems: "il faut violer pour un moment la langue, afin de peindre des travers nouveaux que partagent quelques femmes" (p. 45).

A strange constellation of words forms from the description of Madame de Bargeton: literature is linked to madness, as well as to revolution. Part of this juxtaposition of words is explicable by an invocation of Rousseau: "Elle adorait lord Byron, Jean-Jacques Rousseau, toutes les existences poétiques et dramatiques" (p. 46). Rousseau's distrust of the written text, and especially that of the "modern" genre of the novel has become rather a commonplace in literary history. The novel, dangerous supplement to nature and to the chaste order of things is especially harmful for impressionable women: "Jamais chaste fille n'a lu de Romans: et j'ai mis à celui-ci un titre assés décidé pour qu'en l'ouvrant on sût à quoi se tenir. Celle qui, malgré ce titre, en osera lire une seule page est une fille perdue: mais qu'elle n'impute point sa perte à ce livre, le mal était déjà fait d'avance."[5] But for Rousseau, along with the dangerous evil of the written text, there remains a positive quality, a representation of exemplary behavior (Julie, for example) to serve both as a model and as a means of finding one's way back from "une vie déréglée": "Ce recueil avec son gothique ton convient mieux aux femmes que les livres de philosophie. Il peut même être utile à celles qui dans une vie déréglée ont conservé quelque amour pour l'honnêteté."[6]

For Balzac, however, there is no redemption by letters, no exemplary return: "A beaucoup de personnes, elle paraissait une folle dont la folie était sans danger: mais, certes, à quelque perspicace observateur, ces choses eussent semblé les débris d'un magnifique amour écroulé aussitôt que bâti, les restes d'une Jérusalem céleste, enfin l'amour sans l'amant. Et c'était vrai" (pp. 46–47). But these remainders are not enough of a counterweight against madness. They have been replaced, in fact, by a very concrete materialism, typified throughout the entire first portion of *Illusions Perdues* as "life in

Paris": "Puis, après avoir reconu que la vie de Paris, à laquelle elle aspirait, lui était interdite par la médiocrité de sa fortune" (p. 47), Madame de Bargeton retreats into the illusory world where the poet's work gives her life-sustaining nourishment. Thus, through her illusion, Madame de Bargeton creates a place for Lucien, a reason for his existence, a void for him to fill: "il ne se trouvait autour d'elle aucun homme qui pût lui inspirer une de ces folies auxquelles les femmes se livrent, poussées par le désespoir que leur cause une vie sans issue, sans événement, sans intérêt" (p. 47). Enter Lucien.

Balzac's introduction and description of Madame de Bargeton clarifies our perception of two epistemological models. The materialist model, of which she does not partake, involves the structures of a capitalist society. More generally, participation in this model involves awareness of a system in which the written word (the signifier as general equivalent) is no longer bound to a presence of meaning and is a commodity like any other. Accession into a full comprehension of the system depends not on a transcendental ego but on a perspicacity and ability to use commodities and to invest in them the least amount of concrete value for the largest return. The second epistemological system is the illusory one in which David, Lucien, and Madame de Bargeton all function. Contrary to the materialist system, it is reminiscent of an idealism in which concrete value is attached to objects, by virtue of a transcendental signified or meaning that anchors the entire system. For David, it takes the form of the invention of a new type of paper, one which, he erroneously believes, will be worth more because of its abundance and accessibility. For Lucien, it means becoming fully integrated into Angoulême's high society, by means of his poetry, his genius. Finally, to Madame de Bargeton, it means transcending the banal by means of art, ascending to the sublimes of aesthetic delight. For her, Paris is not capitalism, but the apotheosis of art.

M. du Châtelet is a character who functions entirely by the materialist model and ethic. He already has crossed the border into a fully-functioning capitalist mode of production; he is a parvenu, "venu au monde Sixte Châtelet tout court" (p. 49). As long as he functions according to this system, he can only go on to greater successes. Perfect representation of this system, his production has a zero investment of real value and consists entirely of profit:

> Monsieur du Châtelet possédait toutes les incapacités exigées par
> sa place. Bien fait, joli homme, bon danseur, savant joueur de
> billard, adroit à tous les exercices, médiocre acteur de société,
> chanteur de romances, applaudisseur de bons mots, prêt à tout,

souple, envieux, il savait et ignorait tout. Ignorant en musique, il accompagnait au piano tant bien que mal une femme qui voulait chanter par complaisance une romance apprise avec mille peines pendant un mois. Incapable de sentir la poésie, il demandait hardiment la permission de se promener pendant dix minutes pour faire un impromptu, quelque quatrain plat comme un soufflet, et où la rime remplaçait l'idée…. Enfin il avait tous ces petits talents qui étaient de si grands véhicules de fortune dans un temps où les femmes ont eu plus d'influence sur les affaires. (p. 49)

Châtelet gives nothing, even poetry, any value or intrinsic worth. By not investing any (illusory) value in a poem, as David or Lucien would have done, he is able to *capitalize* on it totally. Its exchange value is completely and wholly based on surplus-value. He has turned Lucien's gold and treasures into paper money, the quintessential floating signifier of capitalism.

In order to climb the provincial social ladder where Madame de Bargeton is the "reine d'Angoulême" (p. 53), Châtelet insinuates himself into her circle thanks to his ability to turn art into commodities. He buys his way into society, with paper money, with scrip, with the counterfeit notes of a wily sycophant. He reinforces Madame de Bargeton's illusory ideals with his scrip in which he has invested nothing. "Ils s'extasiaient ensemble sur les œuvres des jeunes poètes elle de bonne foi, lui s'ennuyant, mais prenant en patience les poètes Romantiques, qu'en homme de l'école impériale il comprenait peu" (p. 53). He is able to complete his coup by telling Madame de Bargeton of the existence of a great poet—Lucien—in Angoulême. In catering to her illusions about poets and poetry, "il crut alors faire merveille" (p. 53). Châtelet transforms his paper money into gold for Madame de Bargeton. Instead of the black and white of paper, there is an image of blinding light: "il existait à Angoulême *un autre enfant sublime*, un jeune poète qui, sans le savoir, surpassait en éclat le lever sidéral des constellations parisiennes" (p. 53).

Totally unaware that he is the future commodity in the marketing of literature, Lucien is unable to maintain a sufficient distance from his work, for he has invested not only time and energy but also himself. In Paris, Lucien will learn to live by continually deferred payments. But here it is still gold that counts, flower of an older system of exchange, one that depends on the transcendental signifier of power—the *louis d'or*, the golden coin, the coin of the Sun-King: "en bonne ménagère, en divine devineresse, Ève sortit quelque louis du tresor pour aller acheter à Lucien des souliers fins ... un habillement neuf" (p. 55).

The narrator insists on the golden illusion in a very striking *segue*: "Lucien chez Madame de Bargeton, e'était pour Ève l'aurore de la fortune. La sainte creature, elle ignorait que là où l'ambition commence, les naïfs sentiments cessent. En arrivant dans la rue du Minage, les choses extérieures n'étonnèrent point Lucien. Ce Louvre tant agrandi par ses idées était une maison bâtie en pierre tendre particulière au pays, et dorée par le temps." (p. 55). The text passes without a break from the golden dawn of Ève's fortune (*aurora*, not *alba*) to Madame de Bargeton's house, gilt by time. Even the first views that Lucien and Madame de Bargeton have of each other prove to be entirely caught in the web of this golden illusion. Lucien has invested himself so entirely in his work that "le poète était déjà de la poésie"; in that he is distinct from Châtelet who puts nothing of himself in his verse. Madame de Bargeton has a coiffure that "comporte un souvenir du Moyen-Age, qui en impose a un jeune homme en amplifiant pour ainsi dire la femme; il s'en échappait une folle chevelure d'un blond rouge, dorée à la lumière, ardente au contour des boucles. La noble dame avait le teint éclatant par lequel une femme rachète les prétendus inconvenients de cette fauve couleur. Ses yeux gris étincelaient.... Le nez offrait une courbure bourbonienne, qui ajoutait au feu d'un visage long en présentant comme un point brillant où se peignait le royal entraînement des Conde" (p. 56). And for Lucien, "son imagination s'empara d'abord de ces yeux de feu, de ces boucles élégantes où ruisselait la lumière, de cette éclatante blancheur, points lumineux auxquels il se prit comme un papillon aux bougies" (p. 57). Such metaphors of blinding fire, light, and gold continue throughout the descriptions and point to the blinding illusion in which both Lucien and Madame de Bargeton are caught. Moreover, this gold, as reflected in the "folle chevelure" of Madame de Bargeton, recalls the folly of her romanticized view of the world and of its (or her) redemption through Poetry (pp. 46–47). Blind to the exigencies of the real world, Lucien and Madame de Bargeton prefer to stay down in their cave with the flickering light given off by the candles.

Lucien is immediately accepted by Madame de Bargeton as her poet. For her, but only for her, he has crossed the boundary separating their two worlds, and all that remains for him to do (in her eyes) is a ritual change of names. To show him her total acceptance, "elle lui conseilla de répudier audacieusement son père en prenant le noble nom de Rubempré, sans se soucier des criailleries soulevées par un échange que d'ailleurs le Roi légitimerait.... Elle soulève l'une après l'autre les couches successives de l'Etat Social, et fit compter au poète les échelons qu'il franchissait soudain par cette habile détermination" (p. 65). Lucien, to whom this idea is infinitely appealing "mordit à la pomme du luxe aristocratique et de la gloire. Il jura d'apporter aux pieds de sa dame une couronne, fût-elle ensanglantée; il la conquerrait à tout prix, *quibuscumque viis*" (p. 65). The same play of forces is at work here as in all his previous relations to the printed word. The aristocratic particle, golden key to fame and fortune is invested with value; for Lucien, and for the aristocracy it has intrinsic worth. On the other hand, for Châtelet, no such fanfare is necessary; he has simply prefixed the particle to his name. Lucien abjures any democratic ideals he still harbors and is completely taken by the mythic power and glory of the aristocracy. Madame de Bargeton "lui montra la haute société comme le seul théâtre sur lequel il devait se tenir" (p. 65).

In the idealism of his illusion he can only react negatively to his own, worthless name. Or more exactly, to the name of his father, *written* for all to see: "Lucien éprouvait depuis un mois une sorte de honte en apercevant la boutique où se lisait en lettres jaunes sur un fond vert: Pharmacie de Postel, successeur de Chardon. Le nom de son père, écrit ainsi dans un lieu par où passaient toutes les voitures, lui blessait la vue" (p. 70). That is to say, in the written word there can be a negative value as well as a positive one.[7] But once again, it is apparent that this investment could only happen within Lucien's onto-theological illusion. It comes about in a situation in which the word, not a floating signifier, is an anchored logos, tied to a transcendental sign. The name of "Chardon" which springs from the *vulgus*, which springs from the earth rather than descending from the heavens in the form of an aristocratic name, becomes for Lucien an anti-logos, containing a negative value, one which hinders him and poses obstacles. In his quest for a true logos, he is only attracted to the eschatological logos. As Balzac notes so well, Lucien "planait sur le Sinaï des prophètes sans voir au bas la mer Morte, l'horrible suaire de Gomorrhe" (pp. 66–67).

The next section of "Les deux poètes," entitled "La soirée dans un salon; La soirée au bord de l'eau" is a series of tableaux. In description after description, Balzac presents characters, would-be dilettantes, who use art simply as a means of currying favor. For them the art has no value whatsoever in itself, except in its function in society. If art does not have the reified status of a commodity that it has in the Parisian market, it is for de Brebian, de Bartas, and de Saintot the *passe-partout* given a separate and somewhat exalted status by a decadent dying society. In contradistinction to Lucien, these fawning aristocrats have invested nothing of themselves in their art. They see it more a serious toy than a valuable substance. M. de Saintot, for example:

> employait en niaiseries tout le temps qu'il demeurait dans son
> cabinet: il y lisait longuement le journal, il sculptait des bouchons
> avec son canif, il traçait des dessins fantastiques sur son garde-
> main, il feuilletait Cicéron pour y prendre à la volée une phrase
> ou des passages dont le sens pouvait s'appliquer aux événements
> du jour; puis le soir, il s'efforçait d'amener la conversation sur un
> sujet qui lui permît de dire: Il se trouve dans Cicéron une page
> qui semble avoir été écrite pour ce qui se passe de nos jours. Il
> récitait alors son passage au grand étonnement des auditeurs, qui
> se redisaient entre eux:—Vraiment Astolphe est un puits de
> science. (p. 88)

Apeing reading and mimicking writing, much like Borel's monkeys at their
typewriters, de Saintot perversely employs the printed word as a means of
drawing attention to himself, of being admired. It is a trap "to catch the
conscience" of his listeners. At the same time, it is a means of seeing his own
reflection in the others' eyes. M. de Bartas whose "amour-propre l'avait assis
sur le solfège" desires to have himself talked about as well, and he
accomplishes this by singing and then speaking only of (his) music: "il allait
néanmoins de groupe en groupe pour y recueillir des éloges." Finally, there
is de Brebian who is "le héros de la sépia, le dessinateur qui infestait les
chambres de ses amis par des productions saugrenues et gâtait tous les
albums du département" (p. 88).

   If, for Lucien, art is an investment of himself intended in part to enable
him to accede to the position of the other, for these jaded aristocrats it is
merely a means of making the other desirous of the self. The two positions
are complementary, even though they do not appear to be at first. The
aristocrats see each other as *alter egos*. But Lucien, despite his difference in
social status, is also in the position of the other, and wants what the other has.
Lucien is in a position of rivalry with this aristocracy and is resented by the
elite group because his desire is perceived as a threat to them. Thus the ideal
solution, for them, is to stem the flow of desire by appropriating Lucien's
text, just as M. de Saintot has appropriated Cicero's, and then, subsequently
to reject Lucien: " 'Puisque ses vers ... sont imprimés, nous pouvons les lire
nousmêmes,' dit Astolphe" (p. 96), who is none other than the manipulator
of Cicero. His line of reasoning is followed by the rest of the company,
who, only playing at the game of desire, in no way understand Lucien's
labor: "—Travaillez-vous promptement? lui demanda Lolotte de l'air dont
elle eût dit à un menuisier: Etes-vous longtemps à faire une boîte" (p. 102).
Lucien is defended by the bishop, and thanks him: "répondit le poète en

espérant frapper ces bêtes d'imbéciles de son sceptre d'or" (p. 103). In the end, the entire evening is disastrous for Lucien, wounding him "comme le taureau piqué de mille flèches" (p. 105). Having hoped to gain access to the magical world of the aristocracy by his poetry, he finds himself used, rejected, a discarded plaything. He had been greeted by a group of self-protecting, selfish people, afraid of his desire, people who treat his valuable art as a worthless toy, from which he must first be separated and then cast off:

> —Votre accouchement sera laborieux, dit monsieur du Hautoy en l'interrompant.
> —Votre excellente mère pourra vous aider, dit l'évêque. Ce mot si habilement préparé, cette vengeance attendue alluma dans tous les yeux un éclair de joie. (p. 104)

At first sight, it would seem that Lucien and the aristocrats do not maintain the same illusions. On one hand, Lucien imbues literature with a value that for him is equivalent to gold: on the other hand, the aristocrats, proud of their social standing and noble heritage (their gold) refuse to accord any value to Lucien's poetry. But the difference between the two models is purely formal, depending on the choice of valuable objects. But the systems' structures are the same. The variables (poetry, nobility) are changed, but never the parameters or the structures.

The model proposed for the evening at Madame de Bargeton's can be reduced to a system of rivalling desires founded and grounded in a definite conception of the absolute, wherein a specific determination of the Other (generally, the transcendent, meaningful signifier) is fundamental. It is the crystallization of the basic illusion of which the characters will sooner or later be disabused if they are to survive.

After describing Lucien's evening, Balzac recounts David's and Ève's stroll, during which a proposal of marriage is made and the art of printing is described. David and Ève subsequently tell Lucien of their engagement, but he reacts negatively because he feels David unworthy of being Madame de Bargeton's brother-in-law. For Lucien fantasizes marrying her: "il habitait un de ces rêves d'or où les jeunes gens montés sur des 'si,' franchissent toutes les barrières" (p. 123). But after the initial shock, "Lucien, charmé par la voix de David et par les caresses d'Ève, oublia la blessante couronne d'épines que la société lui avait enfoncée sur la tête. Monsieur de Rubempré reconnut enfin David" (p. 123).[8] Finally, before David's interview with his father about his upcoming marriage, the three go to tell Madame Chardon about their hopes and projects. "Les trois enfants s'empressèrent alors de raconter à leur mère étonnée leur charmant projet, en se livrant à l'une de ces folles causeries de famille où l'on se plaît à engranger toutes les semailles, à jouir par avance de toutes les joies" (p. 124). Magical, charmed illusion, their project is reflected in the metaphor of sowing and reaping. Here, just as for David, just as for Lucien, there is a direct relationship between material and investment, between labor and ultimate gain. And it is madness to be bound in this illusory and antiquated value system, says the narrator, and not to know it.

The final section of "Les deux poètes" is Balzac's means of precipitating the move of Lucien and Madame de Bargeton to Paris. The section is constructed to that end, and developed around an event that compromises Madame de Bargeton. We find action and little analysis. Monsieur de Chandour sees Lucien kneeling at the feet of his beloved. Gossip that he is Chandour pretends that the two have been seen in a "situation équivoque" (p. 147). Monsieur de Bargeton defends his wife's honor against Chandour, and in a duel wounds him. Following this incident, Madame de Bargeton goes to Paris a few days before the wedding of David and Ève, presenting Lucien with an ultimatum: either he goes with her (missing the wedding), or he must leave her forever. Lucien opts for the first alternative and follows his beloved Madame de Bargeton to Paris.

As a transitional chapter, "Catastrophes de l'Amour en Province" is useful as a means of thickening the plot and bringing about a change in locale. Two points should be noted, however. First, is the introduction of Lucien's own texts, which will now serve as pre-texts for his life in Paris: "il apercevait le jour où le roman historique auquel il travaillait depuis deux ans, "L'Archer de Charles IX," et un volume de poésies intitulées "Les Marguerites," répandraient son nom dans le monde littéraire, en lui donnant assez d'argent pour s'acquitter envers sa mère, sa sœur et David" (p. 134). In its most concise form, Lucien's illusion again comes to the fore: investment of two years' time and labor will be directly transformed into money. His texts are magic machines that change work into gold. Reinforcement of this motif at the end of the first part of the novel serves as a contrast to the massive disillusionments occurring in "Un Grand Homme de province à Paris." Second, the narrator turns his attention to Paris for the first time: "Paris et ses splendeurs, Paris, qui se produit dans toutes les imaginations de province comme un Eldorado, lui apparut avec sa robe d'or la tête ceinte de pierreries royales, les bras ouverts aux talents. Les gens illustres allaient lui donner l'accolade fraternelle. Là tout souriait au génie … Après avoir lu les premières pages de "L'Archer de Charles IX," les libraires ouvriraient leurs caisses et lui diraient:—Combien voulez-vous?" (p. 153). Envisioning all this gold, Lucien, "ce Fernand Cortès littéraire" (p. 158), goes off in search of a fabulous Eldorado, the key to its gates the novel he has written. But the golden bubble of Lucien's illusion is not without a tinge of reality: capital finally appears to him, clearly and distinctly: "Postel, dit madame Chardon en entrant sans voir David consent à prêter les mille francs, mais pour Six mois seulement, et il veut une lettre de change de toi acceptée par ton beau-frère, car il dit que tu n'offres aucune garantie" (p. 156). Postel, a Homais before the fact, a money-lender to boot, does not have faith in the gold mine of Lucien's poetry and will only exchange money for a legal text, one that is not anchored, but one that gives its bearer power. Capital has at last reared its head.

NOTES

1. Honoré de Balzac, *Illusions perdues*, ed. A. Adam (Paris: Garnier, 1961), p. 114. Subsequent parenthetical page references are to this edition.

2. Georg Lukács, *Studies in European Realism* (New York: Universal Library, 1964), p. 49.

3. One might object to the presence of Victor Hugo in this list, for he did not really make his revolutionary presence felt until the "Bataille d'*Hernani*" (25 February 1830). However, the reference may be to the more classical odes of 1822.

4. Again, one thinks of the famous "Bataille d'*Hernani*," in which even the anti-Hugoliens, despite their counter-revolutionary behavior, succeeded in drawing attention to their art and thereby forced a revaluation of it and its position vis-a-vis the new wave.

5. Jean-Jacques Rousseau, "Préface à *La Nouvelle Iléloise*," in *OEuvres complètes* (Paris: Gallimard, 1964), II, 6.

6. Ibid.

7. Following this line of thought, it is tempting to see the written word as a *pharmakos*, especially since the late M. Chardon was a pharmacist. However intriguing this might be, it is only tangential to the present study. See however, not only the *Phaedrus* 274c–275b and Derrida's "La Pharmacie de Platon," in *La Dissemination*, but also the *bon mot* repeated at Madame de Bargeton's reception for Lucien:

> —Puisque le père vendait des biscuits contre les vers, dit Jacques, il aurait dû en faire manger à son fils. —Il continue le métier de son père, car ce qu'il vient de nous donner me semble de la drogue.... Drogue pour drogue j'aime mieux autre chose. (p. 101)

8. This crown of thorns of course could be the same bloody crown (p. 65) that Lucien would offer Madame de Bargeton. As becomes evident in the last part of the novel and in *Splendeurs et misères des courtisanes*, Lucien's sacrifice, the ultimate continuation of his illusion, is the total investment of himself into what he does, makes, and creates. Steadfast in his "rêve d'or," his belief in value, he is the "victim" of a society that has no real/absolute value. See pp. 701–19 for Lucien's conversation's with Carlos Herrera, alias Vautrin.

WILLIAM W. STOWE

Systematic Realism

O ne clue to the similarity between Balzac's project for the realistic novel and James's can be found in their common understanding of the place of subject matter in the novel-writing process. Both writers seem to have believed they had found the appropriate subject matter ready to hand in the world. In fact, they created the "reality" they claimed to have discovered.

In the preface to *Une Fille d'Eve* Balzac explains his choice of subject matter this way:

> The author does not yet know of any observer who has noticed how much French manners excel those of other countries, literarily speaking, for variety of types, for drama, for wit, for movement; in France everything can be said, everything can be thought, everything can be done. The author here does not judge, he does not reveal the secret of his political thought, entirely opposed to that of most people in France, but which we will perhaps reach before long. The time is not far off when the costly trickery of the constitutional government will be recognized. He is an historian; that is all. He congratulates himself on the grandeur, the variety, the beauty, and the fruitfulness of his subject, however deplorable it is made, socially

From *Balzac, James, and the Realistic Novel.* ©1983 by Princeton University Press.

speaking, by the confusion of the most opposing facts, the
abundance of materials, the impetuosity of movements. This
disorder is a source of beauties. Therefore, it is not out of
national vainglory or patriotism that he has chosen the manners
of his own country, but because that country offered, more than
any other, *social man* in more numerous aspects than anywhere
else. (II, 264)

Two things strike us in this passage: Balzac's insistence on "disorder" as a
"source of beauties," and his apparently gratuitous interpolation of his
political opinions in the midst of a literary discussion. He clearly values the
great variety he perceives in French society: he is interested in the sparkling
surface, in wit, as he says, in animation, and in spontaneity, all of which,
together with a certain freedom of thought, of expression, and of action, he
finds in the Paris of his day. More important for his literary project, however,
is his perception of this society as formless. "Formerly," he writes,

> everything was simplified by monarchical institutions: social
> types were clearly defined: a bourgeois was a merchant or an
> artisan, a nobleman was entirely free, a peasant was a slave. That's
> European society as it used to be. It didn't provide much material
> for novels. (II, 263)

Nowadays, however,

> Equality is producing infinite nuances in France. At one time
> caste gave everyone a set of features *(une physionomie)* which took
> precedence over individual characteristics. Nowadays, the
> individual creates his own features *(physionomie)* on his own
> authority. (II, 263)

The implication is that if there is to be any order in Balzac's portrayal of a
society that seems to be a large and various group of self-defining individuals,
he must provide it himself.

This notion will come as no surprise to the reader of the "Avant-
Propos" to the *Comédie humaine*, in which Balzac insists as much on the
active, interpretive role of the writer as on the faithful representation of
experience. Here he claims first that the task of the would-be historian of
manners is syncretic rather than simply mimetic. Balzac wants to be the
"secretary of French society," it is true, but the kind of secretary he has in

mind would spend more time organizing and interpreting data, and putting them in shape for publication, than he would spend taking minutes:

> French Society was going to be the historian, I only had to be the secretary. By drawing up the inventory of vices and virtues, assembling the principal facts of the passions, painting the characters, choosing the principal events of Society, composing types by putting together the traits of several homogeneous personalities, I could perhaps succeed in writing the history forgotten by so many historians, the history of manners. (I, 11)

Moreover, if the relatively disorganized social scene of post-revolutionary France provided a suitable body of material for this kind of secretarial activity, it was also especially liable to the kind of political and moral interpretation which Balzac thought the novelist obliged to undertake. "'A writer must have steadfast opinions in morals and in politics,'" he quotes the conservative politician Bonald as saying, and then declares that he himself writes "in the light of two eternal Verities: Religion and Monarchy, two necessities that contemporary events proclaim and toward which all right-thinking writers should try to steer our country" (I, 12, 13). If Balzac intended simply to observe preexisting "facts" in order to draw deductive conclusions from them, he should ideally have been without prejudicial "steadfast opinions." If, on the other hand, he intended to write polemics in favor of the King and the Catholics, he had no business claiming to be the secretary of a formless society. If, however, his literary project required a society apparently formless, but whose hidden form he thought he had discovered, he could have it both ways, masquerading as Society's scribe, while revealing at the same time the pattern of historical development, that "political thought, entirely opposed to that of most people in France," whose secret he claimed not to intend to reveal. In the passages from the preface to *Une Fille d'Eve*, Balzac is simultaneously creating and observing such a society, projecting his desire for a suitable subject on the world around him, and claiming to have found that subject in that world.

James proceeds similarly in the preface to *The Awkward Age*. In France, he writes, the social complications which provide such a fertile field for *his* imagination could never arise, because the awkward situations which produce them have been eliminated by a strict code of social behavior. "On the other hand," he goes on,

> nothing comes home more ... to the observer of English manners
> than the very moderate degree in which wise arrangement, in the
> French sense of a scientific economy, has ever been invoked; a
> fact indeed largely explaining the great interest of their
> incoherence, their heterogeneity, their wild abundance. The
> French, all analytically, have conceived of fifty different
> proprieties, meeting fifty different cases, whereas the English
> mind, less intensely at work, has never conceived of but one—the
> grand propriety, for every case, it should in fairness be said, of just
> being English. (x–xi)

English manners, it seems, with "their incoherence, their heterogeneity,
their wild abundance," offered James just the kinds of socially awkward
situations he found artistically stimulating. The "fifty different proprieties"
of the French might be a great many, but the mind that was trained to
distinguish among them was likely to be satisfied that those fifty had
exhausted the moral possibilities, and to devote its energies to classification
and description rather than to fresh and sensitive perception. In a society
which lacks such an array of ready-made categories and proprieties, one is
forced to deal with each situation as if it were totally new. One must resort
to a kind of moral *bricolage*, using whatever methods, tactics, and notions are
at hand, compromising a principle here, manipulating a person there,
overlooking this and emphasizing that in an attempt to bring the facts of the
specific situation into some acceptable relation with the general standard of
propriety.

"The consequent muddle," James tells us, though "a great
inconvenience for life," offered "an immense promise ... for the painted
picture of life" (xii), and we have abundant evidence in the *Notebooks* and the
prefaces of his own enthusiastic encounters with the muddle and his
exploitation of the promise. Time and again James describes a situation
susceptible not to organization "in the light of two eternal Verities," but to
development into a complex moral and aesthetic text. In the preface to *The
Princess Casamassima*, for example, James says this about the experience of
walking the London streets:

> One walked of course with one's eyes greatly open, and I hasten
> to declare that such a practice, carried on for a long time and over
> a considerable space, positively provokes, all round, a mystic
> solicitation, the urgent appeal, on the part of everything, to be
> interpreted and, so far as may be, reproduced. "Subjects" and

situations, character and history, the tragedy and comedy of life, are things of which the common air, in such conditions, seems pungently to taste; and to a mind curious, before the human scene, of meanings and revelations the great grey Babylon easily becomes, on its face, a garden bristling with an immense illustrative flora. Possible stories, presentable figures, rise from the thick jungle as the observer moves, fluttering up like startled game, and before he knows it indeed he has fairly to guard himself against the brush of importunate wings. (I, v)

And in the preface to *The Spoils of Poynton* he explains at some length the relationship between the "germ" of his novels and stories and their necessarily untrammeled development in his imagination. Even more important, perhaps, we have the record of James's characters' encounters with the muddle, and of its more or less successful interpretation by the likes of Christopher Newman, Isabel Archer, Maisie Farange, Lambert Strether, and Maggie Verver.

Like Balzac, James knew precisely what kind of society his novelistic art required, and like Balzac he simultaneously projected it on the world around him and claimed to find it in that world. Balzac saw himself cataloguing and interpreting a post-revolutionary society, giving form and meaning to a formless and as yet incomprehensible welter of cases and distinctions. James saw himself following the development of the individual consciousness faced with a rich complexity of social, emotional, and, above all, moral conditions. Both writers stress the apparent priority of the phenomenal world, and the novelist's responsibility to represent it faithfully, yet neither abdicates for a moment his own privileged position as a mediator between the world and the reader. Both are conscious, deliberate "realists," who are at the same time conscious, deliberate artists and interpreters of experience. They use common concepts of reality to produce literary texts that will call the validity of these concepts into question. To do this, they choose subjects which might well be extensions of the world readers ordinarily perceive, and, without destroying the metonymic *vraisemblance* of the subjects, the sense that they are slices of life, transform them into metaphorical analogues for the readers' experience, related not by contiguity but by resemblance.

The combination of these two tropes suggest a threefold definition of what might be called "systematic realism." James and Balzac both work methodically (systematically) to present a convincing picture of life in the world. Their realistic intentions naturally lead them to describe and analyze systems of behavior, communication, exploitation, and so on, that structure the world, and to rely, consciously and unconsciously, upon these systems to help structure their texts and to provide them with figurative language. Finally, their desire to create literary analogues for life in the world leads them to elaborate textual systems of great complexity, of purposeful particularity, and of ample power both to reproduce something like the density and the texture of experience and to involve the reader in an active process of reading and interpretation.

It is not likely to be controversial as a statement of superficial fact that both James and Balzac did intend to produce texts which created the illusion of an extension of the phenomenal world. Similarly, it seems clear from their descriptions of the societies they portrayed that James and Balzac chose their material with an eye to the social structures and systems of behavior that material contained or exemplified. These two metonymic features of their novels require and will receive some exemplary illustration, but no lengthy theoretical explanations. This is not the case with the peculiar metaphoric nature of the novels, which needs further elaboration.

One very helpful way of approaching this notion of the text as metaphor is to imagine the author creating a *model* of the world in his writing. "The vast majority of works of art," writes Claude Lévi-Strauss, "are *modèles réduits*," versions of actual phenomena which do not reduce their subjects' essential complexity, but eliminate inessential and, for the moment at least, irrelevant complications. Every art sacrifices some aspect of its subject in order to concentrate on others: painting gives up volume to concentrate on line and color; both painting and sculpture give up the temporal dimension to concentrate on spatial relations. For Lévi-Strauss, the virtue of this reduction is twofold. First, it makes its subject less formidable than it would be in the phenomenal world, and guarantees its intelligibility. At the same time, it insists upon its own artificiality, its status as the product of an artist's choices and of his craft.

Furthermore, as Lévi-Strauss elsewhere argues, the transformation from the sensible to the intelligible entails a transformation of the phenomenal into the systematic. The scientist, for example, in order to understand the phenomenal world as it presents itself to his senses, must first simplify his impressions by eliminating their extraneous aspects, and then relate the results of this simplification to each other, to the corpus of already existing data, and to his theoretical hypothesis. He must, in other words, systematize his simplified sense impressions. The result of his work need by no means be "simple" in the sense that it is easy for the layman to understand, but it should be intellectually more manageable than the welter of sense perceptions which the phenomenal world presents. It is in effect a metaphor for these perceptions and for that world, a declaration of similarity between them and a set of intellectual constructs which science has already created or is in the process of creating.

The artist, like the scientist, does not imitate life in the sense that he creates a substitute for life or a faithful reproduction of life. He rather presents one of many possible complex metaphors for life, homologous to human experience without being identical with any given human experience. These metaphors are "*modèles réduits*" of life in that they eliminate certain aspects of life which the artist considers extraneous to his purposes; they are systems in the sense that they organize the hurly-burly of phenomena into a coherent set of lines, of shapes, and of colors, or, in the case of the fictional text, into plots, into sets of images and themes, and into coherent verbal patterns. "Miniaturization" of experience leads to enrichment of understanding by transforming the nonhuman complexity of phenomena into a man-made complexity. It represents preexisting phenomena, it organizes them by means of independently existing structures, and in so doing it creates a new phenomenon and a new structure. The purpose of the work of art is therefore to render its subject more richly intelligible than it would be as a phenomenon in nature or in society, and at the same time to be richly intelligible itself.

It is this notion of intelligibility that distinguishes Lévi-Strauss's definition of the work of art as a model from similar definitions. Martin Price, for example, outlines the advantages of seeing the literary work as a model of the world in much the same way as Lévi-Strauss. The model, he writes, "encloses a section or isolates a dimension of reality upon which we wish to concentrate our attention, and it frees it of distracting irrelevance." Whereas in scientific practice, furthermore, the model "exists for the sake of studying what it represents," the literary model demands to be enjoyed for its own sake and therefore, like a ship in a bottle, a toothpick cathedral or, to be fair, a painting or a sculpture, produces what Max Black calls a "harmless fetishism" in its admirers.

Where Lévi-Strauss moves beyond Price is in his examination of what makes the model especially susceptible to study and even to fetishistic admiration. "The intrinsic value of the reduced model," he writes, "is that it makes up for the loss of sensual dimensions by the addition of intelligible dimensions." Furthermore, when Lévi-Strauss calls a model intelligible, he does not mean to suggest that it can be understood once and for all, but rather that it invites a process of understanding, an active engagement of intellect. His "intellectual artifact" is not a product ready for consumption, but rather the trace of a process which the perceiver of a work of art is invited to retrace and in effect to relive. The *modèle réduit* is not only an object to be contemplated, but a machine for thinking.

James's notion of the nature of the work of art is inversely related to Lévi-Strauss's. While Lévi-Strauss's definition of the *modèle réduit* would include even the most complex of James's texts, it seems more useful to regard those texts as the traces of a process of elaboration rather than a process of reduction. James begins with a single element—a character, a situation—and develops from it an intelligible textual model. He prefers an organic metaphor of growth to a mechanical one of reduction; he sees the artist as starting with the tiniest "kernel" of a "real" situation and elaborating it into a complex system, rather than starting with all of life and reducing it to such a system. The purpose of the artistic process, however, and its result, are for both quite similar. James's simple "kernel" is no more intelligible in itself than Lévi-Strauss's infinitely complex "reality": in both cases the artist's job is to make them so.

The process of rendering his small subject intelligible involves for James the realization that "the art of interesting us in things ... can *only* be the art of representing them," and that "this relation to them, for invoked interest, involves his accordingly 'doing'; and it is for him to settle with his intelligence what that variable process shall commit him to." Once "the subject is found and ... the problem is then transferred to the ground of what to do with it the field opens out for any amount of doing." "Doing" a subject, for James, means presenting it, elaborating on it, and, most important, transforming it from futile local fact into a metaphor for more general human experience.

Perhaps the richest record of the "doing" of such a kernel begins with a morsel of gossip "related to me last night at dinner at Lady Lindsay's by Mrs. Anstruther-Thompson," and ends, triumphantly, in "the little drama of my 'Spoils,'" *The Spoils of Poynton*. The case of the sensitive "deposed" mother making off with those prized possessions that now legally belong to her son "is all rather sordid and fearfully ugly," James writes, "but there is surely a story in it." It lends itself, "this case (the case I should build on the above hint)," to the most artful *doing*, the provision of "circumstances, details, intensifications, deepening it and darkening it all," the rendering intelligible of "the terrible experience of a nature with a love and passion for beauty ... domiciled in ... the kind of house the very walls and furniture of which constitute a kind of *anguish* for such a woman as I suppose the mother to be."

From the merest hint, therefore, from a few idle words at dinner, there springs into James's mind the sense of a possible text, of the representation of just the right house and just the right lady to convey just the right sense of futile anguish. The necessarily *textual* nature of such a conception is underlined by James's retelling of the anecdote in his preface to the novel. Here his interlocutor enters into the actual details of the situation, details for which James "had absolutely and could have, no scrap of use," which reminded him once again of "the fatal futility of Fact," the "classic ineptitude" with which life never fails to develop "the excellent situation" in just the wrong way.

The anecdotal kernel, then, is meaningless in itself, and can produce the stupidest, most banal "factual" developments. The artist's work, for James as for Lévi-Strauss, is to make this kernel intelligible by constructing around it a text which is an ideally ordered whole, and an invitation to active participation in a process of intellection.

The emphasis in both James and Lévi-Strauss is on the possibility and the process of rendering experience intelligible. Although Balzac was not so active a theorist as James, and is therefore a little harder to pin down on these matters, it seems clear from his ambition to emulate the great natural scientists Buffon and Saint-Hilaire by writing the natural history of French society of his day that he, too, wished to provide his readers with an intelligible version of the world as he saw it. Whether the realistic artist thinks in terms of analysis, systematization, and classification, or of the representation of life and the intensification of consciousness, his problem is how to accomplish this goal while remaining faithful to experience itself. To *render* experience is difficult enough: to render it intelligible is even harder. To do both, simultaneously, was Balzac's goal in the *Comédie humaine*, and James's in all his fictions.

To accomplish this goal, both writers developed systematic versions of realism: they made texts the experience of which is analogous to, but in Lévi-Strauss's sense simpler than, the experience of life, and they did so by reflecting, creating, and deploying certain cultural, social, and textual systems. As it happens, the novels whose prefaces helped us understand their authors' general goals also provide schematic examples of their novel-writing practice. *Une Fille d'Eve* and *The Awkward Age* are not their authors' best works, but in them Balzac and James develop certain characteristic techniques more fully and more explicitly than anywhere else.

In *Une Fille d'Eve*, Balzac presents an historically verifiable analysis of the structure of social systems in France around 1830, and uses this analysis to help create a particular kind of textual intelligibility. He does this by describing the three social milieux that the main character knows and finds oppressive in such a way as to suggest the possibility, even the logical necessity, of a fourth, whose actual existence she discovers and whose temptations bring her close to ruin.

Madame de Vandenesse, née Marie-Angélique de Granville, has left the frigidly pious home of her mother, a great magistrate's wife, to preside over her new, titled husband's more liberal, elegant establishment. In Félix de Vandenesse she finds an affectionate partner who has enjoyed his grand passion and his youthful extravagances and is ready to devote himself to his wife's happiness. Her sister, meanwhile, has made a less fortunate match, accepting the great *arriviste* banker, "un sieur Ferdinand *dit* du Tillet" ("a gentleman who calls himself Ferdinand *du* Tillet" [II, 275]), and a very large marriage settlement, in part as a means of compensating the family for the large dowry it gave Marie-Angélique. "Thus," as Balzac puts it, "the Bank had repaired the damage done to the Magistracy by the Nobility" (II, 275). The result for Madame du Tillet, however, is unhappy. True, her establishment is luxurious, but it is as loveless as her mother's; it is rich but tasteless, characterized by the kind of factitious elegance that can be purchased *en bloc* from a fashionable interior designer.

The Bank, then, is vulgar and loveless, the Magistracy, or at least its female manifestation in Madame de Granville, puritanical and loveless, and the Nobility moderate, cultured, and affectionate. This ternary system of oppositions would seem complete and satisfactory as it is presented in the first three chapters of the tale if it were not for three things: the hint that Madame de Vandenesse is not so happy as she ought to be, the fact that a whole segment of rich Parisian society is missing from it; and the fact that the ternary system is actually a quaternary system with one quadrant missing. The model here is simple. Whenever two sets of mutually exclusive qualities are used to describe a field of possibilities, each of which must be characterized by two terms (x or not-x and y or not-y), four categories result: x and y; x and not-y; not-x and y; not-x and not-y. Suppose, for example, that Professor W is stodgy and a profound thinker, Professor X is stodgy and superficial, and Professor Y lively and superficial. These three characterizations suggest the possibility that there exists a Professor Z who is both lively and profound. Similarly, in the first three chapters of *Une Fille d'Eve* Balzac describes three ménages, two as cold and loveless, the first—du Tillet's—in terms of objects and surfaces, and the second—Madame de Granville's—in terms of moral ideals, and one—Vandenesse's—as warm and loving, also in terms of moral ideals. What is missing from this array of possibilities, and from Balzac's description of Parisian society so far, is a warm, loving milieu described in terms of surfaces and objects. Balzac presently fills this lack with an account of the demimonde of journalists and actresses personified by Raoul Nathan and his mistress, Florine, and symbolized by her magnificent establishment. Florine's world is opposed to the world of Madame de Granville as Vandenesse's is opposed to du Tillet's. It combines the concern for objects, surfaces, and display of the banker with the affection of the nobleman, and has no room for either the moderation or the cold morality of the judge's puritanical wife. Its passionate vulgarity attracts Marie-Angélique much as the empty quadrant tempts the logician, analyst, or reader to fill it in. Furthermore, the process by which she learns the truth about this world's place and her own in the Parisian social system parallels the task that the text asks the reader to undertake in order to do its richness justice.

Madame de Vandenesse falls in love with Raoul Nathan, demimondain and journalist, out of boredom and curiosity: Balzac represents her fascination with this figure from a foreign social and moral milieu as the inevitable result of her own unmixed purity and her husband's generosity and elegance. Fallen by chance into the perfect marriage with a man who has exhausted his first violent passions but retains his youth and his capacity for affection, Marie-Angélique becomes under his direction the perfect wife. She has freedom and security, good taste and unchallenged social position, but she is bored. In his scheme for wedded happiness, Félix has left the dynamics of desire out of account. By anticipating and fulfilling all his wife's wishes, he has only heightened for her the allure of the unknown, and made her infatuation with its representative all but inevitable.

Luckily, Félix de Vandenesse discovers his wife's infatuation in time to show her its folly and realize his own shortsightedness. As a result of her husband's enlightened reaction to her flirtation, Marie-Angélique gains that mature marital happiness of which her earlier state was only an imitation.

The lesson of Balzac's four-part analysis of society is not that one quadrant or another should or could exist independently, but that we can only appreciate any possible way of life in the context of other possible ways. His text moves from static analysis reminiscent of his own earlier "*physiologies*" to narrative, from the social taxonomy which he thought was his special strength to the dynamic description of social process at which he really excelled. At the same time it demands progressively more of the reader. Content in the first few chapters with our recognition of its acute analysis of various social milieux, it soon demands to be seen not only as a representation of social structure and personal growth, but as a demonstration in purely literary terms of the process of maturation that its protagonist undergoes. Like Marie-Angélique de Vandenesse, the reader of *Une Fille d'Eve* is presented with an oversimple view of the world, and taught how to supplement it, to make up for its inadequacies. In addition—and here lies Balzac's genius—he is presented with a text which asks to be read first as simple analysis, then as narrative, which demonstrates the inadequacy of its own apparent first assumptions as it demonstrates the inadequacy of its characters' first views of the world. The experience of reading *Une Fille d'Eve* resembles the experience that the text describes: the text is not only a picture of reality; by demanding to be read in progressively more complex ways it provides its readers with a literary analogue for the experience of learning. It renders experience intelligible by recreating it in its own literary medium.

The Awkward Age, too, makes experience intelligible, but despite the care it takes to present a believable picture of an unmistakably *fin-de-siècle* London milieu, it focuses on the development of the interpretive faculty rather than on the outcome of any particular interpretation. In *Une Fille d'Eve* the reader and main character arrive in analogous ways at suitably sophisticated views of society and of the text. *The Awkward Age* leads the reader to reflect on the process of interpretation by creating a model in which various kinds of interpretation can be tested.

A great deal of the interpretation in *The Awkward Age* is idle, trivial chatter, the vapid pastime of the bored rich, with Mrs. Brookenham using her skill at this game to get what she wants out of the people she interprets. Against this background of trivial and/or interested interpretation, however, two sincere interpreters stand out, one successful and one a failure.

The successful interpreter, Mr. Longdon, an elderly gentleman and former admirer of Mrs. Brookenham's mother, is at present marveling at the phenomenon of that lady's daughter, a girl who, at the awkward unmarried age of eighteen, is by necessity emerging from the security of the nursery and schoolroom just as he is by choice emerging from the security of his country retreat. Mr. Longdon finds London's new, breezy informality awkward at best, in comparison with the customs of an earlier age. Comparing Nanda Brookenham and her grandmother, Longdon admits to the young lady that "'nothing could be less like her than your manner and your talk.'"

> Nanda looked at him with all her honesty. "They're not so good, you must think."
> He hung fire an instant, but was as honest as she. "You're separated from her by a gulf—and not only of time. Personally, you see, you breathe a different air." (152)

The gulf yawns as wide, of course, between Nanda and Mr. Longdon as it does between Nanda and her grandmother, but the young woman is confident it can be bridged. "'You'll get used to me,' she said with the same gentleness that the response of her touch had tried to express; 'and I shall be so careful with you that—well, you'll see!'" (154) As it turns out, Nanda is right. The gulf is bridged, and she and Mr. Longdon meet on her side of it, determined to cope with their modern circumstances in an unprejudiced, even an unprecedented way.

Mr. Longdon is the novel's great success because he interprets a strange world boldly, discarding an outdated set of proprieties and recognizing the true value behind Nanda's "modern" freedom. Mr. Vanderbank, on the other hand, is its great failure. The first few lines of the book humorously depict him "interpreting" the weather according to a set of fixed principles:

> Save when it happened to rain, Vanderbank always walked home, but he usually took a hansom when the rain was moderate and adopted the preference of the philosopher when it was heavy. On this occasion he therefore recognised as the servant opened the door a congruity between the weather and the "four-wheeler" that, in the empty street, under the glazed radiance, waited, and trickled and blackly glittered. (3)

While James and his readers enjoy a masterful sketch of a London scene— that waiting, trickling, glittering four-wheeler is magnificent—Vanderbank "recognizes a congruity" between atmospheric conditions and a mode of conveyance. Unfortunately for him, furthermore, his attitudes toward people are no more imaginative than his fixed, categorical perception of the weather. Despite his exposure to modern ways, he cannot rid himself of a combination of hereditary delicacy and rigid self-confidence which is his great strength and his great weakness. He cannot, more specifically, bring himself to propose marriage to a young person who he thinks has been spoiled by her precocious knowledge of the world of loose talk and French novels, and therefore retreats into official busyness at the end of the novel, leaving the scandalous world behind, and abandoning his friendship with Nanda and Mr. Longdon, who comment sadly on his failure, and illuminate for the reader their own special success:

> "Everything's different from what it used to be."
> "Yes, everything," he returned with an air of final indoctrination. "That's what he ought to have recognised."
> "As *you* have?" Nanda was once more—and completely now—

enthroned in high justice. "Oh, he's more old-fashioned than you."
"Much more," said Mr. Longdon with a queer face. (544)

Nanda and Mr. Longdon and, to some extent, Mitchett, interpret the chaotic world, its incoherent heterogeneity, its "wild abundance" just the way James thought the modern English novelist had to, by using a kind of moral *bricolage*, based on sincerity rather than on fifty different proprieties. Vanderbank attempts to impose a preexisting set of values on this world, and he fails.

Une Fille d'Eve teaches the reader *what* Balzac believes experience teaches his characters, by inviting him to live their experiences with them, vicariously. *The Awkward Age*, on the other hand, demonstrates *how* experience teaches, and how best to profit by its lessons. Considering these novels as examples of their authors' systematic realism does not preclude interpreting them in other ways, as vehicles for philosophic views, signs of economic developments, expressions of individual anxieties, or whatever. It does, however, help us focus at one and the same time on their representational claims and their status as textual models which, by opening themselves to a particular kind of interpretation, can teach readers alternate ways of understanding events in the world. It is also, I would claim, a generous kind of reading, granting each novel's claim to be telling a certain kind of truth, and acceding to each text's demands for careful, serious attention to the program it sets out for its readers.

Balzac and James share a common set of literary traditions, forms, and purposes; they are both concerned with the faithful representation of the world as they see it, with the textual simulation of systems in that world, and with the production of literary systems which are convincing analogues of worldly experience and contribute through their superior intelligibility to a new and an active interpretation of the world. Like all representational works of art, their texts are models of the world, and since models by their nature eliminate some elements in order to concentrate on others, they are selective, emphasizing and exploring particular structures of experience rather than attempting to reproduce experience itself.

I hope that so far even those readers—certainly the majority—who are skeptical about the need for yet another discussion of realism will find my formulation of systematic realism plausible. Its great advantage, to my mind, is precisely that it does *not* propose a new definition to rival those of Auerbach or Lukacs, Fanger or Levin. Instead, it suggests a general understanding of realism which can accomodate various ideological positions and provide workspace for the interpretive tools of various schools of literary criticism.

My own original purpose in wielding these tools in this context was simply to demonstrate how particular texts function as intelligible models of experience, to show how several complex realistic novels work. In the course of my investigation, though, I discovered something else: that the shapes of Balzac's career and of James's are congruent, and can be defined by their choosing to explore similar patterns of experience at similar stages of their artistic development.

I have chosen three such patterns to discuss here; they are important throughout Balzac's and James's oeuvres, but I examine them in pairs of texts which help me trace the course of their authors' careers, as well as their use of particular structures of experience. In *Le Père Goriot* and *The American*, both in their ways *Bildungsromane*, experience is seen in terms of the process of *interpretation*, while in *Illusions perdues* and *The Princess Casamassima* the crucial process is *representation*. In *La Cousine Bette* and *The Wings of the Dove*, Balzac and James develop their visions of experience as *drama*: the characters in these novels are seen as consciously or unconsciously playing conventional roles, and the action is conceived as a series of dramatic scenes. In their progress from examining how characters come to understand their experience to studying how some parts of experience can stand for other parts to seeing life as a series of more or less consciously enacted scenes, Balzac and James describe intriguingly parallel courses, reflecting as it seems to me a common sequence in the ways people come to understand their worlds.

JANET L. BEIZER

Victor Marchand: The Narrator as Story Seller Balzac's "El Verdugo"

—*La dénomination (dist Epistémon à Pantagruel) de ces deux vostres coronels Riflandouille et Tailleboudin en cestuy conflict nous promect asceurance, heur et victoire, si, par fortune, ces Andouilles nous voulaient oultrager.*

—*Vous le prenez bien (dist Pantagruel) et me plaist que par les noms de nos coronels vous praevoiez et prognosticquez la nostre victoire. Telle manière de prognosticquer par noms n'est moderne.... Voyez le* Cratyle *du divin Platon.*

—*Rabelais*, Quart Livre

[Félicité exclame:] "Sterne a raison: les noms signifient quelque chose, et le mien est la plus sauvage raillerie."

—*Balzac*, Béatrix

"'S̲ouvent,' [dit Louis Lambert], en parlant de ses lectures, 'j'ai accompli de délicieux voyages, embarqué sur un mot dans les abîmes du passé.... Quel beau livre ne composerait-on pas en racontant la vie et les aventures d'un mot?'"[1] This "fine book" dreamed of by Balzac's mad genius is in fact an anachronistic projection, an intertextual reference to a previously completed project, for the author of *Louis Lambert* (written in 1832) had

From *Novel* 17, no. 1. ©1983 by Novel Corp.

already recounted such a linguistic journey when he wrote "El Verdugo" three years earlier.[2]

"El Verdugo" juxtaposes a temporal and spatial journey, a quest for origins which traverses geographical lines as it reverts in time. The text, then, operates as a motor force which we might more aptly call a *vehicle*[3]—a narrative vehicle whose itinerary, moreover, shuttles the reader between two stories.

The more prominent of the two is the drama of a Spanish nobleman's son who murders his father and thereby earns the eponymous title "El Verdugo," translated by the narrator as "le Bourreau." The parricide, however, is presented from the point of view of a young French soldier, the son of a Parisian grocer, whose story is alluded to but suppressed in favor of the Spanish drama it introduces. So the Spanish castle is constructed upon the ruins of a Parisian grocery store, and the text, from the beginning, is structured by a series of substitutions: a *transfer* from France to Spain, a *translation* from French to Spanish, a *transference* (that is, a playing-out of the French soldier's story through the Spanish nobleman's), and a *metaphor* (the title "El Verdugo" replaces the young nobleman's proper name, "de Léganès"). The common etymological source of these terms, which all have to do with conveying, or displacing, affirms the text's vehicular status, and reflects the thematized voyage—or more accurately, perhaps, is reflected by the voyage motif. For the narrative emphasis upon displacement exhibits the means of textual production, points to the rhetoric of displacement as more fundamentally the displacement of rhetoric, rhetoric *as* displacement. The text which represents a quest for origins is inherently reflexive, since the language of interrogation is doubled by an interrogation of language, a quest for narrative origins in language. As we turn to "El Verdugo," it will become evident that the itinerary it follows describes a rather particularized journey through language which might well be subtitled "Voyage en Cratylie."[4]

The text opens with the presentation of Victor Marchand, a young French soldier in Napoleon's service, who is stationed in the small Spanish town of Menda dominated by the Marquis de Léganès' château. Victor, posted on a terrace overlooking both the sea and the château, is charged with surveying both sites: the sea, for a threatened British debarkation, the château, for a suspected indigenous uprising in collaboration with the British. But Victor is absorbed in a contemplation of the land and seascape (and we are told that his revery is perhaps inspired by a romantic interest in the Marquis' daughter, Clara). He therefore notices all too late that the town is resplendent with light (contrary to curfew orders), and that the sea is covered with sails. Then one of his soldiers, struck by a bullet, falls dead at his feet, and a cannon thunders over the ocean. While Victor rapidly realizes that his soldiers have been attacked, that the British are about to land, and that he is therefore dishonored, Clara approaches him in the night and offers her brother's horse, urging him to flee. So Victor is saved, and delivers himself in shame to his general, who immediately sets out with his soldiers to suppress the rebellion. The general agrees to spare the population of Menda in exchange for the rebels' death, and the château inhabitants' surrender.

The second part of the story is marked by a decelerated rhythm as the narrative closes in on the fate of the Marquis' family. Victor Marchand, acting as mediator between the noble family and the French general, requests three favors on the Marquis' behalf. First, he asks that the sentence imposed on the nobles be revised to provide for a more aristocratic death, by decapitation rather than by hanging. This request is accorded. Then he presents a double plea: the family asks for the privilege of religious succor, and for permission to be released from their fetters, promising in exchange that they will not attempt to escape. This appeal duly complied with, Marchand conveys the third proposal. The Marquis offers his entire fortune in exchange for the life of his son. But the general, who comprehends the import of this last request, strikes a harder bargain. He will allow the Marquis to *buy* the eternity of his name: he will spare any one of the three sons who will purchase this privilege by serving as executioner of the remaining family members.[5] Determined at all cost to preserve his name from extinction, the father first orders, then implores his eldest son and namesake to take on the office of executioner. Juanito inevitably concedes, compelled by the supplications of the entire family. At the penultimate moment, Victor procures a pardon for Clara if she will, in exchange, agree to marry him. She refuses; we then proceed to what is literally a blow-by-blow account of Juanito's murder of his two sisters, his two brothers, and his father. The Marquise leaps to her death from the terrace to spare her son a last impossible blow. The final paragraph is a kind of epilogue, written from an unspecified later point in time, spoken in a distanced narrative voice. It informs us that the Marquis' successor (and executioner) lives a dark and solitary life, forestalling death only to await assurance of his own posterity.

Now, the title, "El Verdugo," reflects the narrative focus upon the second part of the text, at the expense of the first, which then becomes a kind of introduction, or background, for the essential drama (which critics have named the "real" story) contained in the second part.[6] But I would suggest that the narrative highlighting of the second half of the text, and more specifically, the emphasis placed on the parricide, represents a transfer, or displacement of interest, which should be challenged on several counts. If we dismiss the first part as introductory or as "background," we are in effect suppressing half the text. But if the first part is truly insignificant, how can we explain the apparently superfluous inclusion of the character Victor Marchand? Why does Clara cross over the boundary of significance, entering the devalorized first section to introduce romantic implications for Victor? Once we recognize that the course of the narrative diverts our attention from the first part of the text, and more specifically, from Clara's role within it, it becomes clear that what has been called the "real" story is in fact the manifest story; this story is important, but it should not prevent us from asking where and what is the latent story.

I wish to approach these questions through a rather enigmatic comment on "El Verdugo" made by Félix Davin, commonly recognized as Balzac's spokesman. Davin says: "'El Verdugo' représente l'idée de dynastie mettant une hache dans la main d'un fils, lui faisant commettre *tous les crimes en un seul*."[7] Like the modern-day critics of this text, Davin stresses a single crime, the horror of which he expresses by a hyperbole: "tous les crimes en un seul." But I think we need to realize that rhetoric is never empty, and that we have to question this figure of speech, question the text as to exactly what it means to "commit every crime," and how it comes to pass that "every crime" is condensed to "a single one." Since the story of Juanito's parricide provides an inadequate answer, we need to reintegrate the two panels of the text. The text in fact offers us a hinge between its two segments in the shape of a forbidden erotic object: Clara.

The opening scene presents a valley lit by "le scintillement des étoiles et la douce lumière de la lune" before the eyes of Victor Marchand (1133). Turning his head, he catches sight of the sea, "dont les eaux brillantes encadraient le paysage d'une large lame d'argent. Le château était illuminé" (1133). Similar images of light and vision pervade the first half of the text; they continue and reflect the original luminous vista which Victor overlooks in the first paragraph, and which distracts him from his surveillance duties and allows the Spanish insurrection to begin undetected. So his crime is essentially one of vision, of seeing so much light that his sight is obstructed. But we need to look more closely at this scene of panoramic contemplation. For we learn the following:

> *Pendant toute cette soirée, l'aînée des filles avait regardé l'officier avec un intérêt empreint d'une telle tristesse, que le sentiment de compassion exprimé par l'Espagnole pouvait bien causer la rêverie du Français. Clara était belle....* (1133–34)

It becomes apparent not only that Victor's distraction is the result of a meditation inspired by the Marquis' daughter, Clara, but that the alluring illuminated landscape is in effect a rhetorical projection, a kind of onomastic fallacy. What occurs here is a metonymic diffusion of the woman to the landscape through the semantic characteristics of her name, "Clara."

So Victor Marchand's visual preoccupation is more fundamentally an erotic one. The scene he surveys is in fact described by a series of feminine metaphors, among which, "une vallée délicieuse qui se déroulait coquettement à ses pieds" (1133). Thus later, in the midst of the "real" story, the avowal that Victor, as he releases Clara from her fetters, "ne put s'empêcher d'effleurer les bras de la jeune fille, en admirant ... sa taille souple" (1139) is no revelation. It is, rather, a deferred recognition of an erotic element which the rhetoric of the text has already disclosed, and which it represents as a crime. Victor Marchand, the son of a petit-bourgeois father (as his patronym emphatically reflects) does not have the right to covet a Spanish noblewoman: "Mais comment oser croire que la fille du vieillard le plus entiché de sa grandesse qui fût en Espagne, pourrait être donnée au fils d'un épicier de Paris!" (1134). The verb "oser" here marks the transgression.

It appears, then, that the two halves of this text juxtapose an erotic crime and a parricide. In order to understand how these two potentially discordant parts of the text are related, we need to look more closely at the parricide. This crime is labeled an "admirable forfait" (1143); the oxymoron reflects the fact that the plot is ambiguously structured. Juanito's parricide is *ordered by his father*; thus the most extreme expression of filial revolt coincides with the most absolute form of filial obedience. Lest we lend too much credence to what the text, for its own purpose of dissimulation, would have us believe, we should regard the paternal command with a healthy dose of skepticism. We can read this apparent contradiction as a textual compromise, as the sign of a conflict between the story attempting to surface and the forces of censorship striving to repress it; as such, this paradox marks a significant affective node of the intrigue.

By analogy with the dream-work, which strives to disguise its disturbing, or forbidden content, the act of writing, as it works to conceal what is actually the son's parricidal desire, makes of desire a necessity. It transforms the paternal prohibition into its opposite: a paternal command. (That the French pronunciation of "Menda"—the site of this drama—makes it the homonym of *mandat*, or mandate, is no accident; every effort is being made to legitimize the crime that occurs here.) It becomes evident that we are dealing with an Oedipal crime, whose erotic component has been expurgated from the "real" story and displaced to the "background" region of the first part of the text. It is as if, by dividing the crime in two thereby attenuated components, each attributed to a different character, the crime might be prevented from bursting forth in its full horror.[8]

But the erotic component is in fact not wholly consigned to Victor's story; Victor's erotic transgression (though to a certain extent veiled) is only more overtly expressed than Juanito's. Juanito's rapport with his sister is, to say the least, equivocal:

> *Clara vint s'asseoir sur ses genoux, et, d'un air gai: —Mon cher Juanito, dit-elle en lui passant le bras autour du cou et l'embrassant sur les paupières; si tu savais combien, donnée par toi, la mort me sera douce…. Tu me guériras des maux qui m'attendaient, et … mon bon Juanito, tu ne me voulais voir à personne, eh! bien?* (1140)

Clara's plea for death is an appeal to her brother's possessive love for her. The murder of Clara is then a lover's crime, except that Juanito is both less and more than a lover to Clara. Now, the rationale behind Clara's death plea to her brother (which might be paraphrased as "since you can't have me, kill me so that no one else can") is repeated by the conditional pardon that Victor Marchand extends to Clara. He offers her life in exchange for the gift of her person, which is tantamount to saying … "If I can't have you, you will die so that no one else can."

Victor and Juanito, by the analogy of their similar erotic relationship to Clara, are doubles—the difference here being, of course, that Juanito is her brother as well. The identification is reinforced by several other factors. The title accorded Juanito, "el Verdugo," alliteratively identifies him with Victor. Victor and Juanito are close in age. Victor escapes from the scene of his crime on Juanito's horse, which serves as a metonymic vehicle connecting the two. Clara is the common denominator; Clara offers Victor her brother's horse, Clara places the two men in a structure of equivalence by making them rivals in love: "Ses yeux veloutés jetèrent un regard de feu sur Victor, comme pour réveiller dans le coeur de Juanito son horreur des Français" (1140).

Now, if we superimpose the two characters, the one (Victor) erotically linked to Clara, the other (Juanito) related to her by blood, the pattern that emerges is one of vicarious incest. Since Victor and Juanito reduplicate each other, each completing the other's erotic crime, it comes as little surprise that Victor's story includes a figurative parricide. His early scene of contemplation (the representation of his desire for Clara) was punctuated by a reflection on his petit-bourgeois origin. His evident contempt for his humble birthright betrays a symbolic rejection of his father, who is clearly the obstacle that prevents him from attaining Clara. Having nonetheless committed the forbidden act, having foiled the paternal prohibition carried in his very name, "Marchand," by rhetorically enacting the erotic transgression, Victor appropriately seeks punishment from two father surrogates: first "le terrible général," and then Napoleon: "Quand l'Empereur saura cela!" (1136).

His paternal repudiation is in fact not confined to this verbal rejection. There is a (displaced) passage from the word to the deed, because Victor's erotic crime (his contemplation) leads to neglect of his surveillance duty, making him a traitor to his general and emperor, and abetting the Spanish insurrection. Victor's negligence culminates in the punishment meted out to the rebels, and so he is indirectly responsible for Juanito's parricide.

The Victor story and the Juanito story are, then, like a photograph and its negative, in an inverted relationship to each other. The two components of the crime—the erotic and the parricidal—are dissociated, but each retains latent elements of the other, so that the two parts of "El Verdugo" ultimately correspond to a disguised retelling of the same tale.[9] Now we begin to understand what it means to commit "every crime in a single one." The expression is a euphemism for the two crimes of Oedipus, who killed his father and married his mother.

As we reintegrate the two crimes and the two stories, it is important to remember that Victor's meditation launches the Spanish uprising and eventually creates Juanito's drama. The castle of Menda, then, is a synonym for Victor's "château en Espagne," and the drama which unfolds there is a wish-fulfilling projection of his phantasies. For although this is a third-person narrative delivered by an anonymous narrator, there is a narrative investment in Victor: we read from his perspective, and he is the figure with whom the narrator identifies. We have seen that the narrative rhetoric of the opening sentence betrays Victor's erotic act; more crucially, it betrays the erotic attitude of whoever is delivering the narrative, whoever is performing the narrative act. Later on, when the drama intensifies (in the second part of the text) Victor begins to fade, and he disappears entirely when catastrophe strikes the dénouement. Juanito approaches Clara with his sword; we see her head roll (the stroke of the sword is elided, and the elision is repeated, on a grander scale, by the averted—or suppressed—matricide). We hear no more of Victor. It is at this point that the narrative voice changes, seems to become detached from the tale it relates; so that Clara's death, Victor's expulsion from the text, and a break in the narrative voice—a kind of narrative castration—all coincide.[10]

Although Victor Marchand is never assigned an overt narrative role, he leaves his signature on the text in a series of "marchandages," or bargainings. I have mentioned that Victor serves as a mediator, an agent of exchange, in a series of transactions between the Marquis and the French general. But I would argue that each of the "marchés" refers to a more significant *narrative* transaction: the exchange of the narrator's story for Victor's, and Victor's story for Juanito's. It is in this context that Victor Marchand's mediating function becomes essential. For his role, as suggested by his patronym, is to "donner le change," to lure the reader toward another's story—the Other's story—which is given in exchange for Victor's own, to fool the reader into accepting this story as the "real" one, when it is in fact a substitute, a projection of Victor's story, of the narrator's, the story of narrative, of writing.

At the core of this imbricated structure of exchange is the verbal merchandise, mediated by the text. The Léganès story represents a series of linguistic transactions, of name-exchanges. That which Juanito inherits through his father's death, "de Léganès," has as its root the Spanish verb *legar*, derived from the Latin *legare*, *léguer*, in French: "to bequeath," "to leave a legacy." Since one must die in order to make a legacy effective, the father's death gives meaning to his name, makes his name signify. By dying, the Marquis de Léganès makes his name a proper one, which subsequently becomes replaceable by a metaphor: "El Verdugo." Thus the father's death opens the possibility of language as signification, as symbolization. Victor's name is similarly realized, appropriated, through the parricidal drama in which he figures as mediator, or "marchand."[11]

Interestingly, the rapport between language and the father, narrative and death, is very much the same for Balzac as for the fictional characters he creates in Juanito and Victor; this is a kind of external evidence that the text is reflexive, representing its own conditions of being. "El Verdugo," Balzac's first tale of parricide, was written in October of 1829, four months after the death of his father. It is the first text signed "H. de Balzac" by the writer, who here appropriates the particule which Bernard-François, his father, assigned himself. Here, then, Balzac accedes to the patronym. It is also among the very first of the texts that were to figure in the *Comédie humaine*.

The text reposes on a gap which is at the same time a plenitude: the real father dies, but his death guarantees his legacy which is his name, his name which is his legacy, his law which establishes a symbolic order capable of generating an infinite series of substitutions. The chain that leads from the dead father, the marquis de Léganès, to his successor, Juanito, the new marquis de Léganès, to his title, "El Verdugo," and then to "le Bourreau," culminates in "El Verdugo"—the text. The symbolic order—a precondition for the generation of the literary text—is attained through the father's name once his literal presence is annihilated.

This narrative, then, closes upon itself like a Möbius strip, for its fictional pretext plays out its textual conditions of being: death makes life narratable. If the origin of narrative is death, its foundation, an absence, we have to re-think the principles upon which "El Verdugo" appears to be based. The father's death engenders a series of substitutions, but since what is being replaced is a lack, a blank, rather than a substantive referent, the substitutions are catachrestic rather than metaphoric, imposed upon an absence, upon an obliterated presence.[12] The concept of narrative as a system of exchange, in which the narrator is replaced by the protagonist and the narration by the story, becomes problematic. Since the exchange of Victor's story for Juanito's in effect trades same for same, it yields a repetition, a duplication of loss in which more turns into less and excess becomes lack.

Victor, the pretended merchant of Menda, the agent of exchange, is, in the course of the narrative, reduced to nothing. Victim of his vision, blinded to his duty, "il était sans épée." When we recall the motto Balzac had inscribed on his bust of Napoleon—"Ce qu'il a entrepris par l'épée, je l'accomplirai par la plume"—we can appreciate what metaphoric implications this swordlessness has for the text, what narrative story is being told (or exorcised) through this scene of military life.[13] Deprived of his honor, his woman, his sword and his pen, Victor is perhaps more a beggar than a merchant. The narrative, tautologically inscribed in a void, relinquished rather than exchanged, thus becomes a gratuitous act, and the narrator, would-be seller of tales, a "victor" ironically "vaincu" by his own narration.

In much the same way, the text ironically subverts the Cratylistic basis—or bias—upon which it would seem to be constructed. The plot is structured upon a metonymic and metaphoric scaffolding which extends the Cratylistic project in two directions: horizontally, through the drama which unfolds as an acting-out (and, hence, a realization) of names (Clara, Victor, Marchand, Menda), and vertically, via the genealogical playing-out (and once again, realization) of proper naming (Juanito's inheritance of the patronym). But the dynamics of plot reshape and displace its foundations. Just as Victor is vanquished, Clara, the purported emblem of light and brilliance, becomes the portent of death and darkness. (She augurs Juanito's retreat into shadow as well as Victor's disappearance.) The "mandate" of Menda is more accurately an arrogation, an illegitimate presumption. So the metonymic representation reveals the non-correspondence of name and named, the radical impropriety of "proper" names. The metaphoric play fares no better, for Juanito's "proper" name is both literally and figuratively only nominal, the illegitimately "appropriated" name of another which can become his "property" only when that other (the father, the original name-bearer, the named) is obliterated—at which point it is no longer proper, but figurative.

"El Verdugo," then, records that "adventure of words" which for Louis Lambert ended in aphasia, perhaps because that journey through language necessarily became—and becomes—the journey of language, the log which inscribes, and is inscribed by, the infinite displacement of the word.

NOTES

1. Honoré de Balzac, *Louis Lambert*, in *La Comédie humaine*, ed. Pierre-Georges Castex, XI (Paris: Bibliothèque de la Pléiade, 1980), p. 591.

2. "El Verdugo," written in October 1829, first appeared in *La Mode* on 28 January 1830. It figures as one of the *Études Philosophiques*.

3. The linguistic connotations of this term project the voyage into a third dimension as they mark the textual itinerary through language.

4. With apologies to Gérard Genette: *Mimologiques: Voyage en Cratylie* (Paris: Seuil, 1976).

5. "Eh bien, qu'il achète l'éternité de son nom …".: "El Verdugo," in *La Comédie humaine*, ed. Castex, X (1979), p. 1138. Subsequent references to "El Verdugo" will be given parenthetically in the text.

6. See, e.g., Diana Festa McCormick, *Les Nouvelles de Balzac* (Paris: Nizet, 1973), p. 105. A notable exception to the otherwise generalized critical dismissal of the first part of "El Verdugo" is to be found in Pierre Citron's excellent introduction to the text in the cited Pléiade edition (pp. 1123–31). Citron aptly points out the incestuous element of the Clara-Juanito relationship, and indicates that it is analogous to the equally impossible Clara-Victor rapport; he also sheds light on the parricidal aspect of the text.

7. "Introduction par Félix Davin aux *Études Philosophiques*," in *La Comédie humaine*, X, 1213; emphasis added.

8. This is strikingly similar to the dramatic device used by Corneille in his *Oedipe*. Corneille, however, splits the crime in two (assigning parricide to Oedipe, incest to Thésée) only temporarily; he eventually reunites the two crimes, reassigning both to Oedipe.

9. This doubling is in fact a frequent phenomenon in Balzac's tales. Leo Mazet has remarked upon "le lien structural métaphorique qui réunit traditionnellement chez [Balzac] l'histoire enchâssante à l'histoire enchâssée, inscrivant dans son texte un jeu de miroirs plus ou moins vertigineux...." "Récit(s) dans le récit: l'échange du récit chez Balzac," in *L'Année balzacienne* (1976), p. 147.

10. See Roland Barthes' commentary on the metonymic force of castration—castration become contagious—in "Sarrasine": S/Z (Paris: Seuil, 1970), pp. 204 ff. In "El Verdugo" as in "Sarrasine," death, sexual loss and narrative detachment are part of the same substitutive chain.

11. On the relationship between metaphor and parricide, see Jacques Lucan's commentary on Victor Hugo's "Booz endormi," in "L'Instance de la lettre dans l'inconscient," *Ecrits I* (Paris: Seuil, 1966), pp. 264–67.

12. It would be interesting to think about the drama of naming, in "El Verdugo," in conjunction with Derrida's essay on writing as violence, as the "obliteration of the proper." See "La Violence de la lettre: de Lévi-Strauss á Rousseau" in *De la Grammatologie* (Paris: Minuit, 1967), pp. 149–202.

13. Cited by Stefan Zweig in *Balzac: Le Roman de sa vie*, tr. Fernand Delmas (Paris: Albin Michel, 1950), p. 110.

ROLAND LE HUENEN AND PAUL PERRON

Reflections on Balzacian Models
of Representation

In a letter to Mme Hanska dated January 1833, Balzac announces a new project for a novel entitled *La Bataille* which he sets out in the following terms:

> I tell you that *La Bataille* is an impossible book. In it, I undertake to make you aware of all the horrors and all the beauties of a battlefield; my battle is Essling, Essling with all its consequences. A cold man sitting in his armchair must see the countryside, the irregularities of the ground, the masses of men, the strategic events, the Danube, the bridges; must admire the details and the whole of that combat; must hear the artillery; must be interested in these chess moves; must see everything. In every joint of that great body, he must feel Napoleon whom I will not show or whom I will allow to be seen in the evening crossing the Danube in a boat. Not a single female, cannons, horses, two armies, uniforms; on the first page, the cannon roars, it is silent on the last; you will read through the smoke and, when the book is closed, you must have seen everything intuitively and must recall the battle as if you had been [there].

From *Poetics Today* 5, no. 4. ©1984 by *Poetics Today*. Translated by Barbara Benavie.

For three months now I have wrestled with this work, this ode
in two volumes which everyone cries out is impossible to write
(Balzac 1967: 27– 28).

This fragment of a letter, which serves to fix a first approximation of
the Balzacian process of representation, and hence that of the realistic novel,
appears more spontaneously revealing on the whole than the prefaces, and
less suspect than the narrative generally devoted to naturalizing its own
procedures of figuration. It is from this perspective that our analysis will be
organized.

The disclosure that *"La Bataille* is an impossible book" has a two-fold
significance: it indicates the ends, and inscribes in filigree the difficulty of the
means. Ideally, to narrate is necessarily to produce an effect of presence
through recourse to the senses, to sight in particular. "A cold man sitting in
his armchair must see the countryside ... admire the details ... hear the
artillery ... see everything... In every joint of that great body, he must feel
Napoleon... You will read through the smoke." In short, to narrate is to
make one see as if one were there or, more precisely, as if one had been there,
for the end of the passage seems to suggest a displacement of effect from
presence to reminiscence: "and when the book is closed, you must have seen
everything intuitively and must recall the battle as if you had been there."
"Seen everything intuitively," a correction *in extremis* that resituates language
in its semiotic context, for the word is neither the thing nor its stand-in, but
an index that points and that causes to point, a signal that releases, as in those
cases of paramnesia, an impression of déjà vu, which revives an imprint
woven into memory by knowledge and experience. To represent is always to
resort to the antecedence of a trace, to invoke a reference; that is, through
the intermediary of the sign, to establish a topological translation affecting
the space of reading. "A cold man sitting in his armchair must see..."
Balzacian description often uses such strategies of interpellation addressed to
the reader or narratee, strategies which are like summations to be
represented through the mediation of an image or a memory. Thus, in *Un
Drame au bord de la mer*, the beginning of Cambremer's portrait: "Try to call
up before you, dear uncle, some gnarled oak stump, with all its branches
lately lopped away, rearing its head, like a strange apparition, by the side of
a lonely road, and you will have a clear idea of this man that we saw" (Balzac
1979: Pléiade X, 1169). Or, in *Le Chef d'oeuvre inconnu*, the setting of
Frenhofer's portrait: "Picture that face. A bald high forehead and rugged
jutting brows above a small flat nose turned up at the end, as in the portraits
of Socrates and Rabelais... Set this head on a spare and feeble frame, place it

in a frame of lace wrought like an engraved silver fish-slice, imagine a heavy gold chain over the old man's black doublet, and you will have some dim idea of this strange personnage" (X, 414–415). Thus, the illusion of a presence, the very nature of representation, is created by the order of language itself.

Yet, "*La Bataille* is an impossible book" and we know that Balzac did not complete his project, did not even write a first draft, despite the important documentation gathered and numerous notices of impending release. Though it is not important here and now to speculate on the objective reasons that led Balzac to abandon his project, it is nevertheless possible to raise questions about the general significance of the opinion expressed concerning this aborted plan. Assessments of the respective merits of painting and literature are frequently found in Balzac's writings. The preface to *La Peau de chagrin* comes out strongly in favor of literature, "the most complicated of all the arts" (X, 51). Now this preeminence granted to writing has less to do with the techniques of expression than with the capacity of narrative to manipulate ideas, to make itself the instrument of visionary thought, a fact which, in any case, does not prejudice the outcome raised by the problematics of representation. Moreover, after the preface comes to a close, the novel is set in motion by an image: Sterne's drawing which, as we know, in *Tristram Shandy* was ironically substituted for the verbal description of Corporal Trim's whirling stick.

As can be seen from Balzac's text itself, the sign is certainly not an image and cannot in any way claim to rival the visual. Nonetheless, the temptation remains, and fascination with the pictorial appears especially powerful in the writing of portraits. As a figure of rhetoric, the aim of the portrait is to show the body and face, to create an impression of life, to render the dynamism inherent in the supposed animate model through phrasing and the choice of images. The exemplary figure of this is hypotyposis. The Balzacian portrait remains essentially faithful to these precepts, and is established along the lines of the pictorial portrait (cf. Le Huenen and Perron 1980: 37–91). As we know, its lexicon is saturated with borrowings from the language of painters, even in the case of prefaces and letters. An example is this quotation from the preface of *Illusions perdues*: "Only once did M. Scribe attempt to do this [denounce journalism] in his light play, *Charlatanism*, which is more a portrait than a scene. The pleasure caused by that witty draft made the author aware of the need to attempt a more ample painting" (V, 113). We should also recall that a pictorial metaphor is the structuring matrix of Davin-Balzac's two prefaces describing the project for writing *Etudes de moeurs au XIXe siècle*: "... in this rich picture gallery, whose great halls stretch to infinity, does one not find frames of a rather remarkable size, such as those of *Eugénie Grandet*, of the *Médecin de campagne* and of *Les Chouans*, which obviously belong to the *Scènes de la vie militaire?*" (X, 1207).

Moreover, concerned with producing visual illusion, novelistic description calls upon the mediation of the image, either by evoking the memory of famous paintings to ground the written portrait,[1] or, less obviously, by the use of the citational relay of an Epinal engraving,[2] or by weighting the verbal signifier with the materiality of the chromatic: Adeline Fischer has "a complexion mingled in the unknown laboratory where good luck presides" (VII, 74). Another characteristic of Balzacian writing is to relate the written face to a specific painter's technique and aesthetic. Thus the portrait of Esther van Gobseck at the beginning of *Splendeurs et misères*: "Esther, excessively strong though apparently fragile, arrested attention by one feature that is conspicuous in the faces in which Raphaël has shown his most artistic feeling, for Raphaël is the painter who has most and best rendered Jewish beauty. This remarkable effect was produced by the depth of the eye-socket, under which the eye moved free from its setting; the arch of the brow was so accurate as to resemble the groining of a vault" (VI, 464). Here, the language of the portrait indexes less the reality of an image than borrowings from a critical metalanguage, that of art. Not only does this language copy the value judgments of art critics, but it also somehow guarantees the possibility of semiotic collaboration and an homogenization of signs. To account for a picture by means of writing is to assume implicitly the compatibility of languages and the admissibility of their mutual transcoding.[3] But, on closer inspection, figurative description is most often reduced to the doxastic declension of semantic fields; for example, the divine, angelic, sublime, virginal grace of Raphaël; the serious and thoughtful integrity or the ingenuous and seraphic candor of Titian.

One could further examine this type of pictorialization of the written portrait. To evoke a picture or to cite the name of a painter is to urge the reader to substitute for the graphics of sentences and the succession of verbal signs a representation belonging to the realm of figures, of simultaneity and of the whole. It is also to posit the ineffectiveness of writing or at least its inferiority vis-à-vis painting, since, in order to describe, writing must resort to the suggestion of the image. It is, finally, to recognize the inevitability of the sign, for if description evokes the character or the object represented, it also evokes its own literariness as well as the constraints inherent in its descriptive status by the very verbal discontinuity which, through sequencing, deconstructs the original unity of the object. Hence the search for palliatives, for stylistic techniques, which are various means of semiotic correlation, striving to simulate, through forced harmony of discourse, the "natural" harmony of the model (cf. Vannier 1972:36–47). Hence the admiration for Walter Scott whose work, all things considered, is praised less (in the terms of the *Avant-propos* of *La Comédie humaine*) for its historical significance than for its aesthetic qualities. Hence Balzac's enthusiasm for Cooper's novel, *Lake Ontario*, whose craftsmanship inspired this comment: "Never has the printed word encroached more on painting."[4] And hence his nostalgia for the image and fascination with the pictorial.

La Bataille really is an impossible book, even more so since the style of the sketch (as reported in the letter to Mme Hanska) seems to suggest a purely visual treatment of subject, which tends to render the description autonomous and to liberate it from explanatory commentary that invariably accompanies so many Balzacian descriptions. This scopic treatment would involve, in sum, focusing on one image, on one setting in the name of and in the search for the irreducibility of figuration. Such an hypothesis is even more probable since, in the wording of the project itself, through a determinative turn of phrase ("*my* battle is Essling"), a sort of intertextuality-effect comes to the fore, tending to limit this battle to the role of representing battles already represented against the background of other battles, which, in this specific instance, could only be the frescoes of the Napoleonic era. It is perhaps helpful to note that Balzac had a precise knowledge of Imperial iconography,[5] as can be attested from close examination of the postface of *Les Paysans* or the military scene which opens *La Femme de trente ans*. In addition, Olivier Bonnard (1969:53 ff) has shown that the description of the battle of Eylau in *Colonel Chabert* presents striking analogies with Gros's painting of the scene. This provides useful insights into the generative function of visual images in Balzacian creation and, more particularly, into the importance the novelist attached to iconographic documentation.[6] Yet, it is at the very moment he undertakes, and expeditiously finishes, *Colonel Chabert* that Balzac gets inextricably entangled in the descriptive aporias of *La Bataille*. Beyond the trite hypothesis concerning the intermittent nature of Balzac's genius, to what can this success and this failure be attributed if not to the formal difference between two descriptive methods? The first method attempts to create pure effects of figures and inevitably comes up against the insurmountable literariness of the sign; the second assumes representation as a mediating necessity, and ends up designating more the absence of the object than the object itself. The summoning up of a picture, or its allusive citation, has no other goal than to further the verbal sign's indexical dimension, its transcendent functionality and its ostensory capacity. However, at one and the same time this capacity to represent imposes itself and is experienced in the unbridgeable distance separating sign from object, a distance which can be bridged only by mirror effects producing the image as presence/absence. "Thus," writes Barthes (1974:55), "realism (badly named, at any rate often badly interpreted) consists not in copying the real but in copying a (depicted) copy of the real: this famous *reality*, as though suffering from a fearfulness which keeps it from being touched directly, is *set farther away*, postponed, or at least captured through the pictorial matrix in which it has been steeped before being put into words... This is why realism cannot be designated a 'copier' but rather a 'pasticheur.'" And so descriptive gesture can only "de-pict" its copy, detach it from its illusorily figural frame, by putting it into the frame of language and rendering it through discourse, the task of which will be to make it signify. The indefinitely renewed configuration of meaning settles in the very gap created between the object and its representation by the gestural nature of the sign. Originally to represent is to show, yet, as was mentioned before, this visualization is reduced to an evocation; that is, to the reiteration of a trace, an imprint left in memory through the imposition of knowledge.

The narrative indexes and postulates this knowledge, but at the same time conceals it; the narrative insists on it, but simultaneously conceals it. Every reader of Balzac is familiar with those introductory descriptions set into play by an image, a picture, a vision that is immediately indexed as a lack of knowledge. The following examples are from *La Maison du chat-qui-pelote*: "In point of fact, this relic of the civic life of the sixteenth century offered more than one problem to the consideration of an observer ... these windows were glazed with small squares of glass so green that, but for his good eyes, the young man could not have seen the blue-checked curtains which screened the mysteries of the room from profane eyes" (I, 39). One will recall the opening scene of *La Peau de chagrin* which introduces an unknown character who is about to bet—we do not know why—his last *louis* in a gambling house of the Palais Royal, or the vision of that female silhouette unexpectedly surprised at the beginning of *Ferragus*, from which emerge both the enigma and the drama: "That She should be in that filthy neighborhood at that hour of night" (V, 797). In short, examples abound.

This veiled indexation of knowledge results in a shift from the descriptive toward a narrative program, the finalistic unfolding of which systematically diminishes the figural substratum of representation along the axis of signification. By its equivocal emergence, the thing seen sets off the necessity for narrative. To narrate is first and always to reveal a secret, to respond to the desire of the other (the narratee, or the reader), declaring that one knows, reporting what one knows, but, also and perhaps especially, constituting oneself before the other as the knowing subject. And it is at this very moment that a reorientation of the concept of representation takes place in the Balzacian novel—from the pictorial to the theatrical, from the picture to the scene and the setting. The narrative cannot do without this ostensory ritual, the principal function of which is to legitimize and authenticate the origin and nature of knowing. For it is not enough simply to disclose meaning; it is also necessary to establish that this meaning is really the right one. It is this representation of knowledge or, more precisely, the positioning of knowledge that we propose to examine in the case of *Colonel Chabert*.

Inevitably the novella opens with an initial image: "Why, there is that old greatcoat again!" (III, 311). Immediately an enigma is formulated, for "if he is a man, why do you call him old greatcoat?" (III, 311–312). From this image emerges a form but an empty form which, simultaneously, will serve as support for various semantic investments which are not simply definitions of the *old greatcoat*, but also ruses and strategies designed to create curiosity, to hold attention, to fix the necessity and the prestige of the narrative by setting into motion the motivating forces of expectation and desire. What does this grotesque apparel conceal: a former concierge, a doorman, a fallen aristrocrat, a brewer of the Ancien Régime who became a colonel under the Republic? To cut these speculations short, the protagonists interrogate and enjoin the stranger to give his name, and the latter replies: "Chabert.—The colonel who was killed at Eylau?—The same, monsieur..." (III, 317). Such a hypothesis is seemingly untenable, the enigma is looked in contradiction, and madness becomes the only possible explanation. That, at least, will be lawyer Derville's first opinion.[7] Yet the narrative voice maintains ambiguity without seeking, either through a change of focalization or by means of an aside, to keep the narratee informed of what the characters are supposed not to know. Quite the contrary, the repeated use of modalizing terms contributes to the naturalization of the assertive function,[8] whereas the appellative paradigm registers indetermination: old greatcoat, a stranger, old litigant, the patient, the man in the greatcoat, the old man. Moreover, Chabert's portrait, in a manner quite rare in Balzacian writing, articulates descriptive features according to an oxymoronic model, of which the following semic contrasts should be retained: mobile/immobile, life/death, natural/supernatural, mystery/evidence, reality/image. Instead of quoting the entire portrait, we will limit ourselves to this sample: "His forehead, intentionally hidden under a smoothly combed wig, gave him a look of mystery ... his face, pale, livid, and as thin as a knife-blade ... was as the face of the dead... This grotesque effect, though natural, threw into relief by contrast the white furrows, the cold wrinkles, the colorless tone of the corpse-like countenance" (III, 321).

In other words, the narrator has chosen to keep an attitude of prudent perplexity. But why? To maintain suspense? Certainly. But is it only for that reason? On closer inspection, it can be seen that his doubt is somewhat methodical, that it entails a kind of demonstrative intent. But let us return to the text: "... an observer, especially a lawyer, could have read in this stricken man the signs of deep sorrow, the tales of grief which had worn into this face, as drops of water from the sky falling on fine marble at last destroy its beauty. A physician, an author or a magistrate might have sensed a whole drama at the sight of that sublime horror..." (III, 322). The commentary concluding Chabert's portrait clearly shows the need to look beyond the windowpane, to go beyond the level of appearance and to follow the potentiality of signs; but it also declares that this privileged viewpoint, and consequently this knowledge, is the prerogative of a specific category of observers: the author, the lawyer, the physician. Hence, it may be assumed that the strategy of the narrative in *Colonel Chabert* consists of exposing the modalities of knowing, and, more especially, of establishing the narrative knowledge guaranteed by science, and in this particular case by medical and legal science. This is somewhat analogous to the mode of thought of the Cartesian philosopher who, in search of evidence, takes a chance on doubt and, once assured of a primary and incontestable truth, reconstructs the world the existence of which had seemed at first uncertain to him. Like the philosopher, the novelist tells the real, but also pretends to proclaim its truth.

An agnostic by artifice, the narrator lets the stranger speak. The latter begins to tell his story to the lawyer Derville, and it is a story whose telling assumes all the characteristics of narration. This chronological narrative, like all narrative, is a reconstruction, a reconstruction made up of personal memories, texts taken from history, various testimonies, relations of scattered events belonging to different periods, re-set in the unitary mold of discourse and endowed with teleological intelligibility.[9] Its logic is that of the plausible: "Allow me to first establish the facts, or explain to you how things must have occurred rather than how they did happen" (III, 324). To narrate is necessarily to rectify, that is, to shape the inventory of facts according to the constraints and conventions of narrative; and therefore, it is less a matter of showing than of demonstrating through recourse to explanatory logic inscribed in the teleological intent of knowledge. Chabert may be insane, but he speaks like a book, and thus, in an exemplary fashion, reproduces the role of the narrator. Moreover, Derville, as emphasized in the text,[10] at first inattentive, is soon caught up by the narrative: "As he heard his visitor express himself with complete lucidity and tell such a probable though strange story, the young lawyer left his files, rested his left elbow on the table, and with his head on his hand stared at the colonel" (III, 324).[11] The narratee is captivated, and although the narrative has produced its effect, as such it cannot be founded in truth, for the *old greatcoat* who becomes a storyteller cannot "procure the documents that could prove [his] story" (III, 327). Derville undertakes to locate the missing documents. He succeeds, and since they are made out by a physician (hence a scientist), "legally stamped to serve as evidence in law" (III, 327), they can confirm the truthfulness of the narrative. Yet even though the narrative is authenticated in this very way, and even though it constitutes the narrator as a subject of knowing, it is still necessary, in the final analysis, to verify the practical truth of this proposition and demonstrate that the narrator can effectively take on the function of guarantor. That becomes the subject of the second part of the novella.

After Chabert's tale is finished, the narrator once again takes up the narrative voice and that is when the episode, related to Derville's dealings with Countess Chabert, who had become the Countess Ferraud by remarriage, takes place. Anxious to force her legally to recognize Chabert's right to a part of his own fortune, the lawyer seeks a means of intimidating her: "She must be frightened. She is a woman. Now, what frightens women most? Why, a woman is afraid of nothing but..." (III, 346). These suspension points are adumbrated by the narrator and replaced by a voice, which, surplanting Derville's dreamy meditations, reveals Mme Ferraud's secret to the reader.[12] This secret, known only by the narrator, is finally guessed at but not uncovered by the lawyer (for he will never acquire formal proof of it): "Without knowing it, Derville had put his finger on the secret wound, put his hand on the cancer that consumed Madame Ferraud" (III, 350). We could not imagine a better example of reversal of function since, henceforth, it is the narrator's knowing which is responsible for guaranteeing and judging, by his own measure, the lawyer's prescience. The novelist has only to push this demonstrative logic to the extreme and to link, by a relation of reciprocal implication in a definitive and absolute way, the mastery of knowledge and that of the narrative. Twenty years later, the epilogue of the novella brings together Chabert, lodged in Bicêtre, and Derville, accompanied by his former clerk, Godeschal. Spotting Chabert, Derville confides to his companion: "That old man, my dear fellow, is a whole poem, or, as the romantics say, a drama ... this opening having excited Godeschal's curiosity, Derville related the story here told" (III, 371–372). The circle is closed, the narrative contract is made explicit at the very moment it is realized: the narrator has been constituted as a subject of knowing and the keeper of knowledge has been constituted as the subject of the narrative.

Many examples of these stagings, making knowledge both the extension of representation and its very object at the same time, can be found in *La Comédie humaine*. One of Balzac's novellas, *Un Prince de Bohème*, neglected by critics because of so-called frivolity, is, however, important if only for the twisted character of the narrative protocol established. Mme de la Baudraye, as a second narrator, reads a narrative to a character, Nathan, that the same Nathan had told her orally a few days earlier in the presence of a third person, the Marquise de Rochefide. The subject of this narrative is the gallant adventures of a certain Count de la Palférine. But the main point is found less in the story than in the peculiarity of its discursive form, noteworthy for several reasons. First, the narrative subordinates *speaking* to *hearing*. Nathan's main function is to listen and he perceives in otherness his own speech rendered to him from a distant and alien enunciative origin. This narrative, which was his initially, exists independently of his founding speech, in a kind of external and impersonal space. Hence the subordination of *speaking* to *hearing* designates the transition from the verbal second person to the third person, from the primary oral narrative which was inscribed in an interpersonal situation of communication to the written and read narrative; in short, from presence to representation. Listening to his own narrative, Nathan is forced to represent it to himself. In the second place, he remains its guarantor: his silence and non-participation during the reading bear witness to his adherence and confirm the truth of the narrative. Finally, once Mme de la Baudraye's narration is finished, Nathan intervenes to reveal the outcome: "The Marquise de Rochefide is infatuated with Charles-Edouard. My story excited her curiosity" (VIII, 328). The oral narrative establishes its illocutionary force and produces an event in the second degree (fictional reality), the existential character of which has repercussions on the written narrative, insofar as the latter is also the product of oral narration. Thus, once again, the representation of knowledge and of its instrumentality is played out in the organizational economy of a Balzacian narrative.

But what is the nature of knowledge? The *Avant-propos* to *La Comédie humaine* and the prefaces, particularly the two prefaces by Davin-Balzac, provide the possibility for a first systematization. Davin's prefaces present the two-fold descriptive metaphor of a picture gallery designating *Les Etudes de moeurs*, and of a monument built stone by stone, the architectural pyramid of which simulates the successive staging of the *Comédie humaine* in its entirety. The *Etudes de moeurs* thus form its base, the *Etudes analytiques* its apex, and the *Etudes philosophiques* its median transition. This schematization, which

Balzac summarizes in similar terms in the *Avant-propos* and the *Lettres à Madame Hanska*, as well as considerations on the unity of composition borrowed from Geoffroy Saint-Hilaire, would suggest an idealized conception of knowledge moving from effects to causes, then to principles; that is, to the entirety of a form. From this perspective, the place of representation *stricto sensu* in which the novelist's talent to become a "painter who is more or less faithful, more or less fortunate," a "teller of the dramas of intimate life," an "archaeologist of the social scene," a "classifier of professions" is, strictly speaking, only the place of accident, chance, contingency which enfolds knowledge within the common limits of observation. Accordingly, true knowledge would be elsewhere, in the elucidation of the "hidden meaning" and in meditation "on natural principles" based on "the eternal rule of truth and beauty" (I, 11–12). There is no doubt that this pseudo-scientific theory of knowledge is inscribed as a belief, as an act of faith whose ideological (that is, imaginary[13]) character is more apparent in the spontaneous and less circumspect formulation found in this letter to Madame Hanska: "Then, after the *effects* and the causes, will come the *Etudes analytiques* of which the *Physiologie du mariage* is a part; for, after the *effects* and the *causes*, the principles must be sought. The *customs* are the spectacle, the *causes* are *the wings and the machinery*. Principles, that's the *author*" (Balzac 1967:270). Nonetheless, taken literally, this theoretical fiction postulates a sharp dissociation between the realm of representation and the realm of knowledge; that is, if it is true that "as the work spirals up to the heights of thought, it becomes more compact and more dense" (p. 270). It remains to be seen if this purely thetic apprehension of knowledge is really the one that the novels set into place. It would seem, rather, that Balzacian practice actually reverses the preceding theoretical viewpoint and constitutes knowledge as a modelling activity *of* and *on* representation.

As was suggested, the relationship between language and the pictorial is infinite insofar as the sign and the image are irreducible to one another. If "*La Bataille* is an impossible book," it is, as was seen, because the place, the topos, the domain from which it emerges—despite the images, comparisons, and metaphors—are not the ones perceived by sight and the other senses, but those evoked in and through the order of syntax. It is also impossible to write because, from the vantage point occupied by "the cold man sitting in his armchair," the cycle of representation, as focalized space, is presented in its entirety.

Consequently, writing *La Bataille* consists of organizing a determined space for an observer so that he "admires the details and the whole," and the following two series of problems involving composition and structure arise.

In order to represent, a framework is required, one which mediates the transition from the formless to the formed, from the indefinite to the finite, from the unlimited to the limited, from "*a* battlefield" to "*my* battle." This process of delimitation leaves traces in the actual linguistic material itself; for example, the accumulation of such deictic determinants as: "*the* countryside," "*the* irregularities" or "*that* combat," "*those* movements." It thus becomes a question of circumscribing, delimiting, assigning a place to all constitutive elements, arranging characters, squaring or gridding space to make the spectator sense the moves of the pieces on the "chessboard" of the battlefield, pieces which are deployed according to rules and principles that remain to be determined.

Thus, description, that spectacle to-be-seen, is not a simple trace of the real, but an enclosed and divided scene, naturalized through the interplay of organic and anatomical metaphors—"every joint of that great body"—and from these analogies a diagram of the battle emerges, a schema of "those chess moves" which, by becoming delineated space, take on meaning. Moreover, the scene so arranged can converge on one of two figures: the chessboard and its pieces, or the absent player whose presence is sensed and felt—"Napoleon whom I will not show." Description can therefore be organized from two centers of focus: the first, an exhaustive ordering, takes the categorical form of a "table,"[14] a grid, while the second, non-represented, is occupied by the Emperor not encompassed within the framework. All lines of the diagram point to the non-circumscribed place of the one not included in the space of representation. And yet a problem comes to the fore since attention is—or must be—fixed simultaneously on the place of representation and on the imagined site where he who manipulates from afar the shifts and moves on the chessboard is thought to be.

The project of the novel unfolds both as the representation of a scene and as the unveiling of its organizational principles; in other words, as product and process. Hence the outline hesitates between two spaces, recognizes them as distinct, but, by superimposing them, attempts to bring them to a single center of focus. This impossible play of perception, fragmented and atomized, but simultaneously framed, centered, and feasible in pictorial organization, dooms the writing project to failure. To superimpose the vanishing point on the chessboard is, on the one hand, to imagine narrative in terms of pictorial representation, but, on the other, to deny the possibility of realistic writing arising from the concatenation of a gridded space and a vanishing point. It is, also, not to recognize the need for a space proper to narrative. Thought of too much in terms of the pictorial to function as narrative, and incapable of articulating two heterogeneous spaces at the same time, *La Bataille* could not be written and remained an impossible book.

Nonetheless, what is the spatial order of the Balzacian novel and how does this process of grid and vanishing point function as a constituent structure of the realistic narrative? From a purely programmatic perspective, we shall limit ourselves to a brief examination of *La Maison du chat-qui-pelote*, the first scene of *La Comédie humaine*, of which it has been written that the misadventures of a portrait are its principal theme. The text opens with the evocation of an abolished, hence imagined, place. Description will attempt to present(ify) this space—rather, re-present it—to a narratee in the form of a house haunted by characters long since disappeared: "Half way down the rue Saint-Denis, almost at the corner of the rue du Petit-Lion, *there once was* one of those delightful houses..." (I, 39). What is given to be seen (visualized) is organized according to the two-fold principle of a progressive focalization on the fictive dwelling and of the positioning of a spatial network that delineates and locates different spatial planes within a clearly determined grid.

This framed, ordered, and classified topos is examined, interpreted, and commented on so that, although certain figures of knowledge are organized according to principles of resemblance ("one of those delightful houses which enable historians to reconstruct old Paris by analogy"), others, on the contrary, arise from a need for classification. Thus, the front of the house, covered with geometrical figures ("the threatening walls ... seemed to have been decorated with hieroglyphics. What other name could the idler give to the X's and V's that were traced on the façade by the transverse or diagonal wooden beams in the plaster"), must be deciphered through recourse to technical knowledge—spatio-temporal measure—for example, that of the "historian" or the "archaeologist,"[15] or by means of classificatory knowledge such as that introduced by "Cuvier [who found] antideluvian debris in the quarries" (I, 95). Such specialized knowledge in the text is contrasted with that of the idler who can identify signs but, unable to reconstitute the laws of their combination, simply stays at the level of effects and appearances.

The same opposition, it will be seen, is sustained in the very case of the sign, that "ancient picture representing a cat winding a ball of wool" which, for a short moment, holds the attention of the stranger standing watch in front of the house. This visual motivation becomes an immediate pretext for the narrator's commentary, displaying his knowledge of painting and graphics: "Sun and rain had worn away ... the letters of that inscription in which U's and V's had changed places in obedience to the laws of old-world orthography" (I, 41). Unlike Parisian merchants for whom "the etymology of these signs seems so whimsical," the narrator is able to reconstitute their origins, the meaning of those "dead pictures of once living pictures by which our roguish ancestors contrived to tempt customers into their shops." A dizzying *mise en abyme* of the process of representation, the nonexistent sign, delimited and organized by means of language, is a dead picture whose code has now been lost, but which once signalled the site of a place long since disappeared, and referred to a model (a living picture) which established arbitrary interplay with the designated space of commerce. This closed and completed universe of correspondences, this extinct, centered, and circumscribed world, where frames echo frames and signs mirror one another, is reproduced analogically in the geometric arrangement of the façade of M. Guillaume's house, "this relic of the civil life of the sixteenth century [which] offered more than one problem to the consideration of an observer."

In an article entitled "Balzac and the Problem of the Subject," Fredric Jameson (1980) sees in *La Maison du chat-qui-pelote* the setting into play of narrative strategies preceding the constitution of the bourgeois subject which mark a "blockage of its development." Thus, for Jameson (1980:69) the emblematic M. Guillaume would be presented as a character-sign, that is, as a totality of significations to be revealed, in which, according to Althusser, "each element is expressive of the entire totality, as 'pars totalis.'" Contrary to Jameson, for whom the "blocked subject will find its only possible outlet in madness and insanity," we would like to suggest that this introductory narrative to the *Comédie humaine* nevertheless brings about the formation of a new space, another space of knowledge.

Although M. Guillaume's closed universe is organized as a gridded, rationalized, ordered, and measured space, it is presented from the outset not only as vanished but also as closely linked to a transitional period, namely the end of the First Empire. The fictional observer who notes and describes in detail the house's geometric façade catches a glimpse of Augustine, the beautiful younger daughter of the family, who suddenly appears at a third story window. Then follows the inevitable Balzacian portrait which contrasts the fragility, whiteness, and grace of the girl to the roughness, blackness, and decay of the frame. An analepsis of several months allows us to piece together the reasons why the young man happens to be in front of the merchant's house and suggests that just his very presence in that place could cause an accident, a rift, a catastrophe in that totality of signification, a breach which would give free rein to the unfolding of narrative. Passing by chance in front of the darkened shop, the young man unexpectedly glimpses a family scene and remains for "a moment to gaze at a picture which might have arrested every painter in the world" (I, 52). The description that follows is too well known to spend much time on. The main thing to remember here is that the scene, perceived and described as a "natural picture," is framed and organized from a center of focus having as its principal figure Augustine, whose face is completely illuminated by lamplight. The initial verbal representation gives way to an actual setting into painting, executed later on by the young artist. A first canvas, representing the whole interior scene referred to above, and a second one, a separate portrait of Augustine, are both displayed at the Salon to attract the attention of the subjects who unknowingly inspired them. Augustine's portrait—"a life-like work awarded by the public ... the crown which Girodet himself had hung over it"—which is detached from the family setting and made to occupy another space, that of desire, of love, becomes the means by which the excentric painter introduces himself into the centered and organized space of the Guillaume household. The portrait, taken away and removed from its original topos, becomes a vanishing point and its displacement signals a radical disjunction and severance from the space of order and measure which inaugurated and set the narrative in motion. We will recall the emblematic scene of the inventory during which the Guillaume family and all the clerks, except for Augustine, periodically evaluated, assessed, classified, ranked, and listed the objects in a ledger (the *table*, the center of knowledge in the seventeenth and eighteenth centuries, referred to by Foucault), so as to set their exact value: "Every bale was turned over and the length verified ... the retail price was set... How much H-N-Z?—All sold. What is left of that X?... Carry over to three A all of J-J, all of M-P and the rest of V-D-O" (I, 59).

Master of another knowledge, the painter succeeds in giving free rein to his desire by marrying Augustine and introducing her into another milieu where the young woman's original knowledge is worthless and decentered. Soon after his marriage to Augustine, Sommervieux takes the Duchess of Carigliano as his mistress and gives her his wife's portrait as a pledge of love. By accident Augustine learns of the Duchess's existence and decides to pay her a visit, "not to ask her to give back her husband's heart but to learn the arts by which it had been captured" (I, 84). In that world of desire, space and its objects are neither framed nor delineated but rather echo one another through complex and secret correspondences. In the midst of that blurred totality, the object-sign, coextensive with other objects surrounding it and with which it is combined, designates a subject's presence without specifying or even identifying it. Moreover, when Augustine meets the Duchess, the absence of all physical description prevents any focusing on her, since frame and subject, topos and portrait are non-delineated, interchangeable, and, in the final analysis, convertible into one another. The meaning, the significance of the dissolved and hazy space of seduction are inaccessible and remain literally closed to the uninitiated: "... there was here something impenetrable in the disorder as in the symmetry, and to the simple-minded young Augustine all was a sealed letter" (I, 85). Not expecting "the pleasure of seeing the original here face to face with the copy," the Duchess gives the portrait back to Augustine so that, "armed with such a talisman" (I, 91), she can once again be the center of her husband's affections. The young wife shows the picture to the painter who, beside himself with rage, destroys the portrait and frame. In the morning "scattered fragments of a torn canvas and the broken pieces of a large gilt picture frame" (I, 93) are found on the floor. Decentered, indeed unframed and in pieces, the character, deprived of all identifiable spatial support, becomes indistinct, loses all possibility of fixation, and simply fades away into nothingness.

On the one hand, *La Bataille* remains an impossible book for want of a space specific to narrative; on the other, through the interplay of the descriptive and the pictorial, *La Maison du chat-qui-pelote* does, in fact, succeed in constructing a space, the exact status of which is problematical, however. The narrative initially sets into place a completed, ordered, measurable space, which, through untimely fate—that is, an accidental glimpse—is transformed into another, disturbing, unframed, and fragmented space, a vague and undecidable libidinal space where the subject, belonging to another time, another place, cannot be constituted. And, to paraphrase Michel Foucault, if the center of knowledge in the Classical Age is the table, diagrammatical classification, order, and measure which squares space, then the Balzacian text functions as a device which delineates and structures spaces, decomposes and recomposes them according to the general principle of establishing continuity and order, suddenly followed by rift and division.

This process of order and fragmentation, gridding and vanishing point is also the structuring principle of many other of Balzac's texts. Frenhofer, for example, the painter who ends up mad in *Le Chef d'oeuvre inconnu*, refuses to resort to line, drawing, sketch, and produces a formless space of "confused masses of color and a multitude of fantastical lines" (X, 436). Moreover, the narrator takes pains to stress that the painter resembles one of Rembrandt's characters out of frame, in the same way that Chabert is compared to "a portrait by Rembrandt without a frame" (III, 321). A decentered character from the point of view of society and family, Chabert ends up on the fringes of society in Bicêtre and spends his time with a stick in hand "drawing lines in the sand" (III, 372) which are uncontrolled arabesques that can in no way be converted into closed and centered geometric figures. The final picture of

Chabert tracing insane and erratic lines is reminiscent of the clausula in *Ferragus* describing the former leader of the Dévorants, broken and senile, striding along the promenade of the Observatory, an open and undifferentiated space, following, with a "vacant eye" (V, 903) the unpredictable and capricious shifts of the jack of the bowlers who occasionally use the old man's stick as a derisive unit of measure. These indecisive and indeterminable comings and goings are final moments in the constitution of a new space, a new knowledge where the subject cannot find a place; they are the end terms of transformational processes that take archaic spaces and knowledge originally inscribed in the text, redistribute them, and represent them according to an incoherent and incomprehensible logic— troubled and troubling spaces of transition to be reproduced and re-articulated in Balzac's later texts according to modalities that remain to be defined and described.[16]

NOTES

1. Or the example of Adeline Fischer's portrait: "These beautiful creatures all have something in common, Bianca Capella, whose portrait is one of Bronzino's masterpieces; Jean Goujon's Venus... Signora Olympia whose portrait adorns the Doria Gallery..." (VII, 74).

2. Or the example of Montriveau's portrait: "The principal characteristic of his great, square-hewn head was the thick luxuriant-black hair which framed his face, and gave him a strikingly close resemblance to General Kléber" (V, 946).

3. For example, at the beginning of *La Maison du chat-qui-pelote*, the description of the Guillaume family, initially perceived as the written transcription of a genre painting, later on becomes the subject of an actual canvas by Sommervieux.

4. Quoted by Mme Fargeaud-Ambrière (1976) in her critical apparatus for l'*Avant-propos* of *La Comédie humaine*.

5. "You must believe that the author of *Les Paysans* was knowledgeable enough about the times he lived in to know that Cuirassiers did not belong to the Imperial Guard. He would like to indicate, here and now, that in his study he has the uniforms of the armies under the Republic, the Empire, the Restoration, as well as a collection of all the military costumes of the countries that France had as allies or enemies. He also has more works on the wars of 1792 to 1815 than a Maréchal of France" (IX, 1290).

6. In August 1834, precisely with regard to *La Bataille*, Balzac asked Mme Hanska for the following information: "I really need to see Vienna. I must explore the fields of Wagram and Essling before next July. I especially need engravings representing the uniforms of the German army which I must purchase. Be kind enough to tell me if they do exist" (1967: I, 247). He makes the same type of request in January 1844: "I forgot, I was so sorry to leave, when I think that all the uniforms of the Russian army can be found in Petersburg; please use Colmann to do some research on this for me. I need colored engravings and, especially in French, the names of the weapons and the regiments during Russia's wars with France" (Balzac 1968:340).

7. "'Monsieur,' said Derville, 'to whom have I the honor of speaking?' 'To Colonel Chabert,' 'Which?' 'He who was killed at Eylau,' answered the old man. On hearing this strange speech, the lawyer and his clerk glanced at each other, as much as to say: 'He is mad'" (III, 322).

8. "Accustomed, no doubt, to gauge men, he very politely addressed the office boy, hoping to get a civil answer from him" (III, 315).

9. "Allow me here to refer to a detail of which I could know nothing till after the event, which, after all, I must speak of as my death" (III, 324).

10. "… but all the while paying attention to the deceased colonel, he leafed through his files" (III, 323).

11. It should be noted here that the narrator no longer says "the deceased colonel" as he did above.

12. Married under the Empire to Count Ferraud, shortly after Chabert's official death, Rose Chapotel, a former *grisette* at the Palais Royal, is now desperate at the idea of losing her second husband who is beginning to regret this union and, hoping to obtain a peerage, would find it advantageous to have their marriage annulled.

13. Cf. L. Althusser, quoted by Baudry (1968:128): "An ideology is a system with its own logic and rigor of representations (images, myths, ideas or concepts as the case may be), endowed with an existence and an historical role within a given society… Ideology is really a system of representations, but these representations are independent of actual consciousness."

14. Cf. M. Foucault (1970:74–75): "The sciences always carry within themselves the project, however remote it may be, of an exhaustive ordering of the world; they are always directed too, towards the discovery of simple elements and their progressive combination; and in their centre they form a table on which knowledge is displayed in a system contemporaneous with itself. The centre of knowledge in the seventeenth and eighteenth centuries is the *table*. As for the great controversies that occupied men's minds, these are accommodated quite naturally in the folds of this organization."

15. "We also know what methodological importance these 'natural' allocations assumed, at the end of the eighteenth century... And it is in this classified time, in this squared and spatialized development, that the historians of the nineteenth century were to undertake the creation of a history that could at last be 'true'—in other words, liberating from Classical rationality, from its ordering and theodicy: a history restored to the irruptive violence of time" (Foucault 1970:131–132).

16. Some of the ideas expressed on what could be termed "the space of knowledge" in Balzacian fiction develop points made by Fredric Jameson in a lecture, entitled "The Bourgeois Revolution and the Aesthetic Text (Flaubert)," which was given at the University of Toronto, April 1982.

References

Balzac, H. de, 1967 (I); 1968 (II). *Lettres à Madame Hanska* (Paris: Les Bibliophiles de l'Originale). 1976–1981 *La Comédie humaine*, XII vols. (Paris: Gallimard, Pléiade).

Barthes, R., 1974. *S/Z* (New York: Hill and Wang).

Baudry, J.L., 1968. "Ecriture, fiction, idéologie," in: *Théorie d'ensemble* (Paris: Seuil).

Bonnard, O., 1969. *La Peinture dans la création balzacienne* (Genève: Droz).

Fargeaud-Ambrière, M., 1976. "Documents, notes et variantes de l'*Avant-propos* de *La Comédie humaine*," in *Balzac, La Comédie humaine* (Paris: Gallimard, Pléiade).

Foucault, M., 1970. *The Order of Things* (London: Tavistock).

Jameson, F., 1980. "Balzac et le problème du sujet," in Le Huenen and Perron, eds. *Le Roman de Balzac* (Montréal: Didier).

Le Huenen, R. and P. Perron, 1980. *Balzac, sémiotique du personnage romanesque: l'exemple d'"Eugénie Grandet"* (Montréal/Paris: Didier érudition).

Vannier, B., 1972. *L'inscription du corps* (Paris: Klincksieck).

D. A. MILLER

Balzac's Illusions Lost and Found

For F. M.

It has become easy to show how the closural decorums set up by a text are exceeded by the disseminal operations of language, narrative, or desire—so easy in fact that the demonstration now proceeds as predictably as any other ritual. Whenever a text makes confident claims to cognition, these will soon be rendered undecidable, and whatever ideological projects it advances will in the course of their elaboration be disrupted, "internally distanciated." Full, focused psychological subjects will be emptied out and decentered as invariably as desire will resurface at the very site of its apparent containment. Altogether it would seem as though the possibility of a fixed, settled closure were recovered in the fixed, settled character of the arguments against it.

Yet the point of remarking the orthodoxy of recent thinking about closure is not to dismiss the considerable productivity of such thinking, and far less to deny the textual phenomenon to which it so profitably calls attention. Rather, to the extent that the "failure of closure" has been transformed into a compelling, even compulsive critical success, it may well be a text's most powerful and seductive effect. In recent criticism, for instance, sometimes despite the most rigorous intentions to the contrary, the effect has operated to preserve for literature—as the very category of the literary—an almost or even frankly ontological difference from the worldly discourses in which it would otherwise be implicated. Whether the failure of

From *Yale French Studies* 67. ©1984 by Yale University.

closure is greeted with philosophical melancholy (over the fact that meaning can never be pinned down), political relief (that a work's suspect ideological messages don't finally cohere), or erotic celebration (of a desire that erupts when and where it is least wanted), it always gives evidence of a process which is, on one hand, inherent in textuality and, on the other, radically outside and subversive of all that a given text mundanely "wants to say." Capable of demystifying the official projects to which it is inevitably committed, literature would thereby transcend them and constitute itself as a distinct and separate category with its own peculiar privilege. What this privilege allows is suggested if we consider the quasi-political values that implicitly invest its affirmation. As the contest is usually staged, closure enfolds the modalities of a massive, right-thinking repression, while its various "others" carry the more delicate, but also lighter burden of subtle, unconventional subversion. Due allowance made for the newly bleak and "disturbing" values to which it now plays host, literature thus tends to remain what it has been since the category first came into its own in the nineteenth century: a sanctuary for values seeking refuge from an inhospitable world.

Suppose, then, we understand the failure of closure as a textual ruse designed to produce, among others, this very effect: the "literature-effect." Suppose we take that coming-to-fail not as a negative phenomenon, but as a positive strategy, not disruptive but constitutive of a text's social implication and usefulness. Suppose we assume, in other words, that a text has "always already" put to use that which appears to bring the order of its discourse into question. Our attention would shift accordingly from the "problem" of closure to the various textual-cultural interests involved in producing and maintaining the problem. And once the dimension of power were thus introduced into the discussion of closure, then the enterprise of the traditional novel, for instance, which may be situated precisely at the threshold of the modern problematics of closure, would also have to be redefined. It would no longer (or not just) be the doomed attempt to produce a stable, centered subject in a stable, centered social order, but rather (or in addition) the more successful task of forming a subject habituated to displacement and psychic mobility, in a social order whose power is secured through a series of "more or less cunning decompositions."[1] The phrase comes from Balzac, whose work (specifically, the so-called Vautrin trilogy: *Père Goriot*, *Illusions perdues*, and *Splendeurs et misères des courtisanes*) will be used to broach such a redefinition in what follows.[2]

We begin with an ending:

Rastignac, resté seul, fit quelques pas vers le haut du cimetière et vit Paris tortueusement couché le long des deux rives de la Seine où commençaient à briller les lumières. Ses yeux s'attachèrent presque avidement entre la colonne de la place Vendôme et le dôme des Invalides, là où vivait ce beau monde dans lequel il avait voulu pénétrer. Il lança sur cette ruche bourdonnant un regard qui semblait par avance en pomper le miel, et dit ces mots grandioses: "A nous deux maintenant!"

Et pour premier acte du défi qu'il portait à la Société, Rastignac alla dîner chez madame de Nucingen. [*PG* 309]

Thus left alone, Rastignac walked a few steps to the highest part of the cemetery, and saw Paris spread out below on both banks of the winding Seine. Lights were beginning to twinkle here and there. His gaze fixed almost avidly upon the space that lay between the column of the Place Vendôme and the dome of the Invalides; there lay the splendid world that he had wished to gain. He eyed that humming hive with a look that foretold its despoliation, as if he already felt on his lips the sweetness of its honey, and said with superb defiance,

"It's war between us now!"

And by way of throwing down the gauntlet to Society, Rastignac went to dine with Madame de Nucingen. [*OG* 304]

Earlier in *Père Goriot* Balzac told us that "l'étudiant n'était pas encore arrivé au point d'où l'homme peut contempler le cours de la vie et la juger" (245) ["the student had not yet reached that stage in his development when he could stand aside from the current of life, and consider it with detachment" (242)], but now, as Rastignac stands on the heights of Père Lachaise above the *beau monde* of Paris that submits obligingly to his gaze, he appears to have attained that promised position of raised consciousness and total vision. As Peter Brooks comments, "society and city have been seized in their totality and essence, in a gathering together of essential structures, relations, meanings made legible."[3] The scene thus stages a moment of truth, in which, having relinquished his illusions about the world, Rastignac comes into possession of the knowledge that will unlock for him the mysteries of Paris. Furthermore, just as the bewildering confusion that society initially presented to Rastignac had its subjective counterpart in his abundantly complicated psychology, so the moment at which Rastignac recognizes the essential orderliness of the social order coincides with a psychological simplification, in which his character, purged of the blurring sentimentality that he sheds as "sa dernière larme de jeune homme," ["the last tear of his youth"] is confirmed in its strength and decisiveness. The completion of education thus involves, in addition to the acquisition of knowledge, a depletion of the subject who comes to know. And on the basis of such cognitive and psychological clarifications, the novel grounds the persuasiveness of its ending: not as an arbitrary end point, but as an appropriate closure. For though the novel closes by conspicuously opening a new narrative sequence—*aller dîner*, as Roland Barthes might have encoded it—such blatant open-endedness only testifies to a career whose direction and final felicitous destiny are so assured that it can go without telling. Confirmation is provided in the rest of *La Comédie humaine*, where this career is alluded to in its various stages, but Rastignac never again appears as its full-fledged protagonist.

All of this would be conventional enough—the traditional novel typically secures its conclusion as a moment of truth whose dominant mode is psychological resolution—if the ending did not simultaneously negate all that it claims for itself as such. For with Paris "tortueusement couché" ["spread out below"] under the gaze that Rastignac "throws" (*lança*) upon it, as though the city were a beehive whose honey he had already begun appropriating, the moment of truth is at the same time a scene of erotic fascination, a dramatic relapsing into an acute state of desire. And if, as Balzac insists throughout the *Comédie*, the possession of knowledge coincides with the renunciation of desire,[4] then Rastignac's vision, though no longer lachrymose, may be none the less blinded. The eroticism of his gaze dictates quite naturally his return visit to Madame de Nucingen, and also makes for the irony of the grandiose challenge that licenses that visit. "A nous deux" can indicate an alliance as well as an opposition,[5] and Rastignac's "bad faith" is rooted in the fact that he can find no better way of beating Society than by wanting to join with it. Much as the truth about the world is revealed to be only the truth of one's desire for the world, the apparently bellicose gesture merely facilitates submission to the world as it is socially given. Similarly, psychological fulfilment—implicitly, the chief goal of desire—will demand for its realization the evacuation of psychology in a subject whose inwardness has been strictly reduced to the internalization of social codes, norms, and practices. In none of Rastignac's subsequent appearances in the *Comédie* is he equipped with a psychology remotely comparable in extent or depth to the one he is given in *Père Goriot*. The ample "point of view" that he has provided in this novel will henceforward be limited to the objectively registered behavior of a role: here the dandy, there the *intriguant*, finally—summing up and rewarding the entire process of "self-discipline"—the Minister of the Interior. It is as though his richly resistant subjectivity had become a function of his own desire for success, a desire which in the course of being realized eliminated the very possibility of its being "his own." Never will Balzac show Rastignac in a moment of gratification, in contented, triumphant possession of the humming Parisian hive he avidly covets here. He may be a brilliant success, but so far as we know, he never *has* a brilliant success, for that success has been permitted by the replacement of a psychological subject by its social functioning. In this light, the apparently superficial open-endedness of the novel's last recorded action becomes more substantial. Unlike, say, in Jane Austen or Trollope, where a character's final identification with the social order issues in a nonnarratable state of affairs, here that identification commits Rastignac to further action in the world, to ongoing narrative. Whether or not the subsequent stories are actually told matters less than the fact that they are necessarily entailed.

The scene thus situates for us a number of paradoxes. The lucid moment of truth is also a blinding moment of erotic fascination. The assumption of a critical distance from Society promotes a thorough-going integration into it. The self comes into its own at the same time as it is voided of its own inwardness. And finally, the moment of closure only signals the displacement of narrative and the necessity of its further production. I shall suggest that what holds these paradoxes together, determining their social value, is the structure of Balzacian "disillusionment." Though Brooks is certainly right to posit Rastignac's "disillusioned consciousness" behind "the gesture of possession" it entitles him to make,[6] this is perhaps a stranger phenomenon than he quite shows. How is it that the disillusioned consciousness—generally thought (and sometimes with Balzac's own novels for examples) to be an unhappy one whose insights doom it to passivity and withdrawal—turns a profit? We need to focus on the pure potentiality of the disillusioned moment here: bounded on one side by Rastignac's release (from the specific commitments and investments he has just foregone) and on the other by his subjection (to the commitments and investments he must now proceed to make). His "gesture of possession" is thus better named his fantasy of possession, of the possibility of all things being possessed: a possibility that must vanish as soon as one thing actually *is* possessed, when the restrictions that this moment derives its euphoria from suspending must be resumed, and when, as a result, the ambiguity of that possession (of it or by it) will come to impose itself. "A nous deux maintenant!" arrests Rastignac, so to speak, on the threshold of exchange: where, having liquidated one set of goods and not yet having fully bargained for another, he seems exuberantly capable of appropriating all qualities insofar as he might appropriate any. This exhilarating moment, therefore, is a projection, an abstract form demanding its content, an empty exchange awaiting its articles. Precisely as such, however, it requires for its completion a sequel—the concrete specification of Rastignac's vision—which must of necessity abolish it and mark the return to the committed, constrained state of affairs preceding it. And already, we note, this return is anticipated in the disproportion that ironizes Rastignac's passage from his grand and universal challenge to the petty and particular "premier acte" that it inspires.

In *Illusions perdues*, disillusionment is worked through beyond the moment of pure potentiality to its necessary aftermath, and at every point where the well-advertised operation of the title is shown to occur, whatever pathos is associated with losing illusions might be more appropriately assigned to the inevitability of finding them again. Since disillusionment is often considered the quintessential nineteenth-century experience, it becomes particularly interesting to observe that, in the very novel that is often considered the supreme representation of this experience, no disillusionment really occurs. Certainly, Lucien de Rubempré repeatedly undergoes what might be called a phenomenology of disillusionment, though the fact of repetition would alone be sufficient to cast doubt on its authenticity. Consistently, moreover, the moment of ostensible disillusion-ment is exposed as a mere phase: a psychological adjustment which permits the transition from one "illusion" to another, structurally identical to it. An exemplary instance of this takes place during Lucien's visit to the Paris Opera. "Doublement éclairé" ["Doubly enlightened"] by the Parisian *monde* and by madame d'Espard, Lucien "vit enfin dans la pauvre Anaïs de Nègrepelisse la femme réelle," ["saw at length poor Anaïs de Nègrepelisse as she really was"] and the real woman proves to be "grande, sèche, couperosée, fanée, plus que rousse, anguleuse, guindée, précieuse, prétentieuse, provinciale dans son parler, mal arrangée surtout!" (*IP* 181) ["a tall, thin withered woman with a blotched complexion, red hair, angular, stiff and affected in her manner, precious in her tastes, provincial in her speech, and, above all, badly dressed!" (*LI* 179)] But this enlightened perception is only an effect of Lucien's dazzled submission to the mediation of Parisian society. On one hand, his evidently disabused vision sees more than is there, for Louise, the text has just reminded us, "était restée la même" ["was still the same."] On the other, it doesn't see enough: "Lucien ne devinait pas le changement que feraient dans la personne de Louise une écharpe roulée autour du cou, une jolie robe, une élégante coiffure et les conseils de madame d'Espard" (182) ["Lucien could not foresee the change that was soon to be wrought in

Louise's appearance by a scarf to soften the line of her neck, a well-cut dress, a different hairstyle, and Mme d'Espard's advice" (180).] The functioning of his ostensible disillusionment *within* an economy of illusion, tenaciously conserving the energy of its cathexes, becomes explicit when we find that "en perdant ses illusions sur madame de Bargeton.... il fut fasciné par madame d'Espard; et il s'amouracha d'elle aussitôt.... [C]ette reine apparaissait au poète comme madame de Bargeton lui était apparue à Angoulême" (190–91) ["as his illusions about Mme de Bargeton faded ... under the spell of Mme d'Espard, he fell in love with her on the spot.... (T)his queen seemed to the poet all that Mme de Bargeton had seemed to him in Angoulême" (*LI* 189).] The same pattern in which a disillusionment-effect serves the displacement of illusion, thus preserving it, can be seen throughout the novel. During the supper at Florine's, thanks to Lousteau's cynical revelations about the world of journalism, Lucien "avait ... vu les choses comme elles sont" (360) ["had seen things as they are."] But the consequence of this insight is that "il jouissait avec ivresse de cette société spirituelle" ["he was intoxicated with the pleasure of being in such intellectually brilliant society." (329).] Far from discouraging a career in journalism, Lousteau's dismal *tableau* actually seduces Lucien into one, and the illusion about literature is simply exchanged—via the delusion of disillusionment—for an analogous illusion about journalism. Not dissimilarly, at the end of the novel, having taken Carlos Herrera's illuminating "cours" on history and ethics, Lucien is simultaneously taken by "le charme de cette conversation cynique" (713) ["the charm of this cynical discourse" (658)], with the result that he is once again willing to undertake the social itinerary he was preparing to abandon forever. An evidently profound disillusionment thus "ends" the novel, as in *Père Goriot*, by laying claim to a new beginning. In the place of an ending, the novel simply declares its intention, along with its protagonist, to *trade places*: "Quant à Lucien, son retour à Paris est du domaine des *Scènes de la vie parisienne*" (752) ["As for Lucien, his return to Paris belongs to the *Scènes de la vie Parisienne*" (695).] What is tendered in exchange for closure is the very fact of exchange itself.

It is hardly a question of denying the social "alienation" as which disillusionment is demonstrably rehearsed. To the extent that he has been committed to the archaic desire for particular objects or persons in a world requiring their perpetual exchange, the Balzacian *ambitieux* regularly encounters a stinging dispossession: of his writing, his success, his lover, etc.[7] But unlike many of its readers, Balzac's fiction never hypostatizes this aspect of disillusionment (as the evidence of a critical consciousness), but places it within a more inclusive process which quickly reappropriates it. Like

Rastignac's, Lucien's disillusionment is the psychological effect and condition of an exchange. In a society rigorously structured on the principle of exchange, therefore, disillusionment cannot be, as Theodor W. Adorno has claimed, "the experience by which men are split off from their social function," but rather the experience in which they are identified with this function most completely.[8] Nor is it even the case that the alienation Adorno finds here serves merely to mask a deep-seated adaptation, since, in a precise sense, the alienation *is* the adaptation. For as much as desire is checked in this experience, it is commensurately freed, unbound from its investment in a particular person or object and rendered once more available for investments to come. Disillusionment "mobilizes" desire in both senses of the word: on one hand, it frees desire into circulation and thereby, on the other hand, in a society whose functioning demands just such circulation (of money, women, roles, stories), it *constrains desire to active duty*. Accordingly, insofar as desire is momentarily decathected in disillusionment, it promotes in the long run an overall libidinal investment in the social processes themselves, dominated by categories of exchange and transfer. It betokens grief, then, only as does Freudian "mourning": in the work of surmounting grief. Hence, though ambition regularly issues in disillusionment, disillusionment regularly issues in renewed ambition, often reshaped as well into a less vulnerable, more adequate form.

It follows that the structure of disillusionment must be misunderstood when approached from the point of view of a character's psychology, which is chiefly determined by its relationship to this structure. It is no more naive to take Lucien's disillusionment at face value than it is, peering into his character, to reduce the social conformism that emerges from his disillusionment to categories of moral psychology such as self-deception, hypocrisy, and the like. The automatic quality of the process by which one illusion is "lost" and almost simultaneously replaced by another suggests that the structural mechanism at work far transcends the grasp of either the psychology of a character or the psychologism of a reader. One notices that Lousteau preaches against journalism from within the practice of it, and by now it should not be hard to see that the preaching is exactly what enables the practice. As, par excellence, the "stock-exchange of the spirit," journalism requires its practitioners to persevere in disillusionment to the point where the "moment" of disillusionment becomes the enduring state of cynicism. Such cynicism, considered as the impoverished, all but depleted psychology of the mechanism of exchange, is the indispensable condition of success in Balzac. If Rastignac succeeds where Lucien fails, it is not on account of the usual differences of character brought forward when this question is raised.

Rastignac's manly decisiveness and Lucien's effeminate abulia are traits which merely reverse, by way of authorial value judgment, the relationship of each to the mechanism in operation. It is rather the determined Rastignac than the flighty Lucien who is the more truly mobile protagonist, willingly identifying himself, not with particular objects on either side of exchange, as Lucien tends to do, but with the sheer process of exchanging them. At all events, the disillusionment of neither ever mounts the slightest resistance to the social order whose good things the one goes on to "possess" only because, unlike the other, he knows when and how to relinquish them. And as we will see in a moment, social conformism motivates even the most disabused and antisocial of Balzac's characters, Carlos Herrera-Vautrin himself. Ultimately, *Illusions perdues* demonstrates that no authentic disillusionment ever occurs in the social world to suggest that no such disillusionment ever *can* occur there. This, I think, is finally how we ought to gloss the novel's curiously tautological title. For if, as Lucien says in a letter to Louise, illusion is the name we give to belief "plus tard" (201), after, that is, it has been given up, then an illusion is always already lost, and a nonredundant rendering of the title would be either *Croyances perdues* or simply *Illusions*. Unless, of course, as I have been suggesting, what is lost is precisely the practicability of losing illusions, in a world which has radically eliminated the possibility of negation.

Splendeurs et misères des courtisanes presents the most extreme version of the loss-of-lost-illusions, which, in the last incarnation of Vautrin, it reenacts as an identification of criminality with the police. But the transformation of the escaped convict into the chief of the Parisian Sûreté does not simply unmask the apparent resistances of criminality, which proves ultimately bound to the very power that is set against it; it redefines the police as well, whose elaborate activities can no longer be plausibly reduced to the repressive task of enforcing the interdicts of the law. The shock of Vautrin's cop-out is mitigated by the fact that what the narrative here realizes has been thematically anticipated from the beginning: "On ne peut devenir que ce qu'on est" (*S & M* 80) ["You can't become what you aren't" (*HHL* 75).] On one hand, the arch-criminal works exactly like the police. Vautrin has no trouble securing for Esther the police document that will confer on the prostitute her official rehabilitation—or even in getting the resume in an agent's dossier from the Prefect of Police himself. At one point, Vautrin's dress and manner can strike passers-by as that of a "gendarme déguisé" (72) ["a constable in disguise" (68)]; at another, he actually does disguise himself as a police magistrate sent by the Prefect to interrogate Peyrade. When the London police rid themselves of a troublesome murderess by sending her to

Paris, she simply enters Vautrin's own service, which the text doesn't hesitate to call a "contre-police" (268) ["counter-police"]. On the other hand, the police work exactly like criminals. Whereas passers-by might take Vautrin for a *gendarme déguisé*, "un homme d'esprit" would intuit the potential thief in Cotenson (127); and whereas Vautrin disguises himself as a policial emissary, Peyrade camouflages himself as a bohemian who loudly proclaims his "horreur de la police" (136) ["contempt for the Judicial Police" (113)]. And their criminality sometimes goes beyond mere appearance, as when Peyrade breaks the rules of the force by hiring himself out as a private detective to Nucingen, or when, on a larger, world-historical stage, he organizes with Corentin and Cotenson a "Contre-Police" for Louis XVIII (143). Continually analogized to one another—Carlos Herrera is the Spanish Corentin, Paccard is Vautrin's Peyrade, etc.—police and criminals are quasi-instinctively brought together "sans le savoir" (179) ["without knowing it" (153)] in the duel that only the name of legitimacy prevents from being a perfect play of mirrors.

The affinity, even the interchangeability of criminals and police is, of course, a commonplace of nineteenth-century fiction, where it typically functions to consolidate the field of delinquency as distinct from the realm of middle-class civil society. The latter can then be qualified as both uncontaminated by crime and unencumbered by the visible and explicit constraints of the police. Preoccupied in chasing one another, cops and robbers thereby seem to leave *us* alone.[9] But Balzac releases the cops and robbers from the quarantine in which they are usually confined by explicitly connecting police practices—technically the same as criminal ones—to the practices of the social world at large. "A Paris, comme en province, tout se sait. La police de la rue de Jérusalem n'est pas si bien faite que celle du monde, où chacun s'espionne sans le savoir" (259). ["In Paris, as in the provinces, everything gets around. The police in the rue de Jérusalem is not so well organized as that of society, where everyone spies on everybody without knowing that he is doing it." (217)] Indeed, the characteristic excitements produced by Balzac's representation of the social world come precisely at those moments when social banality suddenly appears charged with the designs of a vigorous micropolitics: when the Camusots' dull "chambre à coucher" [bed chamber], for example, becomes a lively "chambre de délibération [council-chamber]." The social *milieu* thus ceases to be a "middle" separating two extremes from one another and from itself. And it loses this protective integrity in other ways as well. The theme of prostitution, for instance, scandalously migrates across class barriers from Esther to the society women like Madame de Sérizy and the Duchesse de

Maufrigneuse who embody a similar sexual license; and beyond gender divisions from "ce qu'il y avait de plus femme dans la femme" ["what is most female in the female"] to what is most female in the male as well, when, like Lucien, he is kept by his own kept woman.[10] Similarly, Vautrin's Platonized homosexuality provides the context for a heterosexuality in which sexual relations with women are subordinated to the far more cathected transactions of power between men, or to the narcissistic process of self-affirmation within men. Rather in the way that Freudian psychopathology ends up problematizing "normality," Balzac's representation of Society takes seemingly marginal and relatively external phenomena to epitomize what is central and inherent to it.

One might note that police and criminals express their affinity to one another, just as the social milieu expresses its affinity with both, "sans le savoir." One might suggest, in other words, that the various social continuities between center and circumference, norm and deviation, can only be manifested "unconsciously," cloaked in ignorance or denial. Yet if ignorance evidently makes for the smooth functioning of the social order, so and no less, paradoxically, does knowledge. Despite the many declarations of its supposed rarity, and though it is frequently divulged *in confidence*, as knowledge whose efficacy depends on keeping it secret, cynicism enjoys an extremely wide distribution in Balzac. It surfaces at least sporadically in nearly all his characters, who nonetheless remain incapable of producing or even contemplating any "escape" from the social order that is instead, as we say, cynically maintained. One thinks how, in a novelist like Dickens, cynicism is arrested both by the vague hope of social reorganization and—in the meanwhile, as it were—by the concrete project of reencoding social differences in less arbitrary, more stable moral terms. Or one thinks how, in Dostoevsky, cynicism is transcended in the divine, where such differences, superficial or substantial, no longer matter. If cynicism unfolds in Balzac to a fullness unparalleled in nineteenth-century fiction this is because the possible subversive social consequences of cynicism—feared and contained in the humanism of Dickens or the religion of Dostoevsky—are never in any danger of occurring. The best defense against the dreaded consequences of cynicism, Balzac shows, is cynicism itself: an eroticized knowledge constituted in too near a proximity to its object not to be another one of the latter's seductions. Cynicism finds its truth in conformism for the same reason that it finds its mode in paradox. Intimately bound alongside a *doxa* which provides the entire content of its reflections, it is always prevented from doing anything but pay hommage to the received opinions that, in its paradoxical turn, it too receives and passes on.

If Vautrin's practices do not differ from the police's, or even from those of the worldly on whose behalf the police do their work, why then does he fail to realize his schemes? After all, though these schemes are attributed to his antisocial desire for "vengeance," once Lucien becomes the vehicle of such vengeance, they conform perfectly to the most ordinary world aspirations. The failure to achieve them would be the more striking in proportion to the horrified admiration with which the text insists on Vautrin's social, policial expertise: the penetrating surveillance of his gaze, his unmatched mastery of cultural codes, his protean ability in disguise and plotting, the absolute autonomy of his will. If with all these advantages, Vautrin fails, it is finally because—supremely disillusioned as he imagines himself—he is not disillusioned enough. No less than his "creature," Vautrin is motivated by specular dreams of presence. The desire to be, to have Lucien, fatally attaches him to a specific object rather than to social processes themselves. Until his "conversion," Vautrin is an anachronism: an individualist not only in the obvious sense that his counterpolice must be a small, all-too-private enterprise in comparison to the vaster corporate-bureaucratic organization of the official force, but also because what inspires him are fantasies of individual possession, possession of individual objects by individual subjects. This comes out most clearly in his sexual infatuations, his victimization by types. For though Vautrin is able to see and manipulate "the arbitrariness of the sign" at most other levels, when confronted by a Rastignac or Lucien, he is entirely willing to grant the appearance all the erotic authority of the reality. A semiotician, as such, can never fall in love, for that experience is based on an assumption that the "outside" intrinsically corresponds to the "inside." (In this light, "tricking" would be the semiotician's chosen mode of sexual expression.) To the extent that Vautrin is enamoured, he abdicates his semiotic competence, not because he misreads the signs, but because in this domain he fails to understand them as signs at all. More broadly, Vautrin's untimely possessiveness comes out in his fantasies of power as something to have and to hold. One recalls from *Père Goriot* his dream of becoming a plantation owner in the American South, "avoir des esclaves, gagner quelques bons petits millions à vendre mes boeufs, mon tabac, mes bois, en vivant comme un souverain, en faisant mes volontés" (*PG* 126) ["to have slaves, earn a few nice little millions selling my cattle, my tobacco, my timber, living like a monarch, doing as I like" (*OG* 131).] Perhaps unsurprisingly, it is the arch-criminal in Balzac who entertains the most reactionary ancien-régime conception of power as a monolithic concentration in a single person. In a world, therefore, where he must encounter the elusively dispersed nature of modern power, diffused in techniques and norms, Vautrin is bound to disappointmemt. His creatures slip from his grasp, like Rastignac and Lucien, or play him false, like Europe and Paccard. Only with the loss of Lucien—not just the loss of the specific object of his ambition, but the loss of *ambition for a specific object*—do Vautrin's machinations at last bear fruit. He successfully replays the failed scenario of saving Lucien with Théodore Calvi, an ex-boyfriend from prison, with whom, suggestively, he has been only sexually, not romantically, involved.[11] In several senses, Vautrin ends by becoming Rastignac. Between the cynical detachment he assumes from society and that already built into and required by the proper functioning of that society, there is no longer any distance. Like Rastignac, moreover, Vautrin obstinately maintains an oppositional stance when the very possibility of one is about to collapse. If he now displaces his desire for revenge within the police force itself, proclaiming his intention to get even with Corentin, the emptiness of that desire is revealed in the last sentence of the novel: "Après avoir exercé ses fonctions pendant quinze ans, Jacques Collin s'est retiré vers 1845" (*S & M* 657) ["After having exercised his functions for some fifteen years, Jacques Collin retired in 1845 or thereabouts" (*HHL* 554).] The whole career of Vautrin as head of the Sûreté has been elided, as the sovereign power he fantasized and tried to possess has been attenuated in the exercise of "functions." Once again, the moment of true insight into the world leads to a psychological evacuation as well as a commitment to further narration, both here explicitly coinciding with the activity of policing. And the last incarnation of Vautrin is only the most obvious figure for a functionalism whose triumph, in the name of the police, affects the entire representation. In the same way that Vautrin is now transformed from character into functionary, so the densely woven novelistic texture of *Père Goriot* has been gradually voided to become the feuilletonesque narrative functions of *Splendeurs et misères*, and these functions are implied to be even barer in the elided adventures of Vautrin's police career. Clearing the ground not just for the routinized exercise of policing functions, but also for their routinized representation, Balzac's novel of disillusionment is appropriately concluded at the end of the Vautrin trilogy, but only because it there asks to be completed in a quite different genre which will nonetheless precisely honor its request: the *roman policier*.

It is perhaps already clear why we must extend our thematic discussion of disillusionment to the larger question of the operation of novelistic form. For the theme of disillusionment recurs in the Balzacian novel's own relationship to what it represents. To see the inadequacy of Lucien's perception of his own disenchantment, for instance, is at the same time to be installed within the disenchanted perception of the narration. When this narration disillusions us about disillusionment, it thereby reclaims the validity of the experience for itself. The Balzacian novel discredits the experience of disillusionment within the representation only by this means to rehabilitate it as the basis on which the narration is entitled to speak. No doubt we can say—positioned by the narration as its readers, we cannot but say—that the narration's perception is truly superior to Lucien's, which it deconstructs. But there are several reasons for suspecting that Balzac's narration belongs to the pattern of coincidences that it seems to be betraying and that the representation of the mechanism of disillusionment is in fact its repetition. For one thing, the treatment of disillusionment is the prime thematic means by which the Balzacian novel wins the adherence of its readers. The cognitive clarity of the narration, produced as an effect of its contrast with the mystified perception of the characters, asks to be consumed as part of a libidinal investment. If in order to be read, the novel must be enjoyed, then the narration must continually practice a charm which is perfectly analogous to that of Lousteau's diatribe or Vautrin's pedagogy. Its insights need to seduce us, and insofar as we are seduced, in entranced "possession" of the truth, the novel has succeeded in escaping our critical scrutiny. Cultivating an affective detachment from the world and thus—what is supposed to be the same thing in Balzac—coming truly to know it, we simultaneously cathect that affect onto the novel, desiring it, and thus—what would also be the same thing in Balzac—never quite understanding it.

How is the reader "operated" in Balzac? What processes must this reader necessarily engage? It only stands our seduction by the text's own disillusionment-effect on its head to argue resentfully—as even some of Balzac's most interesting recent critics have done—that Balzacian narration realizes a fantasy of sovereign semiotic power and total narrative control. Clearly, the evidence for such a fantasy can easily be found: in the biographical resumes that are as full as the dossiers of the police; in the ready-to-hand explanations for whatever occurs; in the continual exhibitionistic display of the narration's superior vision, in which we get, and are always reminded of getting, the supreme panoptic privilege of watching the watchers themselves. But if in these ways the Balzacian novel submits to the hold of the same ancien-régime conception of power that motivated Vautrin, it also more profoundly modernizes such a conception: in its espousal of a logic of displacement and dispersion, its willingness to abandon its positions in exchange for new ones, its ultimate obedience to the category of the *functional*. What Fredric Jameson has called, for instance, "a rotation of character centers" in Balzac precludes imaginary identification with characters in favor of an identification with the process of shifting itself.[12] To read a novel like *Splendeurs et misères* is successively to occupy a whole, but not complete, set of social positions, absolutely attached to none. Similarly, there are no grounds for speaking of a narrator in Balzac, if by narrator we understand a simulacrum of a *person*, for this kind of individual focalization is precisely what the narration, by multiplying, works to by-pass. One identifies not with a narrator, but with a narration—or better, no *one* identifies at all, since when the notion of the person is removed from one side of the equation, it is also gone from the other. The same principle that detaches us from identifying with persons makes the Balzacian description, apparently overflowing with detail, ultimately so abstract and even skimmable. The point of such description is only that it always has a point; the specific details are thereby evacuated in a meaning which could be derived from a different, and hence interchangeable, set of details. The suffocating local particularity of the Balzacian novel is only its point of departure, the point which the dynamism of the narrative consists in *leaving behind*, as "one" is assimilated to techniques, procedures, functions.[13] Along the same lines, as Gérard Genette has best demonstrated, the apparently compulsive need to make sense in Balzac produces considerable incoherence if the various explanations are taken together as parts of a unified understanding.[14] What matters in Genette's demonstration, however, is not its somewhat malicious observation, made as it were behind Balzac's back, that the novelist is being inconsistent—a complaint that finally emerges from a rationalist sensibility as Balzacian as the Balzac it finds to snipe at. Rather, what the discrepancies reveal is the ultimate dependency of the Balzacian text on a conception of narrative functionality. Thus, if the same qualities are adduced in different places as causes for opposite effects, this is only to say that for the reader of Balzac, sense has no absolute basis, but changes with the narrative need and the social context. Like everything else in Balzac, meaning too must adjust to the demands of its functional station.

This is finally why the Balzacian novel, committed to processes of circulation and exchange, is incapable of coming to an end, why it must mark its endings by the promise and necessity of further narration. There simply is no principle of arrest, as there would be if a decisive sense could be established, or even a settled personal identification. The lack of such a principle shows up thematically in Balzac's unorthodox representation of the police, who in *Splendeurs et misères* seem less interested in preventing crime and arresting criminals than in merely supervising a wealth of intrigues, as though the efficacy of policing were now carried not in and by means of an ending, but in the smooth facilitation of narrative processes themselves. This is also why it is mistaken to think that the failed closure opens up, as anything more than a masking effect, transcendent possibilities (such as "freedom") which could be used to justify and characterize "liberal society" or, for that matter, "liberal arts" like literature. What social integration means in Balzac, we have seen, is not arrest and settlement (which would either establish our freedom by putting limits on it, or extend its domain by failing to secure them), but an eminently narratable "exercise of functions." There is no reason not to reverse this proposition and say that what the narration's own exercise of functions drills us in are precisely the basic structuring principles of nineteenth-century social order. This is not an order which values or even requires a fixed self, or the sense of an ending, but aspires—as the disillusioned Balzac is the first to admit—to the condition of money: to its lack of particularity, to the mobility of its exchange, to its infinitely removed finality. In its subscription to such principles, the Balzacian novel finds its redeemable social value.

NOTES

1. Honoré de Balzac, *La Peau de chagrin*, ed. M. Allem (Paris: Garnier Frères, 1967), 59: "A l'origine des nations, la force fut en quelque sorte matérielle, une, grossière; puis, avec l'accroissement des agrégations, les gouvernements ont procédé par des décompositions plus ou moins habiles du pouvoir primitif. Ainsi, dans la haute antiquité la force était dans la théocratie; le prêtre tenait le glaive et l'encensoir. Plus tard, il y eut deux sacerdoces: le pontife et le roi. Aujourd'hui, notre société, dernier terme de la civilisation, a distribué la puissance suivant le nombre des combinaisons, et nous sommes arrivés aux forces nommées industrie, pensée, argent, parole. Le pouvoir, n'ayant plus d'unité, marche sans cesse vers une dissolution sociale qui n'a plus d'autre barrière que l'intérêt." *The Fatal Skin*, [FS], trans. Cedar Paul (New York: Pantheon Books, 1949), 59 ["At their birth nations depend to a certain degree on concentrated, brute material force. Then, as settled communities grow, governments proceed more or less skilfully to parcel out primitive power. For instance, in remote epochs, national strength lay in theocracy, the priest held both the sword and the censer. Later, two men functioned as ecclesiastics: the sovereign pontiff and the king. In these our own times, society, which is the last word in civilisation, has distributed power among a number of groups and so we have the forces called business, thought, money and oratory. This disintegration of authority is leading to a social dissolution against which the only barrier is interest."] Yet if the strategies of modern power are thus perceived as at once scattered and

scattering, this exemplary recognition is ultimately surrendered when power's "cunning decompositions" come to be interpreted as "social dissolution," and when, as a result, the molar unity that power has resourcefully foregone is once again put forward as an implied political aim. It is as though the passage ambiguously grounded both operations I have ascribed to the traditional novel above: the desperate centering inspired by the prospect of social disintegration, and the subtle decentering enjoined by—the other face of such disintegration—the diffuse structuration of modern power. At greater length, it could be shown how the first operation is only a provisional maneuver in the service of the second.

2. References will be made parenthetically in the text to the following editions: *Père Goriot [PG]*, ed. P.-G. Castex (Paris: Garnier Fréres, 1963); *Illusions perdues [IP]*, ed. A. Adam (Paris: Garnier Frères, 1961); *Splendeurs et misères des courtisanes [S & M]*, ed. A. Adam (Paris: Garnier Frères, 1964). When unaccompanied by the abbreviations given in brackets above, page numbers will refer to the last work so specified. The English translations are taken from the following editions: *Old Goriot [OG]*, trans. M. A. Crawford (Harmondsworth, Middlesex: Penguin Books Ltd, 1959); *Lost Illusions [LI]*, trans. Kathleen Raine (New York: The Modern Library, 1967); *A Harlot High and Low [HHL]*, trans. Rayner Heppenstall (Harmondsworth, Middlesex: Penguin Books Ltd, 1975).

3. Peter Brooks, *The Melodramatic Imagination: Balzac, Henry James, Melodrama, and the Mode of Excess* (New Haven: Yale University Press, 1976), 140.

4. The best known example occurs in *La Peau de chagrin*, when the antiquary tells Raphael: "*Vouloir* nous brûle, et *pouvoir* nous détruit, mais SAVOIR laisse notre faible organisation dans un perpetuel état de calme" (37). ["To Will scorches us; To Act destroys us; but To Know steeps our frail organism in perpetual calm." (*FS* 36)]

5. As in a toast, or as in this usage from Balzac's trilogy: "A nous deux, nous donnerons du courage à Léontine" (*S & M* 413) ["Between us, we'll give Léontine heart" (*HHL* 347).]

6. Brooks, 139 and 140.

7. The logic underlying such characteristic peripeties of Balzacian ambition has been well described by Richard Terdiman, in his discussion of the initiation process in Balzac: this process "has as its referent, and tests the possibility of domination over, a concrete structure of interests and power-relations.... But the would-be subject, once initiated, finds himself immersed in the structure of relations over which he sought control, discovers that he is involuntarily speaking the referent *as its own object*. The social system the

initiatory process sought to determine in fact thus determines the process even in its seeking; the power over which control was sought turns out to be *power over those who seek power*" ("Structures of Initiation: On Semiotic Education and its Contradictions in Balzac," *Yale French Studies* 63, 1982, 216).

8. Theodor W. Adorno, "Balzac-Lektüre," in *Noten zur Literatur* (Frankfurt: Suhrkamp, 1974), 140 (my translation here and in n. 11).

9. The pattern summarized here is elaborated in D. A. Miller, "The Novel and the Police," *Glyph* 8 (Baltimore: The Johns Hopkins University Press, 1981), 128–37.

10. In the manuscript of *Splendeurs et misères*, the Duchesse keeps Lucien's letters "à cause des éloges données à ce qu'il y a de plus femme dans la femme" (*S & M* 734) ["because of the praise of what is most female in the female"]; in the published version, these eulogies are given "à ce qu'elle avait de moins duchesse en elle" (588) ["upon what was least duchesslike about her" (*HHL* 492).]

11. Adorno writes about Balzac's treatment of homosexuality: "Faced with the irresistible imposition of the principle of exchange, he perhaps imagined in this proscribed love, a priori desperate, something like love's unmutilated image: he ascribes it to the false cleric, who as the head of a criminal gang has renounced the exchange of equivalences (*Äquivalententausch*)" ("Balzac-Lektüre," 142). Yet we do better to under-stand Vautrin's homosexuality as the advance guard of sexual modernism than as this archaic sentimental refuge. The moment when, on Calvi's reappearance, Vautrin recognizes his homosexuality in its desublimated form is also the moment when his character is most attuned to social exigencies and most expert at the operations they require. It is as though the recognition completes the process of modernizing him as a subject of exchange, by casting his unmanageable love into the more negotiable form of sexual commerce. In the end, Vautrin's homosexuality is not opposed to "the exchange of equivalents," which on the contrary aptly defines it. It thus announces the development that, a hundred and fifty years later, will allow sociology to observe: "Parmi toutes les sexualités, l'homosexualité masculine est sans doute celle dont le fonctionnement rappelle le plus l'image d'un marché" ["Of all forms of sexual behavior, male homosexuality is undoubtedly the one whose functioning most recalls the image of the market place"] (Michael Pollak, "L'homosexualité masculine, ou: le bonheur dans le ghetto?," *Communications* 35 [1982], 40).

12. Fredric Jameson, *The Political Unconscious* (Ithaca: Cornell University Press, 1981), 161: "This rotation is evidently a small-scale model

of the decentered organization of the *Comédie humaine* itself." In the light of Balzacian disillusionment, however, we cannot accept his suggestion that this decentered organization *antedates* the emergence of a centered subject. Rather, we should say, this decentered organization has always-already engendered the correlative fantasy of a centered subject, who is therefore on the verge of being emarginated from the outset, and able to defend his "integrity" only through his willingness to be dispersed.

13. "The exclusion of money from circulation would constitute precisely the opposite of its valarization as capital, and the accumulation of commodities in the sense of hoarding them would be sheer foolishness. (Thus for instance Balzac, who so thoroughly studied every shade of avarice, represents the old userer Gobseck as being in his second childhood when he begins to create a hoard by piling up commodities)" (Karl Marx, *Capital*, vol. 1, tr. Ben Fowkes [New York: Vintage Books, 1977] 735). If Balzacian narrative confirms Marx's thesis, it is not so much by illustrating it along the lines suggested in this passage, as by continually enacting it as the principle of its formal construction. See Adorno "Balzac-Lektüre," 148–49; and Fredric Jameson, *Marxism and Form* (Princeton: Princeton University Press, 1971), 10.

14. Gérard Genette, "Vraisemblance et motivation," in *Figures II* (Paris: Seuil, 1969), 81–86.

DAVID F. BELL

Epigrams and Ministerial Eloquence:
The War of Words in Balzac's La Peau de chagrin

The incessant *bavardage* of the narrator in the opening pages of *La Peau de chagrin* might well obscure the fact that the first section of the novel is marked by significant silences. The young man whom the narrator follows into the gambling house refrains from all utterances and maintains an obstinate silence throughout the whole scene around the gaming table. An obvious part of the fascination he exerts upon the others present during the short moment necessary to accomplish his desperate gesture stems from his Sphinx-like demeanor. Moreover, the empty interpretive space provided by his mysterious behavior is precisely the space which the narrator delights in filling with every possible speculation concerning his protagonist. Ultimately, the young man will not utter his first word until he enters the antique store—and then only grudgingly, at best: "Portant sa croix jusqu'au bout, il parut écouter son conducteur et lui répondit par gestes ou par monosyllabes; mais insensiblement il sut conquérir le droit d'être silencieux...."[1] Only the temptations offered by the antique dealer will finally succeed in drawing the young man into a conversation of sorts, although he listens a good deal more than he speaks. His somber demeanor is finally dissipated, at least partially, when he encounters his friends upon leaving the antique store. At that moment, he simultaneously recovers both

From *Nineteenth-Century French Studies* 15, no. 3. ©1987 by *Nineteenth-Century French Studies*.

his name and his tongue, no longer the *enfant* (in the etymological as well as the ordinary sense) he was during the opening scene in the gambling house.

When, at the end of the novel's first section, Raphaël usurps the position of narrator, his mutism undergoes a radical transformation and unexpectedly becomes, for a time, a stubborn volubility. The transition from mutism to volubility as Raphaël begins to tell his story is not only abrupt, it is a locus of difficulty and hesitation as well. Whatever opinion one might have concerning the effectiveness of the narrative device used by Balzac at this point in the story, the reader is clearly faced with a moment of interruption, a textual rift, which, by its very nature, calls attention to itself.[2] For one thing, Emile's bantering rejoinders undermine Raphaël's undertaking to suspend his narration almost before he has begun: "Si ton amitié n'a pas la force d'écouter mes élégies, si tu ne peux me faire crédit d'une demi-heure d'ennui, dors! Mais ne me demande plus alors compte de mon suicide qui gronde, qui se dresse, qui m'appelle et que je salue" (p. 130). Only when Emile himself falls silent is Raphaël finally permitted to enter wholeheartedly into his tale. Moreover, if the beginning of Raphaël's narrative poses problems, about which I shall have more to say below, so also does its end. It turns out to be no less difficult for Raphaël to stop than it was for him to start. His story and thus his discourse apparently end when he is reminded of the talisman, but this reminder instead sets off a wild tirade which Emile must finally interrupt by leading Raphaël out of the room: "Soit que, fatigué des luttes de cette longue journée, … soit qu'exaspéré par l'image de sa vie, … Raphaël s'anima, s'exalta comme un homme complètement privé de raison" (p. 202).

In the course of the second part of *La Peau de chagrin*, then, Raphaël goes from semi-silent observer of the unfolding orgy to raving madman: to begin to speak has meant to trade excesses and to expose himself to a danger, the nature of which is not quite clear. The act of speaking is in no sense simple—it is, on the contrary, fraught with difficulties and can lead in unexpected directions. Indeed, I would like to suggest that the act of speaking is one of the fundamental questions treated in the novel. No simple narrative ploy, the troublesome nature of Raphaël's transition into the enunciative role is, on the contrary, an emblematic moment that is linked in many ways to his development, to his "education" in the world. Pierre Barbéris has called attention to Raphaël's silence in the first part of *La Peau de chagrin* and has demonstrated how Balzac progressively transferred comments made during Taillefer's orgy from him to other characters as the novel evolved through various editions. Raphaël could thus be portrayed as more aloof, more above the fray, more detached and understanding than the other guests at the orgy.[3] My argument, although not necessarily opposed to that of Barbéris, will adopt a slightly different focus. What Raphaël aims for throughout his period of maturation is not simply to speak more or to speak less, but rather to speak *more tellingly*, more successfully, to learn a kind of conversational skill of which he is utterly bereft when his father dies and leaves him alone in the world.

Without entering into the detail of Raphaël's early youth, one might characterize it by insisting on two essential points: the constraining discipline imposed upon him by his father, on the one hand, and his social timidity, on the other. The two are obviously linked. Because M. de Valentin refuses his son the opportunity to engage in amusements of any kind, Raphaël's life is practically devoid of social development. Symptomatic in this context is the scene set in the duc de Navarreins's ball. Instead of mixing with the other guests, Raphaël assumes a posture which is habitual—he stands off in a corner watching the others, far enough away so that he will not be noticed and have to speak, yet near enough to observe and to dream at his ease: "Je me mis dans un coin afin de pouvoir tout à mon aise prendre des glaces et contempler les jolies femmes" (pp. 122–23).[4] The passivity of Raphaël's stance, its infantile nature (eating sweets), is manifest. Raphaël remains unnoticed by everyone, with the significant exception of his father (further emphasizing his infantile status). His eventual bet is described as an impulsive gesture, unaccompanied by even the slightest hint of a conversation with any fellow bettor. He practically throws his money on the table and withdraws to feign indifference to the game. When he wins and is accused of cheating, he does not speak in his own defense, but is instead defended by someone else: "Le bon gros petit homme dit alors d'une voix certainement angélique: 'Tous ces messieurs avaient mis,' et paya les quarante francs. Je relevai mon front et jetai des regards triomphants sur les joueurs" (p. 124).

Although Raphaël succeeds in pleasing his father during the ball (albeit through a dishonest subterfuge) and is thereby granted adulthood, his isolation and social exile continue: "Ainsi, le jour où mon père parut en quelque sorte m'avoir émancipé, je tombai sous le joug le plus odieux" (p. 126). Such is his state when M. de Valentin dies. At the very moment when he most needs the social talents necessary for litigation and negociations, he is helpless and agrees to sign away his family's remaining fortune in order to pay off the family debts, "ce que mon avoué nommait une *bêtise*" (p. 127). Plunged into embarrassing poverty, Raphaël lacks the one thing which, in the absence of money, could resolve his dilemma, namely, a *voice* which could give him some authority, some standing: "le despotisme de mon père m'avait ôté toute confiance en moi; j'étais timide et gauche, je ne croyais pas que ma voix pût exercer le moindre empire …" (p. 128). His sheltered and repressed existence has left him ill-prepared for the difficulties he must face. As Pierre Barbéris has argued, perhaps the major cause of Raphaël's isolation is his poverty: "D'abord, s'il est seul et souffrant, c'est en grande partie *parce qu'il est pauvre.*"[5] However, the *manifestation* of that poverty and isolation is resolutely presented in terms of the impossibility of speaking:

> Malgré ma promptitude à prendre ce regard ou des mots en apparence affectueux comme de tendres engagements, je n'ai jamais osé ni parler ni me taire à propos. A force de sentiment ma parole était insignifiante, et mon silence stupide. J'avais sans doute trop de naïveté pour une société factice qui vit aux lumières, qui rend toutes ses pensées par des phrases convenues, ou par des mots que dicte la mode. Puis je ne savais point parler en me taisant, ni me taire en parlant. (p. 129)[6]

Raphaël attributes his lack of voice to his own purity which he contrasts with the factitious nature of Parisian society. Rousseau's model looms large here, as it does elsewhere in the novel. What is just as interesting, however, is Raphaël's analysis of the complexity of the act of speaking in society. The first thing one must learn is when to speak and when to hold one's tongue, "parler … me taire à propos." This is no easy task, for it already requires a certain diplomatic sophistication. Yet within a Parisian society strewn with potential pitfalls, it is far from sufficient. Success would require of Raphaël another level of analytical complexity altogether. He must, in addition, cultivate a skill which would allow him, as he puts it, to "parler en me taisant … me taire en parlant." In order to find his voice, he would have to rework the simple dichotomy *parler/se taire* and acquire a subtlety in his utterances which would permit him to convey meanings different from his *apparent* intentions. Those who are versed in the ever-so-slight nuances of attitude and intonation present in Parisian salons are able to transform silence into *significant* silence and innocent remarks into *double entendres*: "A bon entendeur demi-mot suffit," goes the French saying. Raphaël's position in the corner of the room at the Navarreins ball marks his exclusion from the group of initiates. Never a simple act, speaking opens a field of dangerous subtleties which can be mastered only with the long practice that has always been denied Raphaël.[7]

His general ineptitude and failure lead him to take the drastic step of retreating into isolation "pour mettre au jour un ouvrage qui pût attirer l'attention publique sur moi ..." (p. 133). The fact that he seeks salvation through the production of a book is of fundamental importance. Whether Raphaël realizes it or not, this exercise in language is linked directly to his search for a voice: authorship will be a rehearsal of authority. His first creation, the little-noticed comedy that fails lamentably, is symptomatic of his problem. No one is more ill-prepared to write such a work than Raphaël. Comedy is an eminently social genre, one that requires a profound grasp of social interaction, of the relation between various voices in society. Raphaël's attempt, thrown together "en peu de jours," can only be "une véritable niaiserie d'enfant" (p. 138), the futile work of one who cannot yet speak. His *Théorie de la volonté*, on the other hand, will require careful preparation and research and will thus afford Raphaël the chance to further his knowledge and to obtain at least a theoretical background in the sources and nuances of social behavior. It is important to note that Raphaël meets Rastignac only when his work is finished, when his study of human nature is well-advanced. "Ton ouvrage est achevé," says Rastignac, "Eh bien, tu arrives à mon point de départ" (p. 145). Rastignac's invitation to return to society is not a betrayal of Raphaël's original project, but rather, its logical continuation. The evening in Fœdora's salon proposed by Rastignac furnishes Raphaël with the necessary opportunity to test his new-found voice.

Entering into Fœdora's salon will resemble a trial by fire. This is no ordinary salon—it is, in fact, the most brilliant social circle in the city: "une maison où va tout Paris" (p. 145). Nor is Fœdora an ordinary woman. She possesses instead the most penetrating intelligence and is capable of seeing to the heart of even the ablest diplomat. Rastignac cautions Raphaël to use his chance wisely, to be on his strictest guard: "prends garde à tout ce que tu lui diras, elle a une mémoire cruelle, elle a une adresse à désespérer un diplomate, elle saurait deviner le moment où il dit vrai ..." (p. 147). A naïve social failure when he withdrew into seclusion, Raphaël now faces a situation which is, in many ways, the polar opposite of his isolated retreat. In order to succeed, he will truly have to "parler en se taisant, se taire en parlant." If not, Fœdora will unfailingly see through him, expose his precarious social situation, and banish him with appropriate irony.

The description of the first soirée in Fœdora's salon attests to the fact that Raphaël's exile at the hôtel Saint-Quentin has been well-spent. After a few minutes of hesitation camouflaged by Rastignac's remarks concerning his modesty, Raphaël "produisi[t] quelque sensation" (p. 148)—and in a very precise manner. He speaks judiciously and well: "sans abuser de la parole quand elle m'était accordée, je tâchai de résumer les discussions par des mots plus ou moins incisifs, profonds ou spirituels" (p. 148). Raphaël would have been quite incapable of incisiveness or wit at the time of his father's death, but he can now confront Fœdora:

> Elle … me questionna sur mes travaux, et sembla s'y intéresser vivement, surtout quand je lui traduisis mon système en plaisanteries au lieu de prendre le langage d'un professeur pour le lui développer doctoralement. Elle parut s'amuser beaucoup.... Les objections de Fœdora me révélèrent en elle une certaine finesse d'esprit, je me complus à lui donner raison pendant quelques moments pour la flatter, et je détruisis ses raisonnements de femme par un mot.... J'eus l'honneur d'amuser cette femme.... (pp. 149-50)

What strikes the reader in this passage is the instinctive mastery of situation and style demonstrated by Raphaël. He is able to distinguish between professorial and gracefully amusing tones and choose the correct one effortlessly. He plays with Fœdora like a toy, leading her on and then demolishing her arguments with a single remark. It is Fœdora who is finally reduced to silence: "La comtesse resta même un instant silencieuse …" (p. 150).

Lest we be tempted to attribute total victory to Raphaël at this point, we would do well to analyze carefully his reaction once Fœdora leaves him to return to her other guests. He soon finds himself in a posture reminiscent of the one he assumed at the duc de Navarreins's ball: "caché dans l'embrasure d'une fenêtre, j'espionnai ses pensées en les cherchant dans son maintien …" (p. 150). Arguably, there is a difference here—Raphaël's intellectual baggage is now a good deal more substantial. Instead of daydreaming absently, as he did at that first ball, he now appeals to his long studies in an attempt to penetrate the enigma of Fœdora: "J'évoquai toutes mes connaissances physiologiques et mes études antérieures sur la femme …" (p. 150). Nonetheless, the fact that he immediately withdraws after the interview with Fœdora is indicative of his as-yet incomplete mastery of the act of speaking—he is unable to sustain indefinitely the level of conversation he has maintained up to that point.

Following this first skirmish, Raphaël's relations with Fœdora will be highlighted by a series of conversations during which he is constantly forced to muster all his skill at speaking, both to please her and to conceal parts of himself (essentially his desire and his poverty).[8] A characteristic example is the moment of the first quarrel between the two characters. Fœdora, angry at Raphaël for approaching her inopportunely at the theater, explains the guiding principle of her conduct—never to love any man. Raphaël's response is both eloquent and revealing: "Si je vous dis que je vous aime, répondis-je, vous me bannirez; si je m'accuse d'indifférence, vous m'en punirez.... Le silence ne préjuge rien; trouvez bon, madame, que je me taise" (pp. 157–58). Here Raphaël himself is reduced to silence. The distance between this silence and the one observed by the young Raphaël when he was still living under the paternal authority may be measured by insisting upon the *strategic* nature of Raphaël's present choice. He is powerless this time not because he understands nothing, but precisely because he understands very well the terms of Fœdora's ultimatum and knowingly selects his only option—his is now a reasoned silence. It is she, however, who obtains the upper hand in this exchange and toys with Raphaël as he earlier did with her: "Fœdora ... brisait ma vie et détruisait mon avenir avec la froide insouciance et l'innocente cruauté d'un enfant qui, par curiosité, déchire les ailes d'un papillon" (p. 157).

Rejected and threatened with a new exile, Raphaël makes a desperate attempt to solve the enigma of Fœdora by spying on her in her bedroom. Toward the end of one of Fœdora's endless soirées, he withdraws and hides "dans l'embrasure d'une fenêtre" (p. 179), a position which seems always to accompany the critical moments of Raphaël's existence. The ensuing scene is absolutely fundamental in the context of an argument focusing on the act of speaking in *La Peau de chagrin*. What Raphaël overhears from his hiding place is none other than a theoretical and practical demonstration of the art of speaking in Parisian society illustrated by someone who reveals how far Raphaël still has to go in order to master that art, namely, Rastignac. Five or six faithful members of Fœdora's inner circle have remained to have tea with her before she retires for the night. Encouraged by the intimacy of such a private setting, Rastignac and the others engage in a witty and ironic exchange which spares no one: "Les calomnies, pour lesquelles la société actuelle a réservé le peu de croyance qui lui reste, se mêlèrent alors à des épigrammes, à des jugements spirituels, au bruit des tasses et des cuillers" (p. 180). There is nothing serene or disinterested about this conversation characterized by three types of remarks: "les calomnies," "les épigrammes," and "les jugements spirituels." All are aggressive attacks on some absent and therefore defenseless party who becomes an object of the general mirth. Thus Raphaël, precisely because he is hidden from everyone's sight, will unfailingly become a subject of discussion, as we shall see in a moment. The point of such personal attacks is the point itself, "la pointe," the penetrating gibe or sally toward which all the speaker's wit is directed and which socially annihilates the victim. Small wonder that the word *epigram* is etymologically related to *epigraph*, to the inscription upon the tomb. For those who, like Rastignac and Fœdora, live only for the exhilaration of social triumphs, to be the target of an epigram is tantamount to losing everything, to experiencing social death. Moreover, he who uses an epigram always runs the risk of becoming the victim of one.

On the one hand, then, the act of speaking is one of brutality and aggressivity. Rastignac is a master at this activity, for, as the narrator informs us, he "excitait un rire fou par de mordantes saillies" (p. 180). His grasp of "l'idiome moderne," as he terms it, does not stop there, however. He has attained a type of perfection in his conversational style that he calls ministerial eloquence. It permits him, through the use of "natural artifices," to attack or defend anything or anyone indiscriminately by adroitly manipulating his interlocutor and preventing him from seeing the obvious:

> Un de vos amis est-il sans esprit? Vous parlez de sa probité, de sa franchise. L'ouvrage d'un autre est-il lourd? Vous le présentez comme un travail consciencieux. Si le livre est mal écrit, vous en vantez les idées.[9] Tel homme est sans foi, sans constance, vous échappe à tout moment? Bah! il est séduisant, prestigieux, il charme. S'agit-il de vos ennemis? Vous leur jetez à la tête les morts et les vivants; vous renversez pour eux les termes de votre langage, et vous êtes aussi perspicace à découvrir leurs défauts que vous étiez habile à mettre en relief les vertus de vos amis. Cette application de la lorgnette à la vue morale est le secret de nos conversations et tout l'art du courtisan. (pp. 180–81)

Rastignac is the recognized master of the very talent that Raphaël had identified from the beginning as essential to success in speaking: "se taire en parlant/parler en se taisant." One always speaks *in order not to say something*, whether it be to avoid calling attention to the faults of a friend or, conversely, to conceal the qualities of an enemy. Because he never appears to be doing precisely what he is doing, Rastignac remains in an impregnable position and is a redoubtable enemy. His tongue is his sword, and, in the rare cases when someone would challenge him, his sword is the equal of his tongue.

The distance between Raphaël and Rastignac is suggestively indicated by the fact that Raphaël, although also armed as he waits behind the curtain, possesses a greatly inferior weapon: "En m'habillant, je mis dans la poche de mon gilet un petit canif anglais, à défaut de poignard" (p. 179). Furnished only with the arm of a child, he is obviously not prepared for serious swordplay. Unable to defend himself, he must rely on Rastignac and therefore remain hidden as he comes under attack during the conversation. And come under attack he soon does. Rastignac's virtuoso lesson is a signal for one of Raphaël's rivals to provide an immediate illustration of yet another kind of calumny: he begins making fun of Raphaël by praising him lavishly. Rastignac, who responds by defending his friend (but haven't we already seen that such a defense is always in some sense insincere?), is soon outnumbered when Fœdora joins the assault. No rebuttal is now possible, and Raphaël, not yet fully able to match wits with his enemies, silently witnesses his own social destruction.

For all practical purposes, Raphaël's quest to win Fœdora is over after the scene in her boudoir, although he does not accept defeat without further struggle. The failure he experiences here will be avenged, however, in a later scene that employs some of the very same premises structuring the scene in the boudoir, albeit with telling modifications. The passage I am referring to is the important evening at the theater that takes place toward the beginning of the final section of the novel, "L'Agonie." Functioning as a key narrative moment, it provides the narrator with the opportunity to bring together practically all the characters of appreciable significance in the story: the antique dealer, Euphrasie, Fœdora, Aquilina, Taillefer, Emile, Rastignac, Pauline, and Raphaël himself.

Inheritor of his mother's family's estate and living in seclusion in order to avoid using the powers of the *peau de chagrin*, Raphaël goes out to view a play, one of his rare public activities. Immediately upon being seated in the theater, he espies Fœdora in her triumphant glory, viewing the rest of the spectators through her opera glasses: "Une joie inexprimable anima la figure de Fœdora, quand, après avoir braqué sa lorgnette sur toutes les loges, et rapidement examiné les toilettes, elle eut la conscience d'écraser par sa parure et par sa beauté les plus jolies, les plus élégantes femmes de Paris…" (p. 224). Her confident and enticing air makes her the center of attention. Suddenly, however, her gaze falls upon Raphaël and an instantaneous change occurs: "elle pâlit en rencontrant les yeux fixes de Raphaël, son amant dédaigné la foudroya par un intolérable coup d'œil de mépris" (p. 224). Fœdora dominates Raphaël no longer. In fact, he now has clear sovereignty over her, and the narrator quickly indicates the source of Raphaël's power, namely, his talent at speaking:

Aussi Fœdora voyait-elle la mort de ses prestiges et de sa coquetterie. Un mot, dit par lui [Raphaël] la veille à l'Opéra, était déjà devenu célèbre dans les salons de Paris. Le tranchant de cette terrible épigramme avait fait à la comtesse une blessure incurable. En France, nous savons cautériser une plaie, mais nous n'y connaissons pas encore de remède au mal que produit une phrase. (pp. 224–25)

Raphaël presently possesses the voice he was lacking prior to this final moment of vengeance. Once a naïve and innocent outsider, he has now become the source of the epigrams which make and break social reputations. Fœdora, who previously wielded the mortal weapon of words with no fear of reprisal, must pay the piper. She is destined to be *upstaged* by Pauline (it is not without importance that these events occur in a theater), and Raphaël, seated in front of Pauline, becomes, along with her, the new center of attention. Even Rastignac, the mentor toward whom Raphaël has always turned, now looks at Pauline and Raphaël with visible longing.

In a significant way, mastery of the act of speaking appears to belong to the one who possesses a *lorgnette* and can use its ability to distort perception. The reader will recall that Rastignac's long monologue on ministerial eloquence closed with a surprising image: "Cette application de la lorgnette à la vue morale est le secret de nos conversations et tout l'art du courtisan" (p. 181). To see things "par le petit bout de la lorgnette" means to focus on certain qualities to the exclusion of others and therefore to support one's arguments by a skillful manipulation of the point of view one is presenting. In the theater scene, Raphaël has become the possessor of an object which, if not precisely a *lorgnette*, is surely its equivalent, namely, a *lorgnon*, a kind of pince-nez. The narrator informs us of its purpose: "il s'était promis de ne jamais regarder attentivement aucune femme et pour se mettre à l'abri d'une tentation, il portait un lorgnon dont le verre microscopique, artistement disposé, détruisait l'harmonie des plus beaux traits..." (pp. 225–26). The master of epigrams and ministerial eloquence distorts reality in order to present it in his own warped manner. Thus the confrontation between Fœdora and Raphaël almost necessarily takes place "à coup de lorgnette." Fœdora uses hers at the beginning of the scene to deform the other spectators by focusing on the ridiculous aspects of their appearances: "un béret gauchement posé sur le front d'une princesse russe ou ... un chapeau manqué..." (p. 224). As she scans the theater, Raphaël, rendered incapable of perceiving harmony and beauty by the distortion inherent in his own pince-nez, meets her gaze with one that is even more twisted and tortuous, the announcement of his epigrammatic superiority.[10]

By accepting the *peau de chagrin*, Raphaël has in fact chosen the strategy of ministerial eloquence—with obvious success. His decision, signified by the scene just analyzed, was preceded, however, by a final attempt to reach Fœdora in a different manner. Following the debacle in her boudoir during which he overhears Rastignac's theoretical lesson, he requests a final interview with Fœdora to petition her one last time. Unlike the other discussions with her when the two sparred in eloquent style while hiding essential facts and feelings from one another, this time Raphaël elects to reveal the truth concerning his desires and his situation. The form his confession takes is that of an emotional narrative describing his life:

> Je lui racontai mes sacrifices, je lui peignis ma vie.… Ma passion déborda par des mots flamboyants, par des traits de sentiment oubliés depuis, et que ni l'art, ni le souvenir ne sauraient reproduire. Ce ne fut pas la narration sans chaleur d'un amour détesté, mon amour dans sa force et dans la beauté de son espérance m'inspira ces paroles qui projettent toute une vie en répétant les cris d'une âme déchirée. (p. 188)

According to Raphaël, this is more than a mere narrative, it is a rather extraordinary enunciative moment—beyond mere memory, beyond art itself. The words Raphaël uses are "flamboyants," their source an overwhelming passion for exceeding the norm. His narrative seems ultimately to escape the realm of representation—it *is* his very life: "ces paroles qui projettent toute une vie en répétant les cris d'une âme déchirée." Caught up in a moment of ecstasy, Raphaël does not merely describe his agony, he lives it, "les cris d'une âme déchirée," and that agony reveals the center of his being, "toute une vie." The verb *reveal* is too passive here—Raphaël does not merely open and expose his life, he literally throws it at Fœdora, "projects" it, his truth strikes her like a blow to the face.

Her answer to Raphaël's intervention is both surprising and characteristic. She reacts with tears, the very same tears she would shed in response to any ordinary fiction: "Ses larmes étaient le fruit de cette émotion factice achetée cent sous à la porte d'un théâtre, j'avais eu le succès d'un bon acteur" (p. 188). The repetition of the word *factice* is significant here. The reader will recall that Raphaël's original explanation of his failure in society attributed that defeat to the factitious nature of social circles he was attempting to penetrate. Once again he contrasts his desperate appeal with the conventional, artificial interpretation Fœdora gives to it. What Raphaël presents as the truth, as the very voice of his soul reaching out to Fœdora without mediation, is ultimately seen by Fœdora as a theatrical voice, not as the truth, but as just another fiction. Raphaël's apparent abandonment of strategy, of the attempt to win Fœdora by matching her in eloquent and worldly exchanges, is interpreted by Fœdora as one more strategy, as yet another of the possible voices one may adopt in a given social context.

The results of Raphaël's aborted attempt to move Fœdora are twofold. First, as we have already seen, he will elect definitively to join the party of epigrams and ministerial eloquence. More interesting still, his failed narrative has a self-reflexive effect: it puts into question the very act of narration itself. For, as Raphaël says to Emile while he is describing his final appeal to Fœdora, "Je lui racontai mes sacrifices, je lui peignis ma vie, non pas comme je te la raconte aujourd'hui, dans l'ivresse du vin, mais dans la noble ivresse du cœur" (p. 188). The act accomplished by Raphaël when he tells his story to Emile in the novel's second section is but a pale replica of the same act performed in the presence of Fœdora ("non pas comme je te la raconte aujourd'hui"). The attempt to transcend language with Fœdora was a rehearsal for an attempt by Raphaël to convey the meaning of his existence to Emile, a failed rehearsal. Small wonder that Emile's response to Raphaël as Raphaël embarks upon his story for the second time matches Fœdora's— he takes it as a fiction: "Confesse-toi, ne mens pas; je ne te demande point de mémoires historiques.[11] Surtout, sois aussi bref que ton ivresse te le permettra; je suis exigeant comme un lecteur et près de dormir comme une femme qui lit ses vêpres" (p. 119). Shortly thereafter, when Emile again interrupts to request that Raphaël get to the point, his complaint is cast in terms of literary criticism, indicating once again his interpretation of Raphaël's tale as fictional and literary: "Oh! de grâce, épargne-moi ta préface ..." (p. 120).

Raphaël's psychological *usure*, the effect of the life of dissipation he has lived since Fœdora's rejection of him, is paralleled by a certain linguistic *usure* produced by his plunge into ministerial eloquence. Whereas in his culminating plea to Fœdora, he believed himself able to communicate without mediation, with the voice of his soul, he now prefaces his narrative directed toward Emile with a statement of doubt concerning the possibility of rendering the truth of his experience through his narrative voice:

> Vue à distance, ma vie est comme rétrécie par un phénomène moral.[12] Cette longue et lente douleur qui a duré dix ans peut aujourd'hui se reproduire par quelques phrases dans lesquelles la douleur ne sera plus qu'une pensée, et le plaisir une réflexion philsophique. Je juge au lieu de sentir.... (p. 120)

Indeed, Raphaël almost loses Emile's attention. The *usure* present in his language ultimately requires an extension of credit, his interlocutor becomes simply another one of his creditors: "si tu ne peux me faire crédit d'une demiheure d'ennui, dors!" (p. 130). But will Raphaël be able to repay the loan? The product of a fragmented society of which a spirited and ironic critique has been provided in the orgy episode, Raphaël's story is a promised explanation of how and why things have gotten out of hand, an exemplary narration that will supposedly plumb the depths and reveal the truth of the present social situation. It is told, however, by one who has accepted and even assumed the duplicitous and violent nature of Parisian social discourse. Can the reader trust Raphaël any more than he or she trusts Rastignac? Raphaël's mastery of the act of speaking, of epigrams and ministerial eloquence, has in fact seriously undermined the claim that his revelations to Emile can bring the listener closer to any truth. He begins his story to Emile haltingly and ends babbling madly, as if his act of narration were a performance of the very difficulties contained in the attempt to find a voice which marked his passage from naïve silence to worldly conversation.

NOTES

1. Balzac, *La Peau de chagrin*, in *La Comédie humaine*, ed. Pierre-Georges Castex, Pléiade (Paris: Gallimard, 1979) 69. All subsequent references to *La Peau de chagrin* refer to this edition.

2. Martin Kanes calls Raphaël's long story to Emile "an extremely weak device which almost spoils the whole tale." See his "The Mythic Structure of the *La Peau de chagrin*," *Studi Francesi*, 46 (1972): 55. Pierre Barbéris, on the other hand, considers Raphaël's narrative to be structurally fundamental to the novel: "Il fallait ce retour en arrière pour que la tragicomédie de Juillet apparaisse comme autre chose qu'un accident, pour qu'elle soit vérification de ce qu'avait fait soupçonner l'aventure personnelle de Raphaël. La composition ternaire du roman n'est pas artificiel découpage, mais moyen de mieux faire sentir le lien qui unit le présent au passé." See his *Balzac et le mal du siècle* (Paris: Gallimard, 1970) 2: 1448.

3. Barbéris, 2: 1438, n. 1.

4. This structure will later be reproduced in Fœdora's boudoir, as we shall see below.

5. Barbéris, 2: 1455.

6. Martin Kanes surely oversimplifies the problem of social integration in his early analysis of *La Peau de chagrin* when he says of Raphaël, apropos of the period following the death of M. de Valentin, "it is clear that a properly conducted social life would have been one way of winning his case." See "Logic and Language in *La Peau de chagrin*," *Studi Francesi*, 41 (1970): 252.

7. See Martin Kanes, *Balzac's Comedy of Words* (Princeton: Princeton University Press, 1975) 177–82, for a discussion of the dangers of language in society in Balzac's work in general.

8. Contrary to Emile Talbot, I would not attribute Fœdora's failure to discover (for a time, at least) Raphaël's true social situation to a lack of penetration on her part. Rather, I would cite it as proof of Raphaël's successful education resulting in his accomplished *voice*. See "Pleasure/Time or Egoism/Love: Rereading *La Peau de chagrin*," *Nineteenth-Century French Studies*, 11: 1–2 (Fall–Winter 1982–83): 77.

9. One cannot help wondering at this point exactly what Rastignac thought of Raphaël's *Théorie de la volonté* and how he defended it.

10. Raphaël's dominance through speaking is, of course, also fundamentally related to his possession of the *peau de chagrin*. Recent critics have pointed out that Raphaël's wishes always take the form of speech acts— "je veux que ...," "je souhaite que ..."—they are never simply formulated mentally. When Raphaël now speaks, he has the potential of doing so with mortal results in a very literal sense (the "duel" in the novel's third section, for example). See Samuel Weber, *Unwrapping Balzac: A Reading of* La Peau de chagrin (Toronto: University of Toronto Press, 1979) 118. See also Martin Kanes, *Balzac's Comedy of Words*, 75.

11. A rather ironic comment, since Raphaël dates his fall into corruption, at least in part, from the moment he agreed to write the false "mémoires historiques" of his aunt for Finot (166). Moreover, these very same "mémoires" furnish Fœdora with the source of a sharp epigram directed against Raphaël during the scene analyzed above in which Rastignac gives his lesson on epigrams and ministerial eloquence (181).

12. The idea of reduction in size, the *rétrécissement de la vie*, combined with a moral context brings us directly back to the problematic of the *lorgnette/lorgnon* which is so fundamental for Rastignac, Fœdora, and Raphaël.

JANE A. NICHOLSON

Discourse, Power, and Necessity: *Contextualizing* Le Cousin Pons

The last two complete novels of the *Comédie Humaine*, *La Cousine Bette* (1846) and *Le Cousin Pons* (1847), were first published in serial form before appearing together in book form under the title, *Les Parents pauvres*. The present discussion will focus on the oppositional nature of Balzac's discourse in his last complete works, both with respect to liberalism as a dominant social ideology in pre-1848 France and with respect to the *feuilleton* as a popular form of literary production. In *Les Parents pauvres*, Balzac's task is less to rewrite history than to bring each of these dramas—the drama of liberalism and the drama of "literature"—up to the eve of the uprising of 1848 with its sense of impending disaster. In reading *Le Cousin Pons* from this dual perspective, one can identify the verbal complexities relating text and context in Balzac's representation of a new consciousness born of the crises experienced among the established institutions of liberal France during the 1840s. Since, arguably, language is primarily a social force, the methodology of discourse analysis can provide new contextualization for *Le Cousin Pons*— that is, a new understanding of this text in its broadest possible discursive relations—by considering it as a form of intertextuality. Indeed, analysis of the discursive context of this work enables the most complete account of its socio-historical determinations.

From *Symposium* XLII, no. 1. ©1988 by the Helen Dwight Reid Educational Foundation.

The most useful and exciting discourse theory for the present purpose is that of M. M. Bakhtin, who reorients the study of the novel from form to function through his notion of "living discourse." According to Bakhtin, discourse exists as the world of stratified, socio-ideological languages that constitute the pluralism of a new, modern linguistic consciousness. He calls this social condition of language *heteroglossia*: "at any given moment of its historical existence, language is heteroglot from top to bottom: it represents the coexistence of socio-ideological contradictions between the present and the past, between different social groups in the present, between tendencies, schools, circles, and so forth, all given a bodily form. These 'languages' of heteroglossia intersect each other in a variety of ways, forming new socially typifying 'languages.'"[1] These forces are not constituted, then, by mere minimal linguistic units, but rather by centralizing ideological tendencies. Thus, the notion of a verbal-ideological world, where verbal and ideological elements are always mutually determining, is crucial to understanding the emergence of the novel as a modern form. Such an approach allows for a study of the discursive elements of any novel as constituting a system by themselves and as forming part of a much larger verbal system.

According to Bakhtin, the prose writer does not purge works of intentions and tones that are not his own: "He does not eliminate those language characterization and speech mannerisms (potential narrator-personalities) glimmering behind the works and forms.... Therefore, the stratification of language—generic, professional, social in the narrow sense, that of particular world views, particular tendencies, particular individuals, the social speech diversity and language-diversity (dialects) of language— upon entering the novel establishes its own special order within it ..." (298–9). Thus, an ever-broadening range of analysis provides the most reliable access to the level of concrete history and establishes context as a key construct in reading novels. In this view, without these broader interrelations, the literary text tends to be seen either as verbally self-sufficient or as mimetically reproductive of reality.

In his recent *Rereading Intellectual History: Texts, Contexts, Language*, Dominick LaCapra takes up Bakhtin's discussions and proceeds to construct the concept of context on analogy with the concept of text.[2] According to LaCapra, the unfixed nature of a context, based on an understanding of the interpenetration of opposing discourses within a given social formation, suggests a new ground for criticism as well as for specific readings. He finds that contextualizing is too often a matter of documentation and too seldom one of "dialogization"—that is, the determination of the interpenetration of discourses. Thus, his approach prevents the establishing of *the* context for any text and opens a dialogue with subordinate strains of past social formations. In addition, LaCapra stipulates that matters of contextualization should not be confined to either simple continuity or discontinuity vis-à-vis the text. In this way, texts are not to be understood as mere signs of their times or as unproblematic expressions of larger phenomena, for such approaches foreclose close readings of texts at the same time they restrict thé complex intertextual relations that comprise contexts. *Les Parents pauvres* thus may be said to represent broad categories of lived social experience which must be constructed and delimited—but not reduced—in order to enable the discussion of particular contexts. For the present study, *construction* is the key term, for contexts must not be merely posited as self-evident explanations of literary texts.

Bakhtin considers the prose of the novel to be a new language that emerges from the specific historical fragmentation of social classes in the modern age. Therefore, he sees it as reaching beyond the formulations of traditional aesthetics. Accordingly, Balzac's novels are of particular interest because they are products of a profound socio-political upheaval. During this period, linguistic and literary norms are unstable, including relations between authors and readers. A new audience is doubly empowered to make demands by its increased literacy and its economic clout in the literary marketplace. Although Balzac's *codes, traités, physiologies, théories*, etc.—essentially nineteenth-century how-to's—were extremely popular in the 1830s, he dedicated himself to the production of the *Comédie* in the 1840s. While this meant a gradual move away from novelized theories and speculations toward realism, Balzac continued to prefer the book-market mode of production grounded in long-term contracts. Moreover, Balzac's last novel must be set against its primary rival literary discourse, as well as against other public discourses:

> A stylistic analysis of the novel cannot be productive outside a profound understanding of heteroglossia, an understanding of the dialogue of languages as it exists in a given era. But in order to understand such dialogue, or even to become aware initially that a dialogue is going on at all, mere knowledge of the linguistic and stylistic profile of the languages involved will be insufficient; what is needed is a profound understanding of each language's socio-ideological meaning and an exact knowledge of the social distribution and ordering of all the other ideological voices of the era. (Bakhtin 417)

Within the context of the dialogue of languages, therefore, *Pons* will be considered as representative of the *Comédie* both in relation to the *roman feuilleton* and to the contemporary public debate on social problems.

As the most famous novelist of his day, Balzac was honored with the first *feuilleton* contract, for which he produced *La Vieille Fille* (*La Presse*, November 1836). This honor proved to be a dubious one since he was obliged to seek such short-term contracts from that time forward. Whereas his long-term contracts had allowed him to add to the cycle of the *Comédie* as he saw fit, rewriting often, the arrival of the mass press placed Balzac's writing practice at odds with the new mode of literary production. From the point of view of production demands, the *feuilleton* required stringent daily deadlines as well as strict limitations of length on each segment and the total number of segments per work. The publication schedule, moreover, dictated many characteristics of the genre, such as beginning *in medias res*, episodic plot, and use of suspense to link segments. While these characteristics were not recognized as constituting a genre until 1842, virtually all literary works appeared in serial before appearing in book form.[3] By that time Balzac's popularity had suffered so greviously that he actually had difficulty placing his texts. Balzac's 1842 "Avant-propos" must therefore be seen as a contestatory statement made in defense of his own literary mode of production and in response to the dominance of the *feuilleton*.

In 1844, when Balzac got a reprieve in the form of a contract from *Les Débats*, a daily with a large circulation, he contrarily chose to write *Modeste Mignon*, a work devoid of crime and intrigue and unlikely to please *feuilleton* readers. In his preface, he harbored hope for the longevity of his own literary practices: "Pourquoi le feuilleton ne vivraitil pas comme le théâtre par les contrastes?" In a letter to Mme Hanska he complained of a lack of freedom to choose his topics: "Décidément, le redoublement de rage contre moi m'a fait renoncer à l'idée de publier ce dont je vous parlais, cette histoire intitulée *La Séparation* où je voulais montrer les taquineries de l'intérieur domestique."[4] Still later, the *feuilleton* edition of *Pons* is preceded by a few paragraphs entitled, "Avertissement quasi littéraire," in which Balzac attacks the commercial character of the *feuilleton* as well as its stylistic limitations: "L'abonné n'est pas un lecteur ordinaire, il n'a pas cette liberté pour laquelle la Presse a combattu! C'est là ce qui le rend abonné.... Tous ceux qui publient leurs ouvrages en feuilletons n'ont plus la liberté de la forme." While Balzac himself had been involved in projects that involved reader subscriptions, he scathingly indicted the press for denying its readers and contributors what it deemed indispensable to its own good. If we consider the sum of Balzac's remarks as cited here, it seems reasonable to conclude that he could not accept the absence of an oppositional discourse in serial publication; moreover, he saw his own work as that contrastive discourse which could undo the *feuilleton*.

The *feuilleton* form brought together a "high culture" and a "mass culture" readership, who had been previously separate. To Balzac the relations resultant from this coupling must have resembled badly contracted marriages: "Lire c'est créer peut-être à deux" (*Physiologie du mariage*). Balzac's notion of the reading process in the communicational circuit of the text was clearly an idealistic and dualistic one that was suited to book production. In the place of a book held in a lily-white hand, materialized newspapers passed from hand to hand. More importantly, the narrow conventions of the *feuilleton* genre denied one partner in the process the liberty of form and the other the liberty of interpretation. In *Pons*, performance—that of musicians and, presumably, the reader's as well—exemplifies the dualistic creative process: "L'exécution, arrivée à ce degré de perfection, met en apparence l'exécutant à la hauteur du poëte, ... un divin traducteur de choses divines" (*CP* 293).[5] For Balzac, the mass reader is not a performer.

In his recent *Discourse/Counter-Discourse*, Richard Terdiman defines newspaper culture as a set of reading and perception practices fostered by the phenomenal success of the daily newspaper in France from the Restoration to the Second Empire.[6] He notes that the daily follows a commercial logic in its layout where discourse is hierarchized according to the price it brings in and, through the generic format of the article, becomes presentationally interchangeable. Accordingly, a high tolerance for confusion is demanded from the reader-consumer, who must foresake notions of organic form in order to cope with the disconnected format of the daily. Moreover, the daily was a highly anonymous form of distribution in comparison to the *Bibliothèque bleue* and the *colportage* that it displaced.[7] Terdiman notes that this same protocol of perception is needed by the shopper in the newly inaugurated department stores with their random presentation of goods. This elaboration of the profound effect of the daily on cultural practices complements Balzac's own view that liberal institutions are inherently disorderly.

While largely commercial motives have been assigned to Balzac's publication of the "Avant-propos" (1842), one could argue that his unwillingness to yield to the *feuilleton* form indicates his commitment to the *Comédie* as a preferred mode of literary discourse, capable of taking on the *feuilleton*. This understanding of the "Avant-propos" and of Balzac's last novels considers their function as an oppositional discourse that engages another form as well as other production and consumption practices. These practices echo the petty commercial mentality of the ruling class. For all this, Balzac's view certainly cannot be considered attuned to the future, since the novel developed increasingly as a popular form and the serial form dominates magazine and television productions even today.

Despite the role of Balzac's last novels in opposing the *feuilleton* genre, both of them were published serially and steeped in *feuilleton* thematics.[8] Like other popular urban forms, the *feuilleton* featured the Parisian lower class, family situations, the occult and crime, as well as the attendant vengeance, secrecy, and greed fostered in such circumstances. *Pons* depicts working class neighborhoods and various sectors of the working poor, while *Bette* features the upper strata in bourgeois Paris except for Bette herself. The topic of Pons's secret art collection functions complexly to orchestrate the thematics of the entire novel and thus can serve further to construct contexts for the novel. Pons's art collection becomes the object of an inheritance plot wherein Balzac highlights proletarian greed and bourgeois self-interest. The two sentiments seem identical, but the means available to each group in acquiring the collection reside in the respective discourses they wield. *Pons* can therefore be reconstructed as a novel of incipient class warfare, situating the discourses of the novel in relation to contemporary public discourses. Bakhtin's notion of ideological discourse is essential here to one's discussion of class discourse. Although industrialization was not complete until the Second Empire, class consciousness was developing slowly but surely in France throughout the 1840s. As we shall see, *Les Parents pauvres* is informed by a particular discourse of *social concerns*—concerns that the eighteenth century labelled as moral and that were soon to be considered as class interests.

In a recent study, William Sewell, the historian, notes that in post-revolutionary France the term "social" refers to suprapersonal institutions rather than to the general definition of social intercourse or to the eighteenth-century notion of voluntary association of individuals in social contracts. The term undergoes further refinement in the 1830s and '40s.[9] New suprapersonal institutions, investigated by new social sciences, produce a discourse of labor and its organization; the adjective "social" most often alludes to these problems, indicating sympathy with the poor (Sewell 222). Because the bourgeoisie benefited more immediately from the Revolution than the budding proletariat, the very terms of the Revolution simply could not take on their full socio-ideological significance until a thoroughly bourgeois regime—the July Monarchy—was installed. Sewell notes that the great preoccupation of liberal French society in the '30s and '40s was the problem of *demoralization*. Because the social had become an arena of investigation, many studies were undertaken in which the discourse of the ruling class had to justify itself and mete out blame elsewhere—hence, the problems of working class demoralization.

In 1835, Louis Villermé, a physician, was empowered to investigate the moral and physical conditions of the working classes. He depicted the poverty and misery of the working poor, inferring a profound moral degradation from these conditions. Such studies were common enough, and Balzac spoke out against their self-righteousness on more than one occasion, notably in the August 20, 1840, issue of *La Revue Parisienne*, where his target was the institution that had supported Villermé's study, the Académie des Sciences Morales et Politiques: "le lieu de déportation inventé pour ces sortes d'esprits. Une fois là, les hommes graves se tiennent tranquilles.... Si Fourier, si Saint-Simon vivaient, ils n'en seraient point."[10] Interestingly, Villermé's description of the demoralization typical of an urban working class pub could have served as a direct source for Balzac's similar description of a peasant cabaret in *Les Paysans* (chap. 12, part 1). Balzac's rural version, however, turns the blame for such demoralization back on liberal society itself. Moreover, the Marais, where Pons lives, is adjacent to streets completely filled with working class establishments. The rue de la Perle as represented in *Pons* is the very elaboration of moral confusion or the "social problem." While Balzac is frequently taken to task for not representing the working classes, *Pons* is set precisely in the milieu of the working poor who were greedy because desperate during the period of the July Monarchy.

In *Pons*, the institutional organization of language—and of law in particular—is the arbiter of destiny: those having access to such discourse will prevail. Pons is an ugly old man, gifted in music, yet having never produced much of importance. Although he has won a competition in his youth, he makes his ends meet in his old age by giving music lessons, by dining with relatives, and by living with his friend and fellow musician, Schmucke, a thoroughly idealized German Romantic type. Pons falls ill when he quarrels with his relatives, the Camusot de Marville family. In order to make amends, Pons offers to find a rich husband for their unmarried daughter. When the marriage falls through, the Camusot family cuts off Pons completely and he becomes bedridden. His concierge, Mme Cibot, takes care of him and discovers, as have the Camusots, that Pons is an amateur art collector. She plots with the lawyer, Fraisier, to defraud Pons of his collections. The lawyer thinks he can do better by allying himself with the Camusot family, and Mme Cibot ends by obtaining the smallest portion among the numerous co-conspirators. In the end, Pons's "work" falls into the hands of the bourgeoisie, and Schmucke, his legal heir, dies of grief over his friend's death.

Mme Cibot, the concierge who betrays Pons, needs an accomplice to defraud him after failing to cajole her way into his will. She goes to Fraisier, a poverty-ridden lawyer, a type already described by Balzac in *La Fille aux yeux d'or*: "Le jeune avocat sans causes, le jeune médecin sans clients sont les deux plus grandes expressions du Désespoir décent, particulier à la ville de Paris." Now, la Cibot, as she is called, prides herself on her smooth talk but plays directly into Fraisier's hands: "Mme Cibot! je connaissais votre affaire, mais je ne savais rien de Mme Cibot! Autant de clients, autant de caractères. ..." Fraisier, the 1847 version of the unsuccessful lawyer, thus proves to be the consummate professional whose manipulation of the law represents the privatization of a public discourse that is meant to serve society. When Fraisier puts himself at the disposal of the Camusots, he does so provided he one day be appointed *juge dè paix*. Such are the manipulations fostered by codified law, an unqualified disaster in the opinion of Balzac's narrator: "Magistrats, conseillers, jurisconsultes, juges, avocats, officiers ministériels, avoués, huissiers, conseils, hommes d'affaires, agents d'affaires et défenseurs, sont les Variétés sous lesquelles se classent les gens qui rendent la justice ou qui la travaillent" (*CP* 203).

In addition to seeking Fraisier's help, Mme Cibot consults the neighborhood cardreader to assure herself that conditions are generally propitious. Like Henry Monnier's "bourgeois campagnards"—in fact, there is a Mme Cibot in one of his series[11]—Mme Cibot longs to retire to the country. Her fortuneteller, who is, according to the narrator, a central figure in the lives of the lower classes, tells la Cibot that she will be murdered by escaped convicts in the retirement village where she will live with her second husband. Mme Cibot hardly knows whether she should be more shocked by the news of her husband's demise than by the news of her own. She is frightened by her horoscope, yet wishing to believe only the positive parts of the message, she decides to go ahead with the plot against Pons, for she must have money above all else. In a chapter entitled, "Traité des sciences occultes," the only lengthy digression in either *Pons* or *Bette*, the narrator discusses fortunetelling in relation to a very broad sense of the occult. In *Pons*, the occult is represented as an arbiter of destiny: the mystery of the exceptional individual capable of making history has ceded to a broad force that mystifies individuals. The occult simply symbolizes that which those who are excluded from power see as inexplicable yet inevitable: the Law. Liberal society fosters countless professionals like la Cibot's cardreader, Mme Fontaine. Pierre François Léonard Fontaine happens to be the name of the architect employed under Napoleon, the Restoration, and the July Monarchy to complete the Louvre project—the sordid site still incomplete at the writing of *Les Parents pauvres*.[12] In the new society causality is both remote and close at hand, buried and on the surface. The liberal order is like any other form of *astrologie judiciaire*: "une alliance de mots excessivement bizarre" (*CP* 145).

Mme Cibot is wise indeed to consult both the law and the occult sciences. The former, however, is outside her ken. Bakhtin has elaborated two types of ideological discourse: authoritative and internally persuasive discourse. Authoritative discourse is above all "prior," carrying influence because it is hierarchically beyond the reach of familiar communicative interaction. Internally persuasive discourse, on the other hand, belongs to the less hierarchized and more accessible realm of discourse that is heteroglot and available for appropriation: "It is not so much interpreted by us as it is further, that is, freely developed, applied to new material, new conditions; it enters into interanimating relationships with new contexts" (Bakhtin 345). More often than not, the utterances of the speaking person are taken precisely from "living hermeneutics," an everyday concern for the "they say" of public opinion. According to Bakhtin, such assertions are always influencing someone else in an anonymous, social way.

The representation of French liberal society in *Le Cousin Pons* reveals the vulnerability of Law to private interests. Balzac sees a dangerous flux in authoritative discourses in the new social formation, approaching the accessibility of Bakhtin's internally persuasive discourse. One accordingly consults one's lawyer much as one would consult one's fortuneteller. In the preface to *Les Parents pauvres*, Balzac attributes the moral confusion of his age to a form of government that fosters only debate: "Aussi le Livre Saint a-t-il jeté cette prophétique parole: *Dieu livra la monde aux discussions*. J'avoue que ce seul passage de l'Ecriture devrait engager le Saint-Siège à vous donner le gouvernement des deux Chambres pour obéir à cette sentence commentée, en 1814, par l'ordonnance de Louis XVIII." The disorder characteristic of liberal institutions thus contaminates all levels of discourse.

The particular conditions of class discourse inflect discourse at other levels. We have seen that power in *Pons* is calculated according to a system of in-/exclusion.[13] Pons's and Schmucke's destinies are sealed by their unwillingness and inability to adapt to the system of self-interest that surrounds them; they represent a delicate countermodel destroyed by the effects of such exclusion. Furthermore, the speech of numerous professionals—doormen, poverty-ridden lawyers and doctors, tradesmen, theatrical people—is foregrounded to represent the cacophony that opposes

the harmony of music for Pons and Schmucke. At one point in the novel the
values of two social groups—artists and bourgeois—are composed according
to their respective abilities to appreciate music:

> Schmucke se mit au piano. Sur ce terrain, et au bout de quelques
> instants, l'inspiration musicale, excitée par le tremblement de la
> douleur et l'irritation qu'elle lui causait, emporta le bon
> Allemand; selon son habitude au delà des mondes. Il trouva des
> thèmes sublimes sur lesquels il broda des caprices…. Cette poésie
> fut interrompue par une affreuse sonnerie. La bonne des
> locataires du premier étage vint prier Schmucke, de la part de ses
> maîtres, de finir ce sabbat. Madame, Monsieur et mademoiselle
> Chapoulot étaient éveillés, ne pouvaient plus se rendormir, et
> faisaient observer que la journée était assez longue pour répéter
> les musiques de théâtre, et que, dans une maison du Marais, on
> ne devait pas *pianoter* pendant la nuit. (*CP* 292–93)

The narrator's language first adopts Schmucke's flowery, artistic prose, then
a straightforward, no-nonsense bourgeois style in the form of indirect
discourse linked by the narrator's transitional sentence ("Cette poésie fut
interrompue …"). The narrator's language is therefore not a unitary
language of mastery, but is inflected with diverse social languages.

In another passage, the narrator reports details from the first interview
between la Cibot and Fraisier:

> Madame Cibot parla pendant une demi-heure sans que l'agent
> d'affaires (1) se permît la moindre interruption; il avait l'air
> curieux d'un jeune soldat écoutant un *vieux de la vieille*. (2) Ce
> silence et la soumission de Fraisier, l'attention qu'il paraissait
> prêter à ce bavardage à casades (3) dont on a vu des échantillons
> dans les scènes entre la Cibot et le pauvre Pons (4), firent
> abandonner à la défiante portière (5) quelques-unes des
> préventions que tant de détails ignobles venaient de lui inspirer.
> (*CP* 208)

Giving examples of a broad tendency that he calls "l'avilissement des mots,"
the narrator has already discussed the legal professional derogatorily
designated as an *homme de loi*, among whom are *les agents d'affaires* (1) "qui
mettent le métier de plain-pied avec la pratique des rues, avec le peuple."
The narrator uses a military as well as popular expression in characterizing

the interlocutors (2, 3). In this short paragraph he also makes several references (in his role of textual orchestrator), to crucial points reader needs to recall (1, 4). The narrator not only includes the various discourses but several registers as well (including irony [5]), carrying out two functions as narrator, by reporting the action and orchestrating the text.

In *Pons* as well there is a distinct project of semantic invention. Pons is an amateur art collector and Balzac coins the words *collectionneur* and *collectionner*, which, along with existent *collection*, constitute a minimal version of the narrative: the agent, the action, and the noun/object. The sociohistorical occasion for raising the topic of collection is Napoleon's nationalization of the Church's art treasures, which flooded the collectors' market. The emperor's policy toward the Church has opened up a new market for expanding personal collections, eventually commodifying art in liberal society. This commodification of course is exemplified for Balzac by the *feuilleton* form of literary discourse. Pons's collection symbolizes an alternative to bourgeois art values, but dangerously close to regressive aristocratic possession. Pons's collecting, moreover, along with his *gourmandise*, gratifies his repressed sexuality and the collection eventually becomes the "heroine" of the novel. Pons is ultimately powerless to prevent his cherished artworks from being converted into so much exchange value for that very bourgeoisie. At the end of the novel, Pons's collection, functioning as the work's heroine, is a figuration of the reduced possibilities of agency and activity in liberal society: "Tout le monde désirera sans doute savoir ce qu'est devenu l'héroïne de cette histoire, malheureusement trop véridique dans ses détails, et qui, superposée à la précédente dont elle est la soeur jumelle (*Bette*), prouve que la grande force sociale est le caractère. Vous devinez, ô amateurs, connaisseurs, et marchands, qu'il s'agit de la collection de Pons" (*CP* 364–65). To counterbalance the importance of force of character in society, the agent and the activity in *Pons* become virtual, depending upon an absolute value rather than upon a mere thing. The end product is thus a heroic object that seeks to reverse bourgeois values through reference to a prior mode of valuation—in this case, the elevated nature of art. Men and their actions have both been made smaller by the liberal system, but Balzac insists that there are yet symbols to impel men toward greatness and to promote social stability.

Speech, however, betrays the existence of Pons's collection and represents the final, most flagrant appropriation of "Pons." The primary object in Pons's collection is a fan, which he presents to Mme Camusot in order to regain her favor. This donation of the fan, however, reveals the existence of the collection (but not its value, for Mme Camusot does not appreciate Pons's expertise). Since the French expression *éventer* means to disclose a secret, the gift of the *éventail* sets the conspiracy in motion. Moreover, it is not only his fan and his collection that are appropriated, but, finally, Pons's word as well:

> "Cet éventail que vous admirez, milord, et qui est celui de madame de Pompadour, il me l'a remis un matin en me disant un mot charmant que vous me permettrez de ne pas répéter." ... Et elle regarda sa fille. "Dites-moi le mot," demanda le prince russe, "Madame la vicomtesse." "Le mot vaut l'éventail!" ... reprit la vicomtesse dont le mot était stéréotypé. "Il a dit à ma mère qu'il était bien temps que ce qui avait été dans les mains du vice restât dans les mains de la vertu." Le milord regarda madame Camusot de Marville d'un air de doute extrêmement flatteur pour une femme si sèche. (*CP* 366)

Pons's creativity has thus been fully turned to serve bourgeois self-interest.

It has been demonstrated that discourse analysis contextualizes both narrow and broad portions of social languages. We have attempted to reconstruct the rival literary discourse of the *Comédie* as a generic language as well as part of a broad tendency in culture consumption and production. It has been noted that the press created a large mass audience, which might exert great control over cultural politics as easily as it might be manipulated by a given program. Because print culture increasingly became mass culture, Balzac's view of the novel (and of art in general) is regressive, but it does not blunt his critique of bourgeois institutions. Interestingly, the serial output of Balzac's novels has been virtually erased by their containment within the *Comédie*. Editors and literary historians have reserved for Balzac the place in literary history that he desired—one where the artist is king.

Contextualizing the broad public debates over social concerns of the era necessitates being attentive to particular words—social, demoralization, occult—as well as to social languages—those of lawyers, concierges, musicians. Bakhtin's fruitful notion that there is a dialogue of socio-ideological languages at any given time within a particular society constructs contexts while it elaborates the necessary conditions for novelistic prose. We are thus forced to realize that textual relations are always sets of intertextual pragmatics due to this interpenetration of discourses. Discourse analysis, then, guarantees that the nature of modern linguistic consciousness always motivates the study of novels as concrete expressions of verbal and ideological life. A novel, moreover, is never the sum of so many social languages, but a further orchestration of their interpenetration within both textual and intertextual verbal systems. In *Le Cousin Pons*, the heterglossia characteristic of society is present in the same degree and functions expressively as well as thematically. The heterogeneous utterances and mixed style characteristic of Balzac's literary practice thus contribute to social heteroglossia rather than deny it.

In our discussion of LaCapra's construction of Bakhtin, it was noted that this approach to contextualization allows for close readings of novels while developing their complex intertextual relations. Contextualization thus offers new ground for criticism as well as for specific readings. Ultimately, Bakhtin rejects what might be called thematic criticism:

> The study of verbal art can and must overcome the divorce between an abstract "formal" approach and an equally abstract "ideological" approach. Form and content in discourse are one, once we understand that verbal discourse is a social phenomenon—social throughout its entire range and in each and every one of its factors, from the sound image to the furthest reaches of abstract meaning. (259)

Thematic tendencies in criticism are not limited to discussions of artistic themes. Rather, they privilege a single determining element in a critical discussion, cutting off the full range of determining elements of cultural phenomena.[14] If one considers René Guise's study of Balzac's relation to the *feuilleton* form, one is obliged to maintain the primacy of commercial factors and to diminish the relative importance of others in order to focus one's study. Because Guise considers the *feuilleton* strictly in its commercial effects, moreover, its function as a generic language is reduced. The fully intertextual analysis of "commercial" considerations must go beyond pecuniary necessity to questions of dominance in modes of literary production and habits of perception. The tendency to thematize detracts from an understanding of the degree of interrelatedness of discourses as a proper context. No single factor or level of any text or discourse can be the goal of criticism. In *Le Cousin Pons*, it is therefore necessary to analyze specific utterances as well as entire discourses and jargons, and explicit themes as well as implicit modes of discourse, for they are all materially verifiable means of representing social life. In fact, the range of analysis accounted for by discourse analysis is its strength. Context in the novel, then, is a discursive consideration of its production rather than an external mode of explanation.

NOTES

1. M. M. Bakhtin, "The Novel as Discourse," *The Dialogic Imagination: Four Essays by M. M. Bakhtin*, ed. Michael Holquist, trans. C. Emerson and M. Holquist (Austin: University of Texas Press, 1981) 291.

2. Dominick LaCapra, *Rethinking Intellectual History: Texts, Contexts, Language* (Ithaca: Cornell University Press, 1983).

3. René Guise, "Balzac et le roman feuilleton," *Année Balzacienne* (1964): 283–338. Cf. André Lorant, *Les Parents pauvres d'Honoré de Balzac, La Cousine Bette, Le Cousin Pons, Etude historique et critique*, 2 vols. (Geneva: Droz, 1967).

4. As cited in Guise 307.

5. Balzac, *Le Cousin Pons* (Paris: Gallimard, 1973). All references are to this edition. Balzac dedicates *La Cousine Bette* to a commentator of Dante in these words: "Comprendre ainsi Dante, c'est être grand comme lui...."

6. Richard Terdiman, *Discourse/Counter-Discourse* (Ithaca: Cornell University Press, 1985).

7. See the discussion in Gérard Delfau and Anne Roche, *Histoire/Littérature: Histoire et interprétation du fait littéraire* (Paris: Seuil, 1977), and David Bellos, *Balzac Criticism in France (1850–1900): The Making of a Reputation* (Oxford: Clarendon Press, 1976).

8. Critical response to *Les Parents pauvres* was overwhelmingly positive; see Guise, 330–32.

9. William H. Sewell, Jr., *Work and Revolution in France: The Language of Labor from the Old Regime to 1848* (Cambridge: Cambridge University Press, 1980) 222.

10. Honoré de Balzac, "Sur les ouvriers," *Revue Parisienne*, 25 August 1840.

11. Henri Monnier, *Scènes populaires, dessinées à la plume de Henri Monnier* (Paris: Dumont, 1835–39). The proliferation of popular genres in France throughout the 1830s was due largely to the advent of the mass press. Among those popular genres figuring in novels were caricature and physiology, made possible by the economical production of lithography.

12. The unfinished Louvre site in Paris is a recurring motif in *Bette*: "Ce ne sera certes pas un hors-d'oeuvre que de décrire ce coin de Paris actuel, plus tard on ne pourrait pas l'imaginer; et nos neveux, qui verront sans doute le Louvre achevé, se refuseraient à croire pareille barbarie ait subsisté

pendant trente-six ans, au coeur de Paris, en face du palais où trois dynasties ont reçu pendant ces dernières trente-six années, l'élite de la France et celle de l'Europe." Balzac, *La Cousine Bette* (Paris: Garnier-Flammarion, 1977) 103.

13. For a full elaboration of a thematics of in-/exclusion in *Pons*, see Lucienne Frappier-Mazur, "Le Discours du pouvoir dans *Le Cousin Pons*," in Françoise van Rossum-Guyon and Michiel van Brederode, *Balzac et Les Parents pauvres* (Paris: SEDES, 1981) 21–32.

14. We should recall Bakhtin's definition of theme: "The theme is determined not only by the linguistic forms that comprise it—words, morphological and syntactic structures, sounds and intonation—but also by extraverbal factors of the situation.... Only an utterance taken in its full, concrete scope as an historical phenomenon possesses a theme" (attributed to V. N. Voloshinov, *Marxism and the Philosophy of Language* [New York: Seminar Press, 1973] 100).

ALEXANDER FISCHLER

Eugénie Grandet's
Career as Heavenly Exile

B alzac liked to suggest to his readers that some of the exceptional men and women of *La Comédie humaine* were exiles, more suited for a realm where categories and gradation are irrelevant than for cramped quarters "ici-bas." The argument was a romantic commonplace. He was able to vitalize it, however, by adding consistently a very literal dimension to exile as metaphor, by suggesting, as he did in *Eugénie Grandet*, that removal from one's habitual environment or sphere of influence is a reality whose effects can be observed,[1] or by arguing, as he did in some of the *Etudes philosophiques*, that the sense of separation from an extraterrestrial sphere is a significant response to a cosmic order perceived by faith and described by theologians and mystics. As illustrated by Eugénie Grandet's career, the assertion that a protagonist is an exile not only provided a pretext for a close look at the place of confinement, but allowed careful distinctions between types and degrees of removal.

Though he used the twin themes of confinement and exile to structure *Eugénie Grandet* from the start, Balzac had some difficulty in positioning his heroine so as to insure that her home, at the top of the "ancienne Grand-Rue," be seen in perspective with a heavenly abode. Part of the positioning problem was due to the author's desire to suggest a very special affinity between the heroine and two of his mistresses, Mme Hanska and Maria du

From *Essays in Literature* XVI, no. 2. ©1989 by Western Illinois University.

Fresnay. Most of it, however, can be shown to have resulted from concern that Eugénie's necessarily limited perception precluded a sense of exile and from the fact that Balzac realized, as evidenced by his revisions, that an ambiguous connection with the world around ultimately served her characterization better than exile from the world beyond.

The novel was written and published in 1833. In the Edition Béchet, which appeared after serial publication the same year but was dated 1834, it was the first of the "Scènes de la Vie de Province" and was allegedly intended to illustrate the fact that great values (material as well as moral) are to be found in the provinces, far from the madding crowds of Paris. The *Tourangeau*, Balzac, was obviously delighted to confront the connoisseurs of value of both realms and to demonstrate from the start that myopia prevails among them. Here was also an opportunity to show that social exile is a condition both assumed and imposed: while Charles, decked out in finery carefully chosen to dazzle his hosts, is compared by the author to a peacock plumetted into an obscure chicken yard (1054), the *Provinciaux*, united for once in their distaste for fashion and their distrust of the *Parisiens*, scrutinize him mockingly as if he were an exotic giraffe (1058). But the impressions of another observer, the innocent Eugénie, are recorded as well: for her, the young man is a seraph come down from heaven, a phoenix among cousins (1058–59). Charles himself is uneasy in the new setting. By the end of the evening, as he sets out to ascend with the rest of the household, the stairwell does indeed look to him like a chicken roost (1069).

Thus, as exile fosters the defensive responses of contempt and conceit, confinement is shown to foster the naive worship of a creature who, being more attuned to heaven than to earth, sublimates what she sees. This naïve response of the innocent is what Balzac chose to set at the heart of his novel, for through Eugénie, appearing as an exile from an extraterrestrial sphere, he could invoke an ultimate metaphysical scale to evaluate action whose course would otherwise seem determined by worldly considerations alone.

The Grandet household is presented as a cloistered realm within a provincial world insulated in time from modern reality. Twice removed from common affairs and ruled by its own tyrannical and earth-bound god, "le Dieu Argent," the money god, the Maison Grandet could easily become a testing ground, a station on the way to a higher reality in a spiritual realm. Certainly the three women in the house were to appear in transit, accepting their grim lot on earth while praying for happiness beyond.

Dealing with the generally submissive and retiring Eugénie, Balzac showed that true character would not emerge out of sheer contrast with those who surround her. Hence he compared her repeatedly to the Virgin

Mary and then drew freely on the many roles the comparison suggested. With much less effect on characterization, he also compared her to a noble statue, specifically the Venus of Milo, to Penelope, Faust's Marguerite, a linnet, a rare bird, the pure lamb with a golden fleece, and the prey of the pack. In early editions of the novel the author involved himself openly and extensively in the presentation of his Virgin and assumed for this purpose the two complementary roles of artist-creator and worshiper of woman perfected in Mary. The presentation was thus quite formal and clumsy, relying both on the text of the novel and on an external framework which consisted of a "Préambule" and "Epilogue" (deleted after 1843) to which a dedication, "A Maria," was added in the Edition Charpentier of 1839.

The fact that the central character was to be viewed as an exile from a higher sphere was established in the preamble of the early editions. After defending his choice of seemingly plain subjects set against a country background, the author calls attention to the moralities ("mythes" in the manuscript) that can be found in country traditions:

> ... aujourd'hui le pauvre artiste n'a saisi qu'un de ces fils blancs promenés dans les airs par la brise, et dont s'amusent les enfants, les jeunes filles, les poètes; dont les savants ne se soucient guère; mais que, dit-on, laisse tomber, de sa quenouille, une céleste fileuse. Prenez garde! Il y a des *moralités* dans cette tradition champêtre! Aussi l'auteur en fait-il son épigraphe. Il vous montrera comment, durant la belle saison de la vie, certaines illusions, de blanches espérances, des fils argentés descendent des cieux et y retournent sans avoir touché terre. (1026)

> [... today, the poor artist caught only one of these white strands that wander with the breeze, playthings for children, young maidens and poets, which concern not the learned, but which, according to rumor, are dropped from the distaff of a heavenly spinner. Take heed! *Moralities* may be found in this folk tradition. As a result, the author takes it for his epigraph. He will show you how, during life's beautiful season, certain illusions, white hopes, silvery threads descend from heaven and return there without having touched ground.]

Gossamer, in French, is "fil de la Vierge," the Virgin's thread. The folk tradition, which assigns to it a divine origin and a heavenly destination, suggests that one does not pluck it out of the air in vain. Eugénie, we thus learn, is a temporary exile from heaven, drifting untainted through the world and recalling, as the text will tell us repeatedly, a model above.

The epilogue fulfills the promise of the preamble and brings together the Marian strands, relating the portrait drawn in the book to those offered by earlier artists in tribute to the Virgin. The author expresses proper humility in his task (in the manuscript he even slights himself by comparison with the great Madonna painters, asserting he is not one of them, "ni Raphaël, ni Rembrandt, ni Poussin"):

> Peut-être a-t-il trop chargé d'or le contour de la tête de sa Maria; peut-être n'at-il pas distribué la lumière suivant les règles de l'art; enfin, peut-être a-t-il trop rembruni les teintes déjà noires de son vieillard, image toute matérielle. Mais ne refusez pas votre indulgence au moine patient, vivant au fond de sa cellule, humble adorateur de la *Rosa mundi*, de Marie, belle image de tout le sexe, la femme du moine, la seconde Eva des chrétiens. (1201)

> [Perhaps he surrounded the head of his Maria with too much gold; failed to distribute light according to the rules of art; or drew too darkly his already dark old man, a wholly material image. Still, do not refuse your indulgence to the patient monk who lives in the depth of his cell, a humble wòrshiper of the *Rosa mundi*, of Mary, fair image of the entire sex, the monk's spouse, the Christian's second Eve.]

The manuscript ended with an assertion of Eugénie's celestial nature; in the published version of the epilogue, however, she is compared instead with a noble statue taken from Greece that falls into the sea in mid-passage and remains forever unknown. Comparison with Mary did not necessarily always support Balzac's argument; when he revised the text for publication, he chose the image of lost treasure in preference to the image of celestial exile, thus stressing in the end, as he had done in the beginning, the theme of the beauty that fades unseen, a more earth-bound cliché. The revisions shift emphasis from celestial origins and destiny to terrestrial confinement.

The third and last item, added to the novel's external frame in 1839, was the dedication "A Maria." Originally it complemented the preamble and epilogue, dedicating the work to woman epitomized in the Virgin Mary and drawing attention to the presentation of Eugénie as exile from heaven. Four years later, when Balzac revised his works again in preparation for the 1843 Edition Furne, he minimized his interpretative involvement and retained only this dedication from the cumbersome external frame of the novel. As a result, despite obviously religious overtones in its wording, the dedication no longer seemed to invoke the Virgin as model for Eugénie, but to address itself to a contemporary:

A Maria
    Que votre nom, vous dont le portrait est le plus bel ornement de cet ouvrage, soit ici comme une brache de buis bénit, prise on ne sait à quel arbre, mais certainement sanctifiée par la religion et renouvelée, toujours verte, par des mains pieuses, pour protéger la maison.

De Balzac. (1027)

[To Maria
    May your name, you whose portrait is the most beautiful ornament of this work, be here like a blessed branch of boxwood, taken from one knows not which tree, but certainly sanctified by religion and always green, renewed by pious hands, to protect the house.

De Balzac.]

The contemporary Maria, we now know, was Maria Du Fresnay, née Daminois, Balzac's mistress, whose daughter, Marie, born in 1834, he recognized as his own. André Chancerel and Roger Pierrot, who are responsible for the identification, argued that Maria du Fresnay was the actual model for Eugénie.[2] More recent editors, however, doubt the possibility of such identification. They also point out that in the dedication, the preamble and the epilogue, Balzac not only offered a tribute to Maria Du Fresnay and "the entire [fair] sex," but also to Mme Hanska whom he gave the manuscript as a Christmas present.[3] The holy branch, he could argue, was the boxwood over her portrait, and the conventional Maria-Eva association was, as she knew, one of his favorites. Interestingly enough, however, in a letter dated October 12, 1833 (i.e., while still working on the novel), Balzac announces to his sister, Laure, that he has fathered a child and describes Maria Du Fresnay in terms that recall Eugénie and gossamer from the distaff of the Virgin: "une gentille personne, la plus naïve créature qui soit, tombée comme une fleur du ciel" (1648) [a gentle person, the most naive of creatures, come down from heaven like a flower].
    Balzac allowed himself considerable margin when he said in his 1839 dedication that the branch, "taken one knows not from what tree," was

renewable; in settling details of the novel's framing text, he could settle domestic accounts as well. Nonetheless, the Madonna worship and the discussion in the epilogue of woman's place in the creation nearer to the angel than man represented genuine concerns going far beyond the little games he might have been playing with his mistresses.[4] Association with the Virgin Mary was his most expedient device for indicating the superiority of a female protagonist on the grounds of heavenly affinities. As a matter of fact, the manuscript variants indicate that during the composition of the novel Balzac was so taken with this device that he even allowed Charles Grandet to join in the Mary cult midway through the farewell letter to his Parisian mistress, Annette:

> Tu auras du moins embelli ma belle jeunesse, orné mon âme des nobles délicatesses de la femme, je ne pourrai jamais voir les madones de Raphaël sans penser à toi qui as coloré ma seconde enfance des feux de ton visage céleste, qui as sanctifié par ton amour la vie désordonnée à laquelle les jeunes gens se livrent, qui as ennobli les passions mauvaises de ton amant en jettant tes douces voluptés dans mon âme. Si je suis bon, si je vaux quelque chose, c'est par toi. (1704)

> [You will at least have embellished my beautiful youth, adorned my soul with woman's noble delicacies; I will never be able to look at Raphael's madonnas without recalling you who lent hue to my second childhood with the flames of your heavenly face, who hallowed with love the unruly life that the young espouse, who made noble a lover's foul passions by filling my soul with your exquisite delight. If I am good, if I am worth anything, it is through you.]

These lines to Annette, however, detracted from the theme of celestial virtue in the country and gave Charles a sensitivity that was in direct opposition to the aridity Balzac wanted him to represent. So he changed the text to eliminate this *Ave Annette* and, in the same revision, introduced into the letter a hint at the possibility of marriage between Charles and Eugénie and followed it with a comment on the coldness of tone manifest in the writing: the naive country girl who reads the letter is unaware of this coldness, but the author marks it as a characteristic of the spoiled, big-city child. Such revisions indicate Balzac's growing awareness of the scale he had adopted by comparing Eugénie to the Virgin—in the final version, only she was to be allowed a hallowing love: "La candeur d'Eugénie avait momentanément sanctifié l'amour de Charles" (1141) [The guilelessness of Eugénie had momentarily sanctified the love of Charles]. Associations with the Madonna were much better suited for her, and, if there were to be extensions to the other virtuous women in the novel, Balzac could handle them just as effectively by reference to feminine angelism and to physical manifestations of the soul's transcendence (notably, in the transfiguration of Mme Grandet before her death). There is only one exception to the rule, an early reference to Nanon, "plus chaste que ne l'était la Vierge Marie elle-même" (1043) [more chaste than the Virgin Mary herself].

Despite her many virtues, however, Nanon is no exile from heaven. What distinguishes her, as the last line of the novel tells us, is that she does not have wits enough to understand the corruption of the world. Eugénie, on the other hand, overcomes her initial naïveté, learns to assess those about her at their worth, and follows her confessor's advice by coming to terms with the world, albeit uneasily. Her heavenly antecedents and destiny, which may have been clichés at the outset, allow evaluation of her career in the world and explain the nature of her compromise with it, notably in her insistence on remaining a virgin.

Balzac's attempt to insure a metaphysical perspective for his heroine is well illustrated in the famous portrait of Eugénie *à sa toilette*, offered early in the novel (1073–76). This scene, set against the melancholy background of the garden on the morning after Charles's arrival, provided an excuse for a detailed physical description enhanced by the author's own estimate of her beauty and some suggestive analogies. Viewing herself in the mirror after discovering the "mystérieuses beautés particulières aux endroits solitaires ou à la nature inculte" (1074) [the mysterious beauties that are particular to solitary places or untamed nature] which had hitherto seemed ordinary to her, Eugénie concludes that she is unworthy of her cousin. But the author, claiming she is unfair to herself, compares her to the recently discovered Venus of Milo, adding that her beauty is actually "ennoblie par cette suavité du sentiment chrétien qui purifie la femme et lui donne une distinction inconnue aux sculpteurs anciens" (1075) [ennobled by that softness of Christian sentiment which purifies woman and gives her a distinction unknown to ancient sculptors]. Such a description supports the theme of the hidden grandeur and offers a parallel to the lost statue at the end of the epilogue. The associations may appear incongruous when we read the description of the rather homely Eugénie which follows immediately, but Balzac was evidently serious: almost in the same breath he went on to compare his heroine's broad forehead with that of the Jupiter of Phidias.

We are told by Pierrot and Chancerel that consideration of the model, Maria du Fresnay, might have been involved here (448). But, more important, we have evidence of Balzac's desire to anchor Eugénie in more than one world: she must represent enduring beauty, celestial beauty in particular, yet remain of this world, and the reference to slight blemishes in her physical makeup, such as the smallpox which ruined her complexion, achieved the secularization and convey the fact of exile. Balzac adds:

> Le peintre qui cherche ici-bas un type à la céleste pureté de Marie, qui demande à toute la nature ces yeux modestement fiers devinés par Raphaël, ces lignes vierges souvent dûes au hasards de la conception mais qu'une vie chrétienne et pudique peut seule conserver ou faire acquérir; ce peintre, amoureux d'un si rare modèle, eût trouvé tout à coup dans le visage d'Eugénie la noblesse innée qui s'ignore; il eút vu sous un front calme un monde d'amour; et dans la coupe des yeux, dans l'habitude des paupières, le je ne sais quoi divin. (1076)

> [The painter who seeks in this world a type for the celestial purity of Mary and asks throughout nature for those modestly proud eyes that Raphael knew, for those virgin lines that may often be due to chance at conception but that are preserved or acquired only by means of a chaste, Christian life; such a painter, enamored of so rare a model, would have discovered on Eugénie's face nobility that is innate but unaware of itself; he would have seen a world of love under a peaceful brow and discovered the divine *je ne sais quoi* in the shape of the eyes, the form of the lids.]

Before dismissing sublimation of Eugénie on the grounds that it catered to the worst of contemporary taste, it is useful to note that hackneyed analogies in this novel, as shown by Ruth Amossy and Elisheva Rosen in *Les Discours du cliché*, far from being reassuring, call attention to departure from convention and result in a multi-layered narrative structure. Amossy and Rosen examine, for instance, the repeated conventional references to birds and show how they allow systematic juxtaposition of aerial and terrestrial, of aspiration and reality, and suggest in the end a heroine who is "un oiseau qui n'aura guère eu l'occasion de déployer son vol" [a bird who will never have had a chance to soar]. They conclude: "la logique du mélodrame se trouve battue en brèche tout au long d'une intrigue qui ne feint de s'y soumettre que pour mieux la démystifier–comme en témoigne un dénouement férocement ironique où sombre toute possibilité de *happy end*" [the logic of melodrama is upset throughout a narrative which pretends to conform to it only to undermine it the better—witness a ferociously ironic dénouement where every chance of a happy ending is lost].[5] Amossy and Rosen feel that the conventional association of Eugénie with the Virgin is intended primarily to show her as a model of feminine virtue. However, if one considers the association as a means of insuring that the heroine has an ultimate stage beyond the terrestrial, where the irony of situation and the irony of fate do not apply, then a happy ending is in fact indicated. There is actually no good reason to read irony into Balzac's conclusion that "Eugénie marche au ciel accompagnée d'un cortège de bienfaits" (1198). [Eugénie strides toward heaven accompanied by a procession of good deeds.]

Although he used her indeed as a model of feminine virtue, Balzac wanted to evoke more than purity by associating his heroine with Mary. Until her brief confrontation with Grandet and afterwards, she is also, like the Virgin, a model of submissiveness and obedience, and long before suffering elevates her, she serves as guiding spirit. Balzac even suggested that her love for Charles brings her a fulfillment that lasts long after his departure. Instead of contaminating her, love consecrates her:

> Avant la venue de son cousin, Eugénie pouvait être comparée à la Vierge avant la conception; quand il fut parti elle ressemblait à la Vierge mère: elle avait conçu l'amour. Ces deux Maries, si différentes et si bien représentées par quelques peintres espagnols constituent l'une des plus brillantes figures qui abondent dans le christianisme. (1147)

> [Before the arrival of her cousin, Eugénie could be compared to the Virgin before conception; once he had left, she resembled the Virgin Mother: she had conceived love. These two Marys, so different and so well represented by some Spanish painters, constitute one of the most brilliant figures that abound in Christianity.]

Eugénie follows her lover on a map and communicates with him via the lovers' star of which Charles had taught her the beauty and the uses. She can continue in her main role since Christianity had substituted Mary for Venus and made the lovers' star into the *stella matutina* or the *maris stella* which guides to the port of heaven. We learn considerably later that during the first voyage she had indeed accompanied him "comme cette image de la Vierge que mettent sur leur vaisseau les marins espagnols" (1181) [like the image of the Virgin which Spanish sailors use to decorate their ship].

Did Balzac realize that Eugénie's association with Mary would, in the end, assume an ironic edge? Clearly she finds no real fulfillment, and her insistence on being allowed to retain her virginity as precondition for interaction with the world only underscores the contrast between her sterile lot and that of the Madonna. All her charity does not compensate for the fact that in the preservation of her purity she mostly recalls her father, the hoarder. Balzac, who had noted the manner in which gold was reflected even in the physiognomy of his miser, notes in his final portrait of Eugénie that wealth came to her at the expense of warmth: "L'argent devait communiquer ses teintes froides à cette vie céleste, et donner de la défiance pour les sentiments à une femme qui était tout sentiment" (1197). [Money was to communicate its cold tints to this heavenly life and make emotions seem suspect to a woman who was all emotion.] Her selflessness may contrast with the selfishness that motivates the world around her, but her purity has worrisome implications betrayed by her appearance.

Balzac knew that purity was so far out of place in the world that it might justifiably seem unnatural: in *La Cousine Bette* he would eventually explore even its monstrous side, like Racine in *Phèdre*. But in the case of Eugénie, he chose merely to concentrate on the manner in which whiteness contrasts with surrounding gold and grey, the colors most notably associated with her father. She remains pure to the end: "Son visage est blanc, reposé, calme. Sa voix est douce et recueillie, ses manières sont simples. Elle a toutes les noblesses de la douleur, la sainteté d'une personne qui n'a pas souillé son âme au contact du monde [ms. qui n'a pas vécu], mais aussi la roideur de la vieille fille et les habitudes mesquines que donne l'existence étroite de la province" (1198). [Her face is white, rested, calm. Her voice is soft, composed, her manner is simple. She has all the nobility of suffering, the saintliness of a person who has not soiled her soul through contact with the world (ms. who has not lived), but also the stiffness of the old maid and the petty mannerisms that come with the restrictions of provincial existence.]

Philippe Bertault has noted that Balzac was subject to the common confusion of the Immaculate Conception of Mary with the Virgin Birth.[6] This is not the case in *Eugénie Grandet*, whose heroine is to appear immaculately conceived, that is, free from the taint of original sin, and whose name, Eugénie, the well-born, suggests this explicitly. Association with gossamer from Mary's distaff remains fundamental in her presentation even after the metaphor itself disappeared with the deletion of the preamble and epilogue; summarized on the last page of the novel, her story is "l'histoire de cette femme qui n'est pas du monde au milieu du monde" [the story of a woman who is in the world though not of the world].[7] But one finds here, as one does throughout the *Comédie humaine*, from *La Peau de Chagrin* to *La Cousine Bette*, that Balzac wants his reader to view characters who have made a conscious decision to remain intact in the world with a sense of awe, that is, with a mixture of admiration and fear.

Bertault documents Balzac's particular interest in virginity as a form of strength or, more precisely, as conserved energy; he cites the discussion of virginity in *La Cousine Bette* which concludes: "cette grandiose et terrible exception mérite tous les honneurs que lui décerne l'Eglise catholique" (7:152) [this grandiose and terrible exception deserves all the honors it is granted by the Catholic church]. Peter W. Lock in his study of Balzac's hoarders and spendthrifts, describes the virgin's place among the hoarders and cites the same passage as well as another a few lines earlier in the text: "La vie, dont les forces sont économisées, a pris chez l'individu vierge une qualité de résistance et de durée incalculable." [Life, whose energy is spared, assumes in the virginal individual an incalculable quality of resistance and duration.][8] Eugénie's virginity suits her both symbolically and physically to become first a match and foil for Grandet and, eventually, a successor. At the same time, however, considered from the point of view of Balzacian hygiene and morality, her virginity and chastity explain also the ironic situation in which we last see her in the novel; for what conserves Eugénie among the living prolongs also her terrestrial exile and underlines the sense of waste which is increasingly associated with her. In the end, she has not only assumed her father's miserly ways and given ground to evil rumor, to the *médisants* who claim she is turning yellow, but, "faite pour être magnifiquement épouse et mère" (1199) [created to be mother and spouse magnificently], she has become an embodiment of wasted vitality and thwarted fruition, justifying the priest's assertion that in denying life she might be guilty of lack of charity. It is interesting to note that the rumor about Eugénie's "yellowing" and the author's expression of a sense of waste, not included in the manuscript, were added in the first edition. Thus, very early, Balzac turned Eugénie's survival into an irony of fate: not only at the expense of the scheming Cruchot de Bonfons, but at her own expense. At best, survival is for her the fulfillment of a religious obligation. Assumption into heaven is indeed to be hoped for her.

The external framework through which Balzac offered his identification of Eugénie with Mary had become cumbersome by the time he was preparing the 1843 Edition Furne. By then, Balzac had also decided to rely within the novel on the more complex and ambiguous aspects of

Eugénie's virginity which—instead of bringing out the "je ne sais quoi divin" in her eyes or her heavenly affinities—served to explain the strength of her character and the tragic element in her fate, the sense of waste. It is indeed possible to argue that he was insuring a more complex characterization when, with the 1843 edition, he eliminated the preamble and epilogue, in which he had insisted on comparing the presentation of his heroine with myth-making (in the manuscript) or with illumination and madonna painting. For in the epilogue, even as he apologized for gilding Eugénie's halo excessively, he was still stressing her heavenly nature. In the preamble, on the other hand, in the Félix Davin preface to the *Etudes de moeurs* (1835), and in the novel itself, he had insisted on a secular design, proving that the ordinary and the seemingly trivial were fit subjects for serious dramatization. By 1843 Balzac found that an excessively Christian emphasis not only detracted from the secular design but could preclude tragedy altogether. Preamble and epilogue were thus dismissed, but the readers' reactions were not much affected.

Balzac became annoyed with the preeminence the public gave this novel among his works.[9] It continues to rank among the most popular, and the reasons have not improved: readers still place Grandet at the center of the story and, ignoring all of Balzac's careful juxtapositions, single Eugénie out for worship. Unfortunately, the pure and saintly Eugénie is doomed to seem less and less tolerable to modern readers unless they can be made to realize that Balzac himself demurred at her canonization and exile in the novel, that he allowed for ambiguity in his final estimate of her position on earth, and that in his design for the novel she represented only one limited touchstone for the reality of Saumur.

Notes

1. After speculating about the glory Grandet might have found if he had exercised his gifts in a larger realm, Balzac notes that he might also have amounted to nothing beyond Saumur: "Peut-être en est-il des esprits comme de certains animaux, qui n'engendrent plus transplantés hors des climats où ils naissent" (1110). [Minds may share the fate of certain animals who stop engendering when transplanted out of the region in which they are born.] All translations are my own, and all page references are to the new Pléiade edition of *Eugénie Grandet*, ed. Nicole Mozet in *La Comédie Humaine*, ed. Pierre-Georges Castex, et al. (Paris: Gallimard, 1976) 3:989–1202, 1644–1748. References to other works by Balzac are to the same edition.

2. "La Véritable Eugénie Grandet," *Revue des Sciences Humaines*, ns 80 (1955): 437–58; cf. Mozet's introduction in the Pléiade edition.

3. Cf. Mozet's introduction in the Pléiade edition. See also Castex's note in the "Classiques Garnier" edition of *Eugénie Grandet* (Paris: Garnier, 1965) 266 and Pierrot's note in Balzac, *Letters à Madame Hanska* (Paris: Bibliophiles de l'originale, 1968) 2:193.

4. In 1833, Balzac is in the midst of a period of intense illuminist concern; see: Lucienne Frappier-Mazur, "Balzac et les images 'reparaissantes': Lumière et flamme dans *La Comédie humaine*," *Revue des Sciences Humaines*, ns 121 (1966): 45–80. Editors usually call attention to Balzac's enthusiasm during this time for the Virgin and angels of the sculptor Bra, to which he himself attributes the inspiration for *Séraphita*; see the letter to Mme Hanska of November 20 and December 1, 1833, the latter being the date on which he sent her the manuscript of *Eugénie Grandet*.

5. *Les Discours du cliché* (Paris: Société d'édition d'enseignement supérieur, 1982) 62–63, 65.

6. *Balzac et la religion* (Paris: Boivin, 1942) 82n.

7. Naomi Schor offers an excellent feminist/Freudian analysis of Eugénie's compromise with the world as a melancholic solution in *Breaking the Chain: Women, Theory, and French Realist Fiction* (New York: Columbia UP, 1985), 90–107. She unfortunately offers only in a note and does not develop her claim that the dedication "A Maria" places the novel "under the sign of Mariolatry" and "serves as a matrix, a master signifier of the fiction" (176 n 18).

8. "Hoarders and Spendthrifts in 'La Comédie Humaine,'" *Modern Language Review* 61 (1966): 33.

9. See the Castex "Introduction" xx.

SCOTT McCRACKEN

Cousin Bette: *Balzac*
and the Historiography of Difference

In recent years post-structuralism has challenged a historically-based criticism. Post-structuralist critics have emphasised textuality and 'difference' where historical critics have used contextual analysis or historical interpretation. Fredric Jameson has described textuality as

> a methodological hypothesis whereby the objects of study of the human sciences ... are considered to constitute so many texts that we *decipher* and *interpret*, as distinguished from the older views of those realities and existants or substances that we in one way or another attempt to *know*.[1]

This approach has been valuable in that it has often opened up totalising or one-sided interpretations to more complex, open, and pluralist readings. A disadvantage has been that the refusal of any one interpretation has sometimes meant that, for post-structuralists, history is just a series of texts with no necessary explanatory value. At the same time, books like Hayden White's *Metahistory* and Fredric Jameson's *The Political Unconscious* have argued the importance of a narrative form in historical criticism.

Balzac criticism has exemplified these debates, from Lukács's classic Marxist account of a general historical approach to the novel in *Studies in*

From *Essays and Studies 1991: History and the Novel.* ©1991 by The English Association.

European Realism to Barthes's minutely detailed 'plural commentary' on Balzac's novella *Sarrasine* in *S/Z*. Both critics have been subjected to a rigorous critique by Fredric Jameson, Lukács in *The Political Unconscious*, and Barthes in Jameson's recently updated essay, 'The Ideology of the Text.' My own essay gives an outline of the debate between the three critics and suggests some ways in which it might be possible to posit a relationship between the narrative structure of Balzac's *Cousin Bette* and 'difference' as it manifests itself in the text.

If history is about dates then *Cousin Bette* is self-evidently an historical novel. The narrative is structured around a specific set of dates and these act as important signifiers in the text. From the opening sentence, 'Towards the middle of July in the year 1838,' to the events in the penultimate paragraph, 'on 1 February 1846,' we are invited to associate actions and time in order to produce a meaningful narrative. Characters date themselves. Crevel's bodily movements, 'by their undisguised heaviness, are as indiscreet as a birth certificate.' The first scene takes place in a room which is dated in two senses. It is both in a state of disrepair and out of fashion:

> The Baroness sat down on a little sofa that must certainly have been very pretty about the year 1809, and motioned Crevel to an armchair decorated with bronzed sphinx heads, from which the paint was scaling off, leaving the bare wood exposed in places.[2]

These descriptive details place the two characters, Crevel and Baroness Hulot, in a historically delimited space, to which each has a different relationship. For Adeline Hulot, the furnishings, from the imperial, Napoleonic period, represent her past, youth, and faded beauty. For Crevel, the room, the historical period it represents, and Adeline herself are all objects to be conquered, or, in the more prosaic terms of the 1830s, to be bought. In *The Age of Revolution* Eric Hobsbawn writes that the 'revolutionary wave of 1830 ... marks the definitive defeat of aristocratic by bourgeois power in Western Europe.' Crevel presents himself with the irony of the ascendant power: 'I am a tradesman, a shopkeeper, a former retailer of almond paste, eau-de-Portugal, cephalic oil for hair-troubles' (p. 16).

This relationship between the character, time, and space, Engels called 'the truthful reproduction of typical characters under typical circum-stances,'[3] opposing it to late nineteenth-century naturalism; and it is Lukács, following Engels, who has done most to develop the idea of typicality in twentieth-century criticism. Characters represent a nexus of contradictory social forces within Lukács's Marxist historiography:

The Marxist philosophy of history is a comprehensive doctrine dealing with the necessary progress made by humanity from primitive communism to our own time and the perspectives of our further advance along the same road [;] as such it also gives us indications for the historical future. But such indications— born of the recognition of certain laws governing historical development—are not a cookery book providing recipes for each phenomenon or period ... but a signpost pointing the direction in which history moves forward.[4]

In so far as this is an evolutionary view of history, it is Hegelian rather than Darwinian (harking back to Lukács's earlier work, published in 1923, *The Theory of the Novel*). The typical is a contradictory category related to a socio-historical totality which the realist novel can only attempt to represent. Lukács follows Engels by putting this in terms of a relationship between Balzac's personal political stance and the representation of history in his novels. According to Engels this was itself contradictory:

Balzac was politically a Legitimist; his great work is a constant elegy on the irretrievable decay of good society; his sympathies are all with the class doomed to extinction. But for all that his satyre [sic] is never keener, his irony never bitterer than when he sets in motion the very men and women with whom he sympathises most deeply—the nobles. And the only men of whom he always speaks with undisguised admiration, are his bitterest political antagonists, the republican heroes of the Cloître Saint Merri [Méry], the men who at that time (1830–36) were indeed the representatives of the popular masses.[5]

Lukács agrees that Balzac, himself representative of the historical contradictions of the time, tries to 'present a totality' in his series of novels, *La Comédie Humaine*.

Typicality has to represent not the average, which is Lukács's criticism of Zola's naturalism, but rather

Balzac builds his plots on broader foundations than any other author before or after him, but nevertheless there is nothing in them not germane to the story. The many sided influence of multifariously determined factors in them is in perfect conformity with the structure of objective reality whose wealth

we can never adequately grasp and reflect with our all too
abstract, all too rigid, all too direct, all too unilateral thinking.[6]

Lukács's concept of realism has subsequently come under heavy attack from
post-structuralists, particularly the idea that there could be 'perfect
conformity' between the plot (despite the 'multifariously determined
factors') and 'objective reality.' Yet, there appears to be a level on which
Cousin Bette works in the way Lukács describes. The plot represents typical
aspects of the eight year period covered by the novel, 1838–46 (the novel was
itself published in 1846); and as such it is typical of the economic and
political changes under the Orléanist regime. The novel centres upon a
typical family established in the Napoleonic period, an origin which is
sufficiently dubious to provide what Lukács calls 'for Balzac the central
problem of French social history.' The family wealth has been accrued
through the Baron's position as Commissary general, and his wife's family
owes its money to foraging contracts during the Napoleonic wars. While no
aristocratic families dating back to before 1789 appear in the novel, and the
representative of the republicanism of '89, Marshal Hulot, is a member of
the establishment, not a leader of the 'popular masses,' the lack of an
established ruling class betrays a crisis of legitimacy, and society is perceived
to be unstable.

The seeds of Hulot's downfall have been sown long before the novel
opens, but it is his inability to compete with the wily financier Crevel which
dramatises his decline. Crevel's skills are more suited to the economic climate
of the 1830s and 1840s and less to the heroic period prior to 1815 to which
Hector so obviously belongs. Hector's desperate attempt to escape from
financial ruin is only a futile attempt to re-enact his earlier career, which
transferred to the new terrain of Algeria exposes the family to the scandal of
corruption. The family's salvation and return to political grace come *via* the
heroic Hector's son, also aptly named, Victorin. Victorin, as attorney and
parliamentarian, represents the new, considerably less charismatic hero of
the age. He is able to negotiate the new state structures in order to extricate
the family from the grip of his father's mistress, Mme Marneffe, and her
accomplice, Cousin Bette.

Hayden White has analysed the narrative tropes of nineteenth-century
historiography as the metaphoric, the metonymic, the synecdochic, and the
ironic, corresponding to romance, tragedy, comedy, and satire respectively.[7]
The metonymic clash between old Napoleonic and new commercial values
in *Cousin Bette* makes Hector's tragedy the dominant narrative trope of the
novel. The Baron's downfall acts as a representative example of the dashing

of an aristocratic ideal in the 1830s; although the illegitimate origin of his title betrays the gap between that ideal and any real possibilities of a return to before 1789. There is a sense of textual play which suggests that rather than nostalgically looking to the past, the novel experiments with the configurations of history on offer. Deprived of a military arena Hulot turns to a 'campaign on women,' which, as he gives it the same energy he once gave to war, assumes an unreal, theatrical quality. In the final stages of his defeat he is helped to disappear by one of his former mistresses, an opera singer, whom he has helped onto the stage and who now admires the operatic quality of his demise:

> 'I'd rather have a proper spendthrift, mad about women, like you, than one of those cold soul-less bankers who are supposed to be so virtuous and ruin thousands of families with their golden railways ... You have only ruined your own family; the only property you've sold is you!' (p. 341)

This dramatic or theatrical element in Balzac's fiction suggests a degree of reflexivity in the text which is not allowed for by Lukács.

Balzac employs a method of dramatic confrontation which is neatly exemplified in the first scene between Adeline and Crevel. The historically delimited space of the drawing room becomes a stage, which the Baroness prepares before the dialogue can take place. As if to underline the fragile and temporary nature of that space we learn, through Adeline's scene-setting, of at least four potential avenues of disruption:

> Only a thin partition divided this room from the boudoir, whose window opened on the garden, and Madame Hulot left Monsieur Crevel alone for a moment, considering it necessary to shut both the window and the boudoir door so that no one could eavesdrop on that side. She even took the precaution of closing the french window of the drawing-room, smiling as she did so at her daughter and cousin, whom she saw installed in an old summerhouse at the far end of the garden. Returning, she left the door of the card-room ajar, so that she might hear the drawing-room door open if anyone should come in. (pp. 13–14)

Adeline's actions develop a number of dramatic possibilities within the scene, helping to relate her dialogue with Crevel to possible actions. The french window holds in stasis the plot lines embodied in Hortense and Lisbeth. In the ensuing discussion Crevel makes declarations of love with menaces to Adeline; one of his threats is that he will not provide any money for Hortense's dowry. The door of the card-room signals the possible entrance of Adeline's husband, while Crevel uses his knowledge of Hector's infidelities in an attempt to break down her resistance.

The scene seems to work because of the artificiality of its dramatic setting rather than through its relationship to any historical truth. The reader's attention is drawn towards the temporal and spatial limits of the representation given. Within the crucible of those limits the 'typical' situation contains the possibility of bursting out of its fragile boundaries and mutating into a new situation. It is only within this context of a provisional conceptualisation of an historical moment, that it is possible to accept the more extreme and melodramatic actions of Balzac's characters, which otherwise would appear to destroy any consensus about the text's realism. Such a moment occurs when the Hulot children throw themselves at the feet of their father, because he has returned (as it transpires only temporarily) to the domestic hearth. This passionate moment of familial harmony has to be interrupted to prevent an embarrassing closure which would prevent the dramatic action from progressing. The temporary nature of the reconciliation is confirmed by the unexpected entrance of the Marshal Hulot, shattering the moment: 'The two young people rose, and they all made an effort to cover their emotion' (p. 270).

The dramatic nature of Balzac's realism and the episodic nature of the narrative raises two related problems with Lukács's historical criticism. The textual play which is an integral part of Balzac's writing does not submit easily even to a 'many-sided reality' and this in turn must complicate Lukács's relationship between the text and a totalising historiography.

Barthes's project in *S/Z* is to decouple the relationship between narrative and totality:

> inventory, explanation, and digression may deter any observation of suspense, may even separate verb and complement, noun and attribute; the work of the commentary, once it is separated from any ideology of totality, consists precisely in *manhandling* the text, *interrupting* it. What is thereby denied is not the quality of the text (here incomparable) but its 'naturalness.'[8]

On this final point there is some agreement between Lukács and Barthes. Both object to 'naturalness' as a category which denies the act of representation. Where they differ is on the relationship of the text to a 'real' history.

Barthes uses 'textuality' to show the text as source of a multiplicity of meanings rather than the narrative's relationship to totality, which must be a reduction of plurality. For Barthes,

> rereading draws the text out of its internal chronology ('this happens *before* or *after* that') and recaptures a mythic time (without *before* or *after*) ... (... there is no *first* reading, even if the text is concerned to give us that illusion by several operations of *suspense*, artifices more spectacular than persuasive); rereading is no longer consumption, but play (that play which is the return of the different).[9]

Now, immersed in the world of criticism post-Barthes, it is impossible not to see the attractions of this approach. In fact, it is easier now to think 'naturally' along Barthesian lines than along Lukácsian. We accept that there is no first reading, that the text can be broken down (*brisé*) into a plurality of socially constructed codes, codes we already know, which we have already read. Lukács, in comparison, appears crude, irrevocably wedded to a formal conception of historical progress. The disadvantage of Barthes's commentary is that if we accept the concept of 'mythic time,' the problem of the relationship between text and history is solved by abolishing history altogether.

To subject *Cousin Bette* to a post-structuralist, plural commentary is to allow aspects of the text to be foregrounded which are subordinated or marginalised by Lukács's historical criticism. Adeline's desire to shut out her husband and her daughter can be read as both a dramatic device and as a textual strategy. Just as Adeline is described as 'suffering as a woman, a mother and a wife,' and is thus defined by three codes of socialised femininity, so Hortense's unmarried state is part of a discourse of feminine sexuality. Hortense's position in the garden with Bette could be read as virginal innocence with Bette as predatory serpent,—Adeline's shutting the french window would then be a futile attempt to protect her. In this reading, sexual desire is a present but unknown force to Hortense, but to Adeline and Crevel, engaged in negotiating her future, its social significance is clear:

> '... There are days when she wanders sadly in the garden, not knowing why. I find her with tears in her eyes.'
> 'She is twenty-one,' said Crevel. (p. 27)

Another reading might see Hortense as having already lost her innocence as it is Hortense who appears to desire Bette's lover (and, in fact, she later marries him). Hortense's majority creates a social crisis which cannot be contained or fully understood in terms of what I have described as the dominant narrative trope of the novel: the metonymic clash of values between Hector and Crevel.

> 'Ought I to send her to a convent?' said the Baroness. 'At such times of crisis religion is often powerless against nature, and the most piously brought up girls lose their heads!' (p. 27)

Hortense's femininity is an unstable element within the text, and as such it allows a deconstruction of the social codes which would define a feminine sexuality as other. Hortense's desire, between girlhood and matrimony, represents an aporia in the narrative structure. Barthes's method of breaking down the text permits us to unknot the codes which cannot explain that desire in their own terms. In contrast, Valérie Marneffe's sexual drive is at one with her drive for wealth, status, and power. This process of decoding does, however, reveal the dominant narrative trope as gendered: Hulot's tragedy is the tragedy of a type of heroic masculinity as much as that of a class created by the Napoleonic period. A plural commentary, as advocated by Barthes, draws out what Derrida calls *différence* in the text, and in Derridean terms this should deconstruct the metaphysic of presence; but, as we have seen, the novel already presents us with a society in which nothing seems certain, further complicating Lukács's attempt to insert history as an explanatory term.

It should be noted, however, that despite the fact that the relationship between text and history is complicated in a plural commentary, it is not absent. There is still an underlying assumption of an historical narrative. Fredric Jameson argues that

> all apparently synchronic or ahistorical analysis depends on and presupposes (for the most part covertly) a diachronic scheme, a vision or 'philosophy' of history, a historical 'master-narrative,' in terms of which its evaluations are processed.[10]

Strictly speaking, to describe Hortense as having an individual sexuality is an anachronism in the 1830s, since the idea of having an identity which is defined by sexual desire belongs to the late nineteenth-century. While Balzac's text does not endow Hortense with an identity defined by her desires, part of the decoding process involves using a more recent concept in order to understand the text as historical. It is, in effect, employing an historical master narrative, here, a history of the subject in relation to desire. The other category of difference which post-structuralist thought has helped to disentangle from the grand narratives which would seek to marginalise it, is that of race. Balzac's pedagogic statements about his characters include significant judgements on the basis of racial or national characteristics. In his representation of Steinbock, the aristocratic Polish artist, Balzac's sense of a French national identity is quite distinct. It places France at the centre of a European civilisation, from which Poland is excluded:

> All Slavs have a childish side, as have all primitive races that have rather made incursion among civilised nations than become properly civilised themselves. (p. 229)

Coming from an even more peripheral quarter (in relation to France), and hence acting as a more powerful source of instability within the text, is Baron Henri Montès de Montejanos, the Brazilian lover of Valérie Marneffe, who returns from his isolated plantation to reclaim her. The Baron's psychology is described in terms of his environmental and racial background:

> Monsieur le Baron Henri Montès de Montejanos, the product of an equatorial climate, had the physique and complexion that we all associate with Othello. (p. 181)

Montejanos is an example of how the text is pluralised by racial difference, but as a character he also has an important role in the resolution of the plot.

While Jameson has criticised Lukács's too ready assumption that Balzac's 'sense of historical realities inflects his [Lukács's] own personal wishes in the direction of social and historical versimilitude,'[11] in his essay, 'The Ideology of the Text,' he argues that content must not be ignored. In his own account of *Sarrasine*, Jameson argues that Balzac's use of the novella—a literary form which originated in the renaissance—demonstrates a logic of content which Barthes cannot escape:

> Barthes' 'hermeneutic code' can now at any rate be seen to be either excessively or insufficiently theorized, insofar as its specific object of study or raw material (what happened? when will we learn what happened?) is a historical form, the art-novella, on the point of artificial revival, and also extinction.[12]

The logic of content of *Cousin Bette* can be described as the relationship between the dramatic scenes described above and the narrative organisation of tragedy. In *Cousin Bette* it is Shakespearian tragedy rather than the art-novella, which structures the narrative. Within Balzac's nineteenth-century novel Shakespeare's tragedies provide a model for a progressive history of the subject in relation to socio-historical change; but the structural limitations of this model are clear.

Baron Hulot's heroic, masculine, and French identity disintegrates on impact with the market values embodied by Crevel, but his son, Victorin, displays an increasing authority in the new political and economic climate. In order to rescue the family's fortunes, Victorin uses the relationship between the legal apparatus of the state and its obverse, the Parisian criminal underworld, to destroy the now married Valérie and Crevel—in that order, thus saving his wife's inheritance. The organisation which mediates between the underworld and families like the Hulots is the police. Although they refuse to intervene directly (we learn that they used to, but this is no longer the policy) they put Victorin in touch with the shadowy Mme Nourisson. She, while representative of criminality rather than the police (legality and illegality often blur in *La Comédie Humaine*, most famously in the figure of Vautrin, criminal turned chief of police), is also an agent rather than an actor. Her skill is in using Montejanos's jealousy to get him to murder the newly-weds.

The murder itself is performed in a manner which marks it as the work of a 'primitive' and 'untamed' sexuality, for Montejanos is 'one of the children of nature.' The method is an obscure tropical poison which cannot be diagnosed and the antidote for which exists only in Brazil. This otherness, which is composed of a plurality of bourgeois fears and the anxieties of class, race, and sexuality, is utilised by Victorin to limit the damage that can be done to future middle-class security by the out-of-control patriarchs of the previous generation, Crevel and Hector. Hector's tragedy is defused, and is itself marginalised because Victorin is able to employ those aspects of social otherness which that narrative trope cannot explain.

This account of the relationship of the narrative structure of the novel to historical change is preferable to the post-structuralist account of a new linguistic freedom under capitalism, which seems to rely on general statements about changes in the mode of production:

The difference between feudal society and bourgeois society, index and sign, is this: the index has an origin, the sign does not: to shift from index to sign is to abolish the last (or first) limit, the origin, the basis, the prop, to enter into the limitless process of equivalences, representations that nothing will ever stop, orient, fix, sanction.[13]

If the limits of this new freedom are not defined, then the valid wish to escape the metaphysic of presence can create more problems than it solves by employing the concept of the free-floating signifier and 'mythic time.' The antipathy of post-structuralist criticism to theories of narrative is demonstrated by Foucault's use of *Don Quixote* to prove the same point that Barthes makes about *Sarrasine*:

> *Don Quixote* is a negative of the Renaissance world; writing has ceased to be the prose of the world; resemblances and signs have dissolved their former alliance; similitudes have become deceptive and verge upon the visionary or madness; things still remain stubbornly within their ironic identity: they are no longer anything but what they are; words wander off on their own...[14]

If it is possible to say the same thing about Cervantes's novel as it is about those of Balzac, written two hundred years later, then it appears that periodisation, which must be one of the tools of the historical criticism, has been rejected out of hand by post-structuralism.

This argument brings us back to Lukács, who notes Balzac's use of older literary forms, but Jameson's argument with Lukács is that he

> is right about Balzac, but for the wrong reasons: not Balzac's deeper sense of political and historical realities, but rather his incorrigible fantasy demands ultimately raise History itself over against him, as absent cause, as that on which desire must come to grief.[15]

Jameson would then replace Lukács's use of typicality with an interpretation of Balzac's characters as allegorical. This is his approach in his early essay on *Cousin Bette*, but while this methodology acts as a way of historicising a post-structuralist, linguistically-based commentary, its heavy use of Freudian psychoanalysis in unearthing the text's 'political unconscious' is of limited use when it comes to an analysis of sexual and racial difference. In this allegorical system, he places Bette in the position of super-ego; Hulot as the id; and Mme Hulot as the ego, 'the place of the *subject*, the rational consciousness that is the battleground between these two buffeting forces.'[16]

While this Freudian system is historicised as part of a narrative of class, Jameson is unable to account for what he sees as the apparently motiveless malevolence of Balzac's women characters, particularly as represented by the character of Cousin Bette herself. Jameson's own account of Lisbeth uses a rather crude, pre-feminist 'psychology of the old maid': her character is 'distorted by repression.'[17]

This must be an inadequate account of the eponymous Bette and of the role of characters like Montejanos. The role of Montejanos as both destabilising, pluralising element and as narrative device demonstrates that it is possible to provide an account of the relationship between narrative structure and the text as *écriture*. An interpretation of, rather than a plural commentary on, the representations of race within the text would have to draw attention to the other use of a racial other within the narrative structure, that is, Hulot's attempt to rescue his fortunes through foraging contracts in Algeria. The events which make up this sub-plot of imperial adventurism are only represented in terms of their effects on the Parisian centre. Hulot fails to bring off the scheme because the techniques of accumulation which worked so well before 1815 are not applicable to the new conditions of North Africa. As with Victorin's success in manipulating the power of the state, there is a relationship between the construction of the subject and the narrative structure. The historical account of Algerian imperialism is related to Hulot's degeneration, not only physically (he appears to age ten years), but also as a viable and coherent centre within the text. This is not to say that the text does not reveal itself as plural, but that the extent of meaning which can be read off depends on an historical approach which reads Balzac not as 'unrelated diversity' (this is Jameson's term for Barthes's rereading) but as a diversity which is related to a narrative structure, implying an historiography. The categories which post-structuralism has helped us to read into literary texts, of race, gender, and sexuality, might then be seen as having their own histories, as categories which become important in textual analysis because of the social movements which have used them as their banners.

If we look at Bette in the same way she appears as both central character and—representative of the drive to ruin the Hulot family—as the most important source of textual incoherence. Her removal from the scene, thanks to a timely chest infection, is an essential pre-requisite for the novelistic closure. Bette is a traditional novelistic device. Her lack of definite social position as poor relation, servant, old maid, allows her to move from stage to stage, while other characters are caught in and defined by the delimited spatial and temporal zones described above. She is a line of communication between Valérie—whose position as bourgeois prostitute is similarly transgressive—and Crevel, as well as between the Hulot family and more peripheral characters such as Steinbock and Montejanos.

Far from being an agent of repression, within the structure of the novel, Bette works as a pluralising device in opposition to the unilateral history of the subject provided by Hulot's tragedy. With an understanding of Bette's role we can see that Balzac's use of Shakespearian tragedy is also plural, incorporating Lear—the tragedy of the family; Antony—the dissolution of heroism into sensuality; and Othello—the tragedy of sexual jealousy and the murder of the object of desire.

The epic-drama of Balzacian narrative means that the social codes of Barthes's plural commentary can be read off more easily than in a naturalist or modernist text. Balzac's realism allows characters to stand out against the narrative structure. There is no easy relationship here between the construction of the subject and narrative, with the result that Balzac's attempted naturalisation of sexual or racial difference is easily denaturalised by the modern reader or historical critic. Bette's 'primitive' nature or Steinbock's 'childishness' are not fully reified into an ideology of racial or sexual inferiority. Reading now, consciously or unconsciously, we read through and against late nineteenth-century naturalism with its scientific categories of race and gender and through and against modernist *écriture*, where ideologies of difference are subsumed, for example in Conrad, into reified subjectivities.

Any historical approach to literature must be inadequate if it cannot account for sexual and racial difference. In *The Political Unconscious* Jameson proceeds too quickly through his own interpretative model to a history of metasynchronous modes of production, bypassing the interrelated complexity of gender, race, class, and sexuality in the history of the subject.[18] There are occasional hints dropped in *The Political Unconscious*, suggesting, for example, a theory of sexuality which sees Freud's project as part of a more general autonomisation of the senses; but while Jameson leaves us with valuable methodological clues, he does not follow them up himself.

A methodology which works better at the micro-level of the history of the subject is Peter Dews's Adornian critique of Derridean post-structuralism. Adorno argues for a history of the subject which recognizes that 'identity thinking' is part of an act of self-preservation in which the 'contingency and difference of nature leaves scars.'[19] Consciousness is unfolded in 'concrete experience,' experience which is part of a socio-historical development. As a text, *Cousin Bette* allows several approaches to an historical understanding, including Lukács's argument for a totality that is directly apprehendable from the text and which conforms to a history of concrete experience; but, while Balzac's realism does allow a neat historical reading, the history of the subject which is made prominent by Baron Hulot's tragedy bears a complex relationship with the novelistic structure. A post-naturalist, post-modernist interpretation would need to draw back from the coherence of Hulot's history and to contemplate the incoherence of Hortense or Montejanos. This need not be a post-modernist celebration of heterogeneity in the name of difference, rather it would be to recognise that the text's own master narrative of tragedy functions in relation to the formal representation of difference in Balzac's dramatic scenes. These scenes construct provisional, discontinuous identities within the text, fixing the construction of the subject in time and space. Lukács is right to see the clash of values which that tragedy exemplifies as the explanatory master narrative of Balzac's fiction, but the provisional nature of Balzac's historical, dramatic moments makes dangerous any attempt to relate them back to even a contradictory historical unity. Accepting that these moments are what Adorno calls non-concepts is not the same thing as saying an objective history does not exist, but that

> history is *not* a text, not a narrative, master or otherwise, but that as an abstract cause, it is inaccessible to us except in textual form, and that our approach to it, and to the Real itself, necessarily passes through its prior textualisation, its narrativisation in the political unconscious.[20]

In philosophical terms, these moments are non-concepts within which a non-identity persists as a necessary illusion, a pre-condition of meaning: 'In truth all concepts, even the philosophical ones, refer to nonconceptualities, because concepts on their part are moments of the reality that requires their formation.'[21] They need to be read historically, that is as non-concepts which are part of Balzac's own nineteenth-century historiography and now as non-concepts which we read through subsequent literary texts as well as through the non-concepts of gender and race which have 'complicated' history as a result of, for example, anti-imperialist struggles and the women's movement. This 'complication' requires a more complex though also much richer historiography, an historiography of difference.

NOTES

1. Fredric Jameson, 'The Ideology of the Text,' in *The Ideologies of Theory: Essays* 1971–1986, 2 vols (London, 1988), I. 18.

2. Honoré de Balzac, *Cousin Bette*, trans. Marion Ayton Crawford, Penguin Classics (Harmondsworth, 1965; 1981), p. 14 (hereafter by page reference in text).

3. Frederick Engels to Margaret Harkness, April 1898, in *Marx and Engels on Literature and Art*, ed. Stefan Morawiski (New York, 1973), p. 115.

4. Georg Lukács, *Studies in European Realism*, introduction by Alfred Kazin (New York, 1964), pp. 3–4 (essays first published 1935–39).

5. *Marx and Engels on Literature and Art*, p. 116.

6. Lukács, p. 58.

7. Hayden White, *Metahistory: The Historical Imagination in Nineteenth Century Europe* (Baltimore, 1973), pp. 31–8.

8. Roland Barthes, *S/Z*, trans. Richard Miller (London, 1975), p. 15 (first published Paris, 1970).

9. Barthes, p. 16.

10. Fredric Jameson, 'The Ideology of the Text,' I. 54–5.

11. Fredric Jameson, *The Political Unconscious* (London, 1981), p. 164.

12. 'The Ideology of the Text,' I. 53.

13. Barthes, p. 40.

14. Michel Foucault, *The Order of Things* (London, 1970), pp. 47–8 (first published Paris, 1966).

15. *The Political Unconscious*, p. 183.

16. Fredric Jameson, '*La Cousine Bette* and Allegorical Realism,' *PMLA*, 86 (1971), 253.

17. '*La Cousine Bette* and Allegorical Realism,' p. 248.

18. *The Political Unconscious*, ch. 1, especially pp. 74–102.

19. Peter Dews, *The Logics of Disintegration* (London, 1988), p. 39.

20. *The Political Unconscious*, p. 35.

21. Theodore Adorno, *Negative Dialectics*, trans. E. B. Ashton (London, 1973), p. 11 (first published Frankfurt am Main, 1966).

LESLIE ANNE BOLDT

The Framed Image: The Chain of Metaphors in Balzac's Le Père Goriot

The goal of realistic narrative has traditionally been to provide the reader with the experience of a fictional reality, with the ultimate intention that the reader become involved in the narrative and gradually lose sight of its fictional status. For this reason, the author of such a realistically portrayed world does not generally draw attention to the representational nature of his work, nor does he usually allude to the creative process engendering the story.

Similarly, the author of realistic narrative usually disguises the presence of boundaries in this created space, a space which nonetheless sets off and frames the reality that it represents. This desire to disguise the limits of the framing implied by all narrative is achieved by centering the reader's vision of a scene on the events described, so that the author's deliberate selection and arrangement of its perspective remain unnoticed. In Bernard Vannier's words: "L'une des feintes du récit "réaliste" entraine ainsi le lecteur à partager la vision du spectateur, à s'attacher à l'énoncé, en oubliant les modalités du discours qui l'y entraînent."[1]

As an author of traditional realistic narrative, Balzac certainly intends that his reader forget the discursive nature of his fiction by concealing his authorial intervention in the selection and arrangement of the scenes he portrays. It is nonetheless true that he refers to the representational status

From *Nineteenth-Century French Studies* 19, no. 4. ©1991 by *Nineteenth-Century French Studies*.

and to the textual construction of his novels more often and more directly than traditional realistic narrative would lead one to expect.

While other critics have noticed this tendency in certain novels of *La Comédie humaine*,[2] in this study, I show that *Le Père Goriot* is also a work in which Balzac refers to his role as author and to the representational status of the novel he has written. It is, however, a novel that represents its discursive origins[3] in a complex and mitigated manner. My analysis of this text will suggest that Balzac was both eager *and* reluctant to refer to the creative process that engendered the story.

Evidence that Balzac was interested in both veiling and revealing authorial control of the narrative is already present in the *Avant-propos à la Comédie humaine*. I will trace the presence of this conflict in the *Avant-propos* and then show how it later manifests itself in *Le Père Goriot* through the deployment of a chain of metaphors, metaphors that have as their unifying principle the notion of the framed image.

Evidence that Balzac should reveal his desire to intervene as an author is found in the *Avant-propos* when he writes:

> En *dressant* l'inventaire des vices et des vertus, en *rassemblant* les principaux faits des passions, en *peignant* les caractères, en *choisissant* les événements principaux de la Société, en *composant* des types par la réunion des traits de plusieurs caractères homogènes, peut-être pouvais-je arriver à écrire l'histoire oubliée par tant d'historiens, celle des moeurs (italics mine).[4]

One could also argue that the very deliberate division of the *Comédie humaine* into *scènes* and *tableaux* is evidence of Balzac's desire to intervene, to impose an order upon his created world. Thus the *frames* and *portraits* that line the galleries of the *Comédie humaine* also reveal his desire to make his authorial presence felt:

> Ce nombre de figures, de caractères, cette multitude d'existences exigeaient des cadres, et, qu'on me pardonne cette expression, des galeries. De là, les divisions si naturelles, déjà connues, de mon ouvrage en *Scènes de la vie privée, de province, parisienne, militaire et de campagne*. (1: 7)

While these passages suggest that Balzac was eager to manifest his authorial control, the *Avant-propos* holds other passages that imply he was subject to the opposing desire of diminishing any reference to the creative process. Such passages suggest that his characters are free of authorial control and may move about without intervention in the world that they populate;[5] Balzac has provided the setting and all the necessary components for an action which could ostensibly propel itself, thanks to its *moteur social*:

> Mon ouvrage a sa géographie comme il a sa généologie et ses familles, ses lieux et ses choses, ses personnes et ses faits; comme il a son armorial, ses nobles et ses bourgeois, ses artisans et ses paysans, ses politiques et ses dandies, son armée, tout son monde enfin! (1: 14)

As I have suggested, evidence of Balzac's desire to both reveal and veil authorial control can also be discerned in *Le Père Goriot* through the deployment of a chain of metaphors that are metonymically linked. An analysis of their function in the text reveals a displacement in perspective from the narrative framework (in which authorial control is veiled) to what could be termed the framework of authorial intervention (wherein such control is revealed).

The narrative framework is supported by structures that fade from the reader's attention in order to permit her* involvement in the tale. It entails a forgetting of the text's status as construct and as linguistic representation. Within this framework, metaphors provide a variant of the *signified*, enriching the reader's experience of the tale.

The framework of authorial intervention, on the other hand, is one in which the reader loses this involvement in the realm of the signified, for her attention becomes focussed on the play of signifiers. The fabrication of the tale, the representative nature of the text, and the writing process upon which the narration depends are all brought to the reader's mind. Within this framework, metaphors are seen to function as *signs*, as the objects of selection on the part of the author.

The move from the narrative framework to that of authorial intervention is one from an experience of the signified in its transparency to an awareness of the signifier in its opacity, from the reader's perception of the fluid uninterrupted flow of imagery, to the disruption of her involvement through the intervention of the author. It is also, in Felman's terms, a return to the "discursive origins of the story,"[6] a displacement from the experience of narrative to the consciousness of discourse.

Balzac's position in *Le Père Goriot* oscillates from one pole of the continuum to the other, in that he alternately chooses to withdraw as a presence within the narrative framework and to emerge, pulling the reader into the framework of authorial intervention. The metaphors that I examine and which facilitate this displacement are that of the framed painting for the textual scene, the framed setting of La Maison Vauquer—settings against which the "drama" of the characters will unfold, and the metaphor of the ocean (and later the labyrinth) for the city of Paris. These metaphors, like all signs, are connected metonymically by a chain which supports the narrative—a chain which, in Le Père Goriot, will lose its transparency as it, in turn, becomes the object of our attention.[7] In addition, the metaphor of the *labyrinth* functions in a way that not only draws attention to authorial control of the narrative, but also reveals the underlying patterns of the linguistic code and of the text as a maze of signifiers awaiting realization through the reading process.

While it is true that narration always implies the framing of depicted events and descriptions, as well as the exclusion of what is not represented within this frame,[8] the *narrative* framework is, however, one which seeks to *veil* its status as a frame, as representation. In Le Père Goriot, Balzac conforms to the tradition in most realistic novels of leaving this veil intact. However, that he should also desire to lift the veil, thus shifting to the authorial framework, is made evident by his metaphorical use of the framed painting for the textual scene.[9]

Balzac's use of the metaphor of the painted scene draws the reader's attention to the framing inherent in the depiction of all textual scenes, thus shifting from the narrative framework, within which such frames are not apparent, to that of authorial intervention. This occurs, for example, when Rastignac enters Delphine's boudoir, as she prepares for Mme de Beauséant's ball:

> Le jeune homme se présenta navré de douleur à Delphine, et la trouva coiffée, chausée, n'ayant plus que sa robe de bal à mettre. Mais, semblables aux coups de pinceau par lesquels les peintres achèvent leurs tableaux, les derniers apprêts voulaient plus de temps que n'en demandaient le fond même de la toile. (2: 1056)

The passage begins to describe Delphine's preparation for the ball, but then shifts suddenly, through a reference to painting, from the narrative framework within which the reader's vision is centered to that of authorial intervention: the "coups de pinceau," the "tableaux" and the "fond de la toile" intrude into the description, reminding the reader that the tale, like a painting, is a representation—the product of signifiers that have been selected and combined to achieve a desired effect. The metaphor of the painted scene pulls the reader from an involvement in the narrative to a consciousness of its discursive origins, to an awareness of the story as "story." In an article in which he discusses, among other things, the "semiotic limits of the different artistic modes of representation," Rickels refers to this shift in focus when he writes:

> [p]ainting is that detour along which literature ultimately confronts its dependence on the sign. For once any literary work has shown that pictures, like words, are signs, it can no longer refrain from reflecting on its own status as sign system. When literature turns its attention to the medium of another art form— in this case to that of painting it ultimately makes a statement about its own medium—language."[10]

This movement from the narrative to the authorial framework, to the awareness of the representative nature of the story, is not infrequent, for Balzac repeatedly makes reference to the art of painting in *Le Père Goriot*. Van Rossum-Guyon observes that Balzac's substitution of "peindre" for "expliquer" and "voir" for "comprendre" is a frequent occurence; in her view, this substitution corresponds to the use of "les deux grands codes mimétiques et cognitifs" that are used to construct *la Comédie humaine* "comme Histoire de la Société et Peinture des moeurs."[11] But in my view, this reference to painting is also evidence of the desire to provide an image which is manifestly controlled by the author; authorial control is thereby no longer veiled and, as it manifests itself, the reader is prevented from engaging in a fluid and uninterrupted perception of the narrated scene.

Other examples of the use of the image of painting for this purpose include the following description of Goriot as a "Christ of Fatherhood":

> Pour bien peindre la physionomie de ce Christ de la Paternité, il faudrait aller chercher des comparaisons dans les images que les princes de la palette ont inventées pour peindre la passion soufferte au bénéfice des mondes par le sauveur des hommes. (2: 1026)

Similarly, Victorine Taillefer had earlier been described as a figure from a medieval painting:

Victorine ressemblait à l'une de ces naïves peintures du Moyen
Age dans lesquelles tous les accessoires sont negligés par l'artiste,
qui a réservée la magie d'un pinceau calme et fier pour la figure
jaune de ton, mais où le ciel semble se réfléter avec ces teintes
d'or. (2:1001)[12]

Balzac's reference to the medium of *painting* is particularly useful in
allowing him to manifest his authorial control, for a painted picture is a static
representation of a scene beheld visually. The textual image, on the other
hand, arises from a graphic description that is meant to evoke an "intellectual
perception" or a "mental image."[13] Thus, though the author may provide
exact details in an attempt to create with words what the painter creates with
the stroke of a brush, the mental image or intellectual perception that arises
will be colored by the imaginative faculties, the whims and the experiences
of the reader. Moreover, not only will the author's words generate à mental
image that is unique to each reader, but the same words will undoubtedly
evoke a different intellectual perception upon successive readings by the
same individual.

The author and painter who depict a scene in a realistic manner
struggle with the limits of representation in different ways. A painter frames
on a two-dimensional canvas a series of objects that would be three-
dimensional and of a different hue if actually seen. An author is at once freer
and more subject to limits than a painter: he is freer in that he may choose
words that will set in motion the characters of a scene without drawing
attention to the limits of its frame—if the story remains within the narrative
framework, the author need not indicate the presence of this frame in any
appreciable way. At the same time, the latter's control is more limited, in that
he must relinquish aspects of the generative act to the reader, who responds
idiosyncratically to the words of a descriptive passage.[14]

That Balzac should both veil and reveal authorial control arises from
the very possibilities inherent in reading and in authorship. When he veils
his control, he takes advantage of the author's freedom to set the story in
motion without reference to the framing inherent in all narration; when he
reveals his intervention, he offsets the loss of control occasioned by the
reader's generation of imagery. While Balzac is certainly willing to set the
narrative of *Le Père Goriot* in motion, thereby relinquishing some of his
control to the reader, he at the same time represents the telling of the story,
thus reasserting his control as an author.

In the passages mentioned above, the reader's perception of the various
characters is arrested by the sudden image of the same scene surrounded by

a frame, and subject to the strokes of a painter's brush. By incorporating the metaphor of the painted scene into his novel, Balzac pulls the reader from the narrative to the authorial framework and thus emerges as an authorial presence, appropriating in a metaphoric fashion some of the control enjoyed by the painter and relinquished to a certain extent by the author.

The conflict between the opposing desires of veiling and revealing authorial control continues to manifest itself in Balzac's deliberate 'framing' of the various descriptions of La Maison Vauquer and in his deployment of two other metaphors for the city of Paris—the ocean and the labyrinth. Of these two, it is only the metaphor of the ocean that represents the desire of veiling authorial presence and of permitting the narrative to proceed without interruption. Unlike the metaphor of the painted scene, and unlike the various framed settings of La Maison Vauquer, the metaphor of the ocean, within the narrative framework, represents the veiling of this authorial presence, a veiling which allows the reader's mental imagery to proceed unimpeded, by dissolving any reference to art as artifice or to representation.

As I have suggested, these various metaphors and framed settings are metonymically linked by a chain that has as a unifying principle the notion of a framed image. The various metaphors that describe the Parisian settings of *Le Père Goriot* are linked to the metaphor of the painted scene not only by the 'framing' that they suggest, but also by their ability to effect a shift in focus from the narrative to the authorial framework. The link between these metaphors is metonymic in that, following Jakobson's theory, their relationship is one of contiguity. Jakobson, it will be remembered, distinguishes between the metaphoric pole, which adheres to the principles of selection and substitution, and the metonymic pole, whose principles are those of combination and contexture.[15]

While each metaphor in the chain conforms to Jakobson's criterion of *selection*, in that Balzac chooses them at the expense of other members of the same paradigmatic axis, the metaphors, all present in the novel, may be combined in various ways (as I have done in proposing their coexistence in a chain whose unifying principle is the notion of the framed image). Thus their linkage in such a chain satisfies Jakobson's criterion of *combination* and the metaphors may therefore be said to be connected in a metonymic fashion.

The interrelatedness of metaphor and metonymy has been the subject of many discussions since the publication of Jakobson's article. Critics such as Genette and De Man, for example, have argued that the principle of metonymy is primordial and orders the functioning of other tropes such as metaphor.[16] While a discussion of their arguments would exceed the scope of this study, the views of Eco on this subject are pertinent and merit some

mention, for they support the notion that metaphors can be metonymically
linked. He would, in fact, state that all metaphors are linked in such a
fashion, asserting that "each metaphor can be traced back to a subjacent
chain of metonymic connexions which constitute the framework of the code
[of any semantic field]."[17] Thus, metonymy would evoke the link between
signifiers, while metaphor the substitution of one signifier for another.

As I have stated, the metaphors for the setting of Paris are linked in
their ability to effect a change in focus from the narrative to the authorial
framework. Like the metaphor of the painted scene, they all evoke or are in
some way related to the notion of the framed image. This becomes
particularly evident when one examines the very focal point of the novel's
action (La Maison Vauquer), a framed setting within whose limits the most
important elements of the drama are centered and whose description
displaces the reader from a position within the narrative framework
(characterized by the uninterrupted flow of imagery) to that of authorial
intervention (art that admits of artifice and of the artist's control).

La Maison Vauquer as the setting for this conflict receives the artist's
strokes at the beginning of the novel. The manner in which the stage is set
for the narration of the story is, itself, most revealing of the chain of
metaphors at work in the novel. The story begins with Balzac's speculation
that the drama in question is likely to provoke tears both "*intra muros* et
extra." This image of walls is made in reference both to the walls within
which various episodes of the drama transpire (Père Goriot's room, that of
Rastignac, the dining room of the Maison Vauquer, the bedroom and great
reception hall of the hôtel de Beauséant, the living quarters of both Delphine
and Anastasie) as well as to the frames within which the reader finds herself.
There follows a direct reference to the reader's sentiments upon completing
the tale, a reference which, in itself, seems to 'frame' the very movement of
which I have spoken—the movement from the narrative to the authorial
framework:

> Ainsi ferez-vous, vous qui tenez ce livre d'une main blanche, vous
> qui vous enfoncez dans un moelleux fauteuil en vous disant: Peut-
> être ceci va-t-il m'amuser. Après avoir lu les secrètes infortunes
> du père Goriot, vous dînerez avec appétit en mettant votre
> insensibilité sur le compte de l'auteur, en le taxant d'exagération,
> en l'accusant de poésie. (2: 848)

What is so fascinating about this intervention on the part of Balzac is
its self-referential quality. Not only does Balzac frame his story by speaking

of its eventual effect once the last page has been turned (the covers of the book thus framing the movement of the story as well as the entire chain of metaphors that this article within its own 'frame' tries to expose) but it invites the reader to visualize another reader—herself as reader, *all* readers, yet no reader in particular—a reader who is perceived intellectually by the reader of Balzac's novel and who, seated in an armchair, also holds a copy of the same novel in her hand, a hand which is unscathed and unthreatened, removed from the pathos of the tale.

The conflict between the desire to reveal and to veil authorial control of the narrative is foreshadowed by the sentences that follow, for no sooner has Balzac evoked the representational quality of his story, by referring to the reader of his book and its author (upon whom accusations of exaggeration will ostensibly fall), than he discounts the artifice of his story as representation by claiming that it is neither fiction nor a novel:

> Ah! sachez-le: ce drame n'est ni une fiction, ni un roman. *All is true*, il est si véritable, que chacun peut en reconnaître les éléments chez soi, dans son coeur peut-être. (2: 848)

The tension between these conflicting desires, evoked and enclosed by Balzac's chain of metaphors, continues as the narration begins in earnest.

The walls within which the reader, real or visualized, is seated, recede as the narrative framework of the novel is entered: the story is situated and, indeed, framed by the following quotation: "Les particularités de cette scène pleine d'observations et de couleurs locales ne peuvent être appréciées qu'entre les buttes de Montmartre et les hauteurs de Montrouge ..." (2: 847).

The setting of Paris, "... cette illustre vallée de plâtras incessamment près de tomber et de ruisseaux noirs de boue ..." holds within it another frame—that of the quarter in which the Maison Vauquer is centered, a quarter delimited by "...ces rues serrées entre le Val-de-Grâce et le dôme du Panthéon, deux monuments qui changent les conditions de l'atmosphère en y jetant des tons jaunes, en y assombrissant tout par les teintes sévères que projettent leurs coupoles" (2: 848). That this setting should constitute a frame is made explicit by the following description:

> Nul quartier de Paris n'est plus horrible, ni, disons-le, plus inconnu. La rue Neuve-Sainte-Geneviève surtout est comme un *cadre* de bronze,[18] le seul qui convienne à ce récit, auquel on ne saurait trop préparer l'intelligence par des couleurs brunes, par des idées graves (italics mine). (2: 848)

The Maison Vauquer itself is situated within a courtyard surrounded by walls: "Le jardinet, aussi large que la façade est longue, se trouve encaissé par le mur de la rue et par le mur mitoyen de la maison voisine, le long de laquelle pend un manteau de lierre ..." (2: 849).

A description of the Maison's exterior and doorframes is followed by a description of the *salon* and *salle à manger*. Throughout these early pages, the description of the setting has projected a static backdrop for the next subject to which the strokes of Balzac's pen will be applied—the characters whose *dramas* he will set in motion. Thus the conflict between the desire to veil and reveal authorial control is inherent in the contrast between the deliberately framed settings in which the narrative is centered (evidence of authorial intervention) and the dramas that will ostensibly engage the reader in the uninterrupted flow of the narrative (narrative that will veil any sense of authorial intervention).

Indeed, Balzac's references to drama are most telling, for drama is an artform that resumes the conflict at the center of our study—it seems to occupy a medial position between painting and the novel. *Like* the painted image, the characters on stage are beheld visually by the spectator; like the characters of a novel and *unlike* the painted subject, the characters of a play are in motion, encouraging the spectator to enter the narrative framework of the play, forgetting her presence in the theatre.[19] It is not surprising, then, that Balzac should refer to the "drama" of his characters, for the representational nature of this artform is both veiled and revealed during the performance of a play. The spectator's awareness of the "framing" of a play— indicated by the lighting, props and closing of the curtain between acts—will both recede and emerge as the play proceeds. This oscillation comes about as the spectator alternately forgets her presence as "spectator," permitting involvement in the drama, or becomes aware of the limits of the site that frames the action—the *stage* upon which the action is centered and that can only *purport* to extend its parameters beyond the limits of the scene.

Balzac alludes to this dual capacity of drama to assert and disguise its representational nature when he writes of the occupants of the Maison Vauquer:

> Ces pensionnaires faisaient pressentir des drames accomplis ou en action; non pas de ces drames joués à la lueur des rampes, entre des toiles peintes, mais des drames vivants et muets, des drames glacés qui remuaient chaudement le coeur, des drames continus. (2:847)

His reference in this passage to both "drames accomplis" and "drames continus" evokes the tension between the conficting desires at the center of our examination. Balzac seems in this passage to undo any sense of a "staged" drama, but cannot suppress the representational quality implicit in the word itself; in his text the word "drama" implies not only the possibility of involvement in the narrative ("des drames continus") but also an awareness of representation, of drama as "drama" ("des drames accomplis").[20]

Whereas this tension implied by the use of the word "drama" is made manifest by the metaphor of the painted scene and by the images of the framed setting in *Le Père Goriot*, the goal of traditional realistic narrative—that of providing the reader with a fluid uninterrupted perception of a scene—is evoked, as I have suggested, by the metaphor of the ocean. Paris, having already been described as "une illustre vallée ... de ruisseaux noirs de boue ..." (2: 847) is later described as an ocean: "Mais Paris est un véritable océan. Jetez-y la sonde, vous n'en connaîtrez jamais la profondeur. Parcourez-le, décrivez-le? quelque soin que vous mettiez à le parcourir, à le décrire; quelque nombreux et intéressés que soient les explorateurs de cette mer, il s'y rencontrera toujours un lieu vierge, un antre inconnu ... quelque chose d'inouï, oublié par les plongeurs littéraires" (2: 856).

When the characters are faced with having to make a decision, of negotiating through the perils of Parisian life, Balzac will use the image of ocean navigation. In the following quotation, he speaks of the hesitations "... qui saisissent les jeunes gens quand ils se trouvent en pleine mer, sans savoir ni de quel côté diriger leurs forces, ni sous quel angle enfler leurs voiles" (2: 872). Once Rastignac has gained confidence in his navigational skills, he is ready to profit from the bounty that the "ocean" of Paris will provide him: "... il avait ainsi quinze mois de loisirs pour naviguer sur l'océan de Paris, pour s'y livrer à la traite des femmes, ou y pêcher la fortune" (2: 918). That the characters should appear to have a "free rein" over the events that take place in the novel is suggested by this metaphor, a metaphor that also evokes the author's wish to *appear* to relinquish control over these events.

This image of Paris as an ocean, a body of water always in motion and "self-governing," in that its tireless movement is entirely and obviously free of human intervention, is in direct contrast with the other metaphor chosen to represent Paris. Unlike the metaphor of the ocean, that of the labyrinth represents a return to the image of a frame.[21]

However, like the metaphor of the Parisian ocean, this new description of the Parisian *labyrinth*[22] is often made in reference to the adventures of Rastignac: "Un étudiant n'a pas trop de temps s'il veut connaître le répertoire de chaque théâtre, étudier les issus du labyrinthe parisien, savoir les usages, apprendre la langue et s'habituer aux plaisirs particuliers de la capitale ..." (2: 871). At another point in the novel, Rastignac's mother writes, begging him to avoid the dangers that his pursuit of Parisian pleasures will entail:

> Mon bon Eugène, crois-en le coeur de ta mère, les voies
> tortueuses ne mènent à rien de grand. Va, mon bien aimé, marche!
> je tremble parce que je suis mère; mais chacun de tes pas sera
> tendrement accompagné de nos voeux et de nos bénédictions." (2:
> 923)

That Rastignac will be faced with temptations and decisions as he chooses his path through the Parisian labyrinth is insinuated by Vautrin: "Voilà le carrefour de la vie, jeune homme, choisissez. Vous avez déjà choisi: vous êtes allé chez notre cousin de Beauséant, et vous y avez flairé le luxe" (2: 935).

The two views of Paris are significant for a variety of reasons: not only does the metaphor of an ocean suggest that the characters who navigate it are in control of their destiny, and that the author's intervention has been apparently reduced, but it provides a view of Paris that permits navigation in any direction. The metaphor of the labyrinth, on the other hand, suggests that the characters' possible routes and decisions, while seemingly the result of their "free" choice, are in fact subject to the pre-determined paths of the labyrinth's very structure—in short, the image of the labyrinth suggests that there exists a "frame" indicative of the author's intervention, for a labyrinth, unlike an ocean, does not permit movement in any direction.

This second metaphor for Paris is evocative of the author's intervention in other more complex and subtle fashions. If the labyrinth, with its pre-determined paths, is more directly representative of authorial control and narrative framing than is the metaphor of the ocean, it is also, by extension, more capable of representing the trace of the labyrinthine linguistic path that the author himself must follow, as it informs all narrative production.

It is thus at this more abstract level that the metaphor of the labyrinth represents the restrictions that *the author* faces in putting his pen to paper: the metaphor suggesting free choice on the part of the characters (ocean navigation) and those suggesting authorial intervention (paintings, frames, negotiation through a labyrinth), while freely chosen by Balzac, are all ultimately and inevitably set against the pre-determined paths of the linguistic code. Thus, while the author is obviously free to combine words and sentences in a manner responding to his intention in writing, he must necessarily respect the linguistic code which pre-determines the order of graphemes and phonemes in words and the grammatical order of these words in sentences.

The image of the labyrinth, which permits freedom of navigation only along a pre-determined set of paths, therefore represents very well both the *possibility* for authorial freedom and the *constraints* this freedom will necessarily encounter. These two competing forces at work in narration combine to produce the conflicting desire at the center of our study. While the element of authorial freedom and the possibility of authorial choice can only be exerted within the structure of the pre-determined and labyrinthine linguistic code, it is this possibility, this element of control that Balzac chooses to alternately veil and reveal in *Le Père Goriot*.[23] When he veils this control within the narrative framework, the reader's perception of a scene proceeds unimpeded by any awareness of authorial intervention, even though the products of the author's selections and combinations, decisions made within the pre-determined structure of the linguistic code, constitute an unobtrusive, but ever-present framework supporting the narrative experience enjoyed by this same reader.

The metaphor of the labyrinth is capable of representing the framework of the narrative and the relative control of the author in yet another fashion as well. As our comparison of the visual perception of the painted scene and the intellectual perception of the textual image showed, the *author's* choice of imagery determines the nature of the narrative experience enjoyed by the reader, though this influence is offset by the *reader's* idiosyncratic response to those same images inscribed by his words on the page. In a sense, graphemes merely enclose potential and various realizations of the signifieds associated with an author's choice of signifiers. Like all authors, Balzac furnishes eventual readers with a *text* that only takes on a life when its potential is realized by the act of reading. The metaphor of the labyrinth not only evokes the pre-determined linguistic paths the author must follow in the creation of his text, but also represents the unrealized potential of the maze of signifiers he inscribes on the page. While the image of the ocean suggests that there are always an indefinite number of possible realizations of a text ("Jetez-y la sonde, vous n'en connaîtrez jamais la profondeur"), the image of the labyrinth is more telling of the structure underlying *all* textual images, for it represents the path of signifiers the reader must follow and which therefore leads the way in the various and potentially different realizations of the author's work. In his "Phenomenological Approach to the Reading Process," Iser distinguishes between the *work*, the *text* and its *realization*:

the literary work has two poles, which we might call the artistic and the aesthetic: the artistic refers to the text created by the author, and the aesthetic to the realization accomplished by the reader. From this polarity it follows that the literary work cannot be completely identical with the text, or with the realization of the text, but in fact must lie halfway between the two. The work is more than the text, for the text only takes on life when it is realized, and furthermore the realization is by no means independent of the individual dispositions of the reader—though this in turn is acted upon by the different patterns of the text.[24]

Iser's use of the terms "artistic" and "aesthetic" to describe the two poles at work in the experience of narrative is linked to the functioning of narrative in what we have termed the authorial and narrative frameworks. Balzac's use of the metaphor of the framed painting, his framing of the various settings for the "drama" of the characters, and his choice of the labyrinth as a metaphor for the city of Paris all indicate, though to differing degrees, a desire to overcome the restrictions inherent in writing and to exhibit authorial control of the narrative. In Iser's terms, Balzac's use of these metaphors and framing devices pulls the reader from a position of apparent autonomy at the aesthetic pole to an awareness of the author's control at the artistic pole.

Both author and reader exert an influence on the actualization of the *work* being read: a close reading of *Le Père Goriot* reveals Balzac's awareness of the relative prominence of these two influences, as well as his desire to both recede as an authorial presence (allowing reader involvement in the narrative) and to emerge, offsetting reader control, by manifesting relative autonomy as an author and ensuring that his controlling presence appear as such when the text is being read.

To put the matter differently, Balzac *opens* his text to successive actualizations by different readers when he adopts the practices of the novelist in the realist tradition, allowing the reader's experience to unfold in an unimpeded fashion within the narrative framework. This *opening* of his text is, as we have seen, linked to the metaphor of the labyrinth to the extent that the printed page, the text that is "entered" intellectually by the reader, is yet another "frame," an entrance to the labyrinth of images chosen by the author and actualized by the reader. The graphemes of these words chosen by the author, when considered on the most opaque level as black marks on a white page, can potentially refuse entry or prohibit access to the mental imagery that they are capable of delivering. Balzac is certainly aware that these graphemes, as "frames" enclosing images, must be opened and relatively unapparent if the reader's involvement within the narrative framework is to be successful.[25] However, he is also aware that the framework of the graphemes and the inscription of a text on a page are both brought to the reader's mind when the image enclosed by the graphemes redirects her attention to the representational quality of language—when, in a move from the narrative to the authorial framework, he interrupts the flow of imagery that he has set in motion by referring, for example, to the art of painting and to the deliberate stroke of a brush/pen.

Thus, while Balzac does guarantees the relative transparency and openness of the graphemes or frames enclosing the images he has chosen, and while his imagery in no way prevents the reader from entering the realm of the signified,[26] the narrative framework in which his imagery is housed does occasionally make a partial move in the direction of its closure. His reference to the art of painting, for example, reveals the framing inherent in all fiction; this allusion to the presence of the frame distances the reader from the realm of the signified experienced in its transparency and effects a partial closure of the narrative framework housing his imagery—the reader, pulled from the narrative to the authorial framework is made aware of the representational status of the tale, of the labyrinthine code upon which all writing rests, and of the potential opacity of linguistic *signifiers*.

By using a metonymically linked chain of metaphors such as the framed painting for the textual scene, the ocean and the labyrinth for the city of Paris, and the various framed settings for the "drama" of the narrative, Balzac intervenes as an author, compensating for what is merely a partial control of his work's realization, by effecting a shift or displacement which pulls the reader from the narrative to the authorial framework. This displacement moves along the continuum from transparent imagery in which authorial control is veiled to relatively opaque narration in which such control is made manifest.

His oscillation between the desire to intervene and to appear to relinquish control of the narrative is perhaps best attributed to his wish to tell the story while at the same time ensuring that the telling be represented in the tale. Balzac, I would suggest, tells another story which doubles that of Goriot and Rastignac: it is the story of narration, the frameworks within which it moves, and the author's control (partial though it may be) of the way in which his imagery is realized in the reading process. This second story shadows the first and can be deciphered at the interstices of the chain of metaphors that weaves through the novel, emerging and receding as the frames of Balzac's images "open" and "close" respectively.

NOTES

*In this article, I use the masculine pronoun to designate the author and the female pronoun when referring to the reader or spectator. Given their mutual influence in the actualization of a work, no sense of hierarchy is meant by this distinction.

1. Bernard Vannier, *L'Inscription du corps: Pour une sémiotique du portrait balzacien* (Paris: Klincksieck, 1972) 23.

2. Françoise Van Rossum-Guyon, for example, examines the "procedures of self-representation, by means of which Balzac's novel takes itself as object and refers to its codes." "Sur quelques aspects du métalangage chez Balzac" in *Le Roman de Balzac. Recherches critiques, méthodes, lectures. Etudes réunies par Roland Le Huenen et Paul Perron* (Montréal: Didier, 1980) 133. Le Huenen and Perron in their discussion of Balzac's *La Bataille* state that "[t]he project of the novel unfolds both as the representation of a scene and as the unveiling of its organizational principles: in other words, as product and process." "Reflections on Balzacian Models of Representation," *Poetics Today* 5 (1984): 723. Shoshana Felman's analysis of "The Illustrious Gaudissart" leads her to assert that while the "realist pretension ... consists in making others believe that language "expresses" something that is not in itself a sign but a reality already there, pre-existing and outside of language," Balzac uses the mad discourse of the salesman in the tale to "despoil that referential illusion, that novelistic mystification. While the realist pretension tries to occult, to hide the discursive origins of the narrative, madness is there to bring the 'story' back to its sole origin in discourse." *Writing and Madness (Literature/ Philosophy/ Psychoanalysis)*, trans. M. Evans (Ithica: Cornell University Press, 1985) 110.

3. Felman, *Writing and Madness (Literature/ Philosophy/ Psychoanalysis)* 110.

4. Honoré de Balzac, *La Comédie humaine* (Paris: Pléiade, 1951) I: 7. All further references to this edition will be included in the text.

5. Other critics have also noticed Balzac's desire to appear to relinquish control. Lawrence Schehr, for example, in noting Balzac's attraction to the theatrical mode, observes that this mode is able to create the illusion of living self-sufficient beings: " ... his characters, which might

otherwise have remained textual figures, are seen to be subjects in their own right, living, breathing human beings, self-sufficient and free of the control of a narrator." "The Unknown Subject: About Balzac's *Le Chef d'oeuvre inconnu,'" Nineteenth-Century French Studies* 12.4 & 13.1 (1984): 61.

6.   Felman, *Writing and Madness* (*Literature/ Philosophy/ Psychoanalysis*) 110.

7.   Lucienne Frappier-Mazur also refers to the metonymic function of the description of La Maison Vauquer when she writes: "Certes, que l'on considère ou non Balzac comme un auteur "réaliste," la signification symbolique du milieu dans la peinture des personnages, telle la description de la pension Vauquer, relève bien d'une relation métonymique." *L'Expression métaphorique dans la Comédie humaine* (Paris: Klincksieck, 1976) 29.

8.   On the subject of narrative framing, Barthes writes: "Toute description littéraire est une vue. On dirait que l'énonciateur, avant de décrire, se poste à la fenêtre, non tellement pour bien voir mais pour fonder ce qu'il voit par son cadre même; l'embrasure fait le spectacle. Décrire c'est donc placer le cadre vide que l'auteur transporte toujours avec lui ..." *S/Z* (Paris: Editions du Seuil, 1970) 61. Le Huenen and Perron describe this phenomenon as well: "In order to represent, a framework is required, one which mediates the transition from the formless to the formed, from the indefinite to the finite, from the unlimited to the limited ..." "Reflections on Balzacien Models of Representation" 722.

9.   Bernard Vannier provides some interesting examples of Balzac's use of the frame: Le texte du portrait, délimité par la mise en page, à tout le moins présenté dans la narration comme morceau détachable, peut se donner à *lire* comme tableau encadré: figure "encadrée" par le papier verni qui décore la salle, par un vêtement (jabot de dentelle, ou bonnet—"cadre festonné de lumière"—sous lequel brille la figure). Le cadre suggère toujours l'idée de tableau, qu'il soit simplement figuré ... ou qu'il soit *réel*, référentiel ... *L'Inscription du corps* 55–56.

10.   Laurence Rickels "Wilhelm Heinse's Media Conception of the Arts," *Semiotics 1984*, ed. John Deely (Lanham: UP of America, 1985) 39.

11.   Van Rossum-Guyon, "Sur quelques aspects du métalangage chez Balzac" 136. Le Huenen and Perron view Balzac's reference to painting as an attempt to "substitute for the graphics of sentences and the succession of verbal signs a representation belonging to the realm of figures, of simultaneity and of the whole ... The language of the portrait somehow guarantees the possibility of semiotic collaboration and a homogenization of signs." "Reflections on Balzacian Modes of Representation" 714.

12. In *La peinture dans la création balzacienne*, Bonard also refers to the portrait-like description of the characters staying at the Maison Vauquer: "Mme Vauquer, Mlle Michonneau et Poiret forment dans cette galerie de portraits une inoubliable trilogie satirique, où le romancier se plaît à dessiner dans de cruelles variations les visages de la laideur. Ce sont, de tous les habitants de la pension, ceux qui ressemblent le plus, ceux qui se sont le plus complètement adaptés à ses murs suintants et pisseux, à son odeur fétide et grasse." Olivier Bonard, *La peinture dans la création balzacienne* (Genève: Librairie Droz, 1969) 170.

Interestingly, Bonard distinguishes between Vautrin, whose "indépendance" and "royauté" result from his being described "ni dans le style proprement pictural, ni dans le style chargé de Balzac" (174) and Goriot who is portrayed by a series of portraits: "Car Balzac ne confine pas à un unique portrait le soin de nous expliquer son personnage. Il nous donne en quelque sorte plusieurs tirages de ce portrait, dans des techniques elles-mêmes différentes (175).

13. Loosely adapted from dictionary definitions.

14. Le Huenen and Perron also suggest that Balzac refers to painting in order to compensate in some way for the limits inherent in writing: "To evoke a picture ... is to posit the ineffectiveness of writing or at least its inferiority vis-à-vis painting, since, in order to describe, writing must resort to the suggestion of the image." "Reflections on Balzacian Modes of Representation" 714.

Vannier refers to Balzac's aspiration to a "pictorial writing" in the following quotation: "Le scripteur se substitue parfois au peintre hypothétique. C'est dans la trame même de la description que se manifeste alors l'ambition d'une écriture picturale; dès le titre qui isole le passage contenant la description, ou dans l'annonce rhétorique du portrait: "tableau," "esquisse" que le narrateur se contente de "crayonner," allusion à un dessin, une palette, ou tout simplement "peinture." L'étiquette ainsi affichée au début du portrait l'associe délibérément, dès la première phrase, à une oeuvre picturale. *L'Inscription du corps* 55.

15. Roman Jakobson, "Two Aspects of Language and Two Types of Aphasic Disturbances," *Fundamentals of Language*, R. Jakobson and M. Halle (The Hague: Mouton & Co., 1956). Among those who have reflected critically on Jakobson's distinction between the metaphoric and metonymic poles, one finds Hugh Bredin, who argues that selection and combination are inseparable (see footnote 23). For a list of articles on Jakobson's distinction see Willard Bohn, "Roman Jakobson's Theory of Metaphor and Metonymy: An Annotated Bibliography," *Style* 18.4 (1984): 534–550.

16. Gérard Genette, "Métonymie chez Proust, ou la naissance du Récit," *Poétique* 23 (1970): 156–173. Paul de Man, *Allegories of Reading* (New Haven: Yale Univ. Press, 1979) 65–72.

17. Umberto Eco, *The Role of the Reader*, quoted in Jonathon Culler, *The Pursuit of Signs: Semiotics, Literature, Deconstruction* (Ithica: Cornell Univ. Press, 1981) 199–200.

18. That a street should serve as a frame is perhaps an instance of what Riffaterre has termed ungrammaticality: "The thematic structure is perceived because of the functional anomalies provoked by its presence in a context. Since the context is generated by one or more descriptive systems, the mechanism of the anomaly is an *interference between structures*. This definition applies to the majority of those phenomena that are usually defined as cases of "ungrammaticality." Michael Riffaterre, *Text Production*, trans. T. Lyons, (New York: Columbia University Press, 1983) 200.

19. Lawrence Schehr presents a similar interpretation of the relationship of the theatrical mode to the narrative and pictorial modes when he writes: "In a narrative or pictorial model, there is a necessary translation from one medium to another ... painting or narrative is not in the same form (medium or dimensionality) as the human beings or objects that each tries to represent. In a theatrical model, however, it is evident that the play with its use of human beings as characters, does not operate the same translation on reality. In fact, under optimum conditions, the theatrical model is conceived as the creation of a simulacrum, a mimetic, non-diagetic copy that is indistinguishable from the original." "The Unknown Subject: About Balzac's *Le Chef d'oeuvre inconnu*" 60.

For a discussion of the representational quality of drama, see Jacques Derrida's "Le théâtre de la cruauté et la clôture de la représentation," *L'écriture et la différence* (Paris: Editions du Seuil, 1967) 341–368.

20. In two separate passages, Lucienne Frappier-Mazur presents a similar interpretation of the significance of "drama" in the evocation of the "real." She acknowledges its ability to be mistaken for the real when she writes of *César Birotteau*: "Ce passage fait ressortir l'ambition de l'auteur: le roman doit se présenter comme un drame pour restituer la vérité du réel. Un pas de plus, et le drame devient plus vrai que le réel." *L'Expression métaphorique dans la Comédie humaine* 112–13. In another passage, she refers to the distinction between drama and the real in *La Comédie humaine*: "Ce n'est pas le théâtre qui imite la vie, mais la vie qui imite le théâtre ..." *L'Expression métaphorique dans la Comédie humaine* 121.

21. François Bilodeau notes Balzac's use of the image of an ocean in *Louis Lambert* and *L'enfant maudit*. While Bilodeau attributes to this image

functions that differ from my view of the same image in *Père Goriot*, in all three interpretations, this image represents freedom from pre-determined and externally defined structures. In all three novels, the characters either freely navigate upon the water's surface or plunge into its depths. In Balzac's *Louis Lambert*, Bilodeau sees thought as a world that acquires the transparency of light or of an ocean into which one plunges with pleasure; in *L'enfant maudit*, Bilodeau sees Etienne, who develops a sympathetic relationship with the ocean, as seeking "un autre lui-même, une autre profondeur en transparence où la lumière se trouve possédée par réflexion. Il s'agit d'une relation de miroir à miroir." F. Bilodeau, *Balzac et le jeu des mots* (Montréal: Les Presses universitaires de Montréal, 1971) 78.

22. Other critics have observed that the labyrinth is a recurrent image in *La Comédie humaine*: "... espace initiatique, le labyrinthe devient l'inflexible spirale que P. Nykrog a bien vue à l'oeuvre, non seulement dans la Physiologie mais encore dans l'ensemble de *La Comédie humaine*." Jean-Claude Fizaine, "Ironie et fiction dans l'oeuvre de Balzac," *Colloque de Cerisy, Balzac, l'invention du roman* (Paris: Pierre Belfond, 1982) 177.

23. In a discussion of Roman Jakobson's "Two Aspects of Language and Two Aphasic Disturbances," Hugh Bredin describes the freedoms and restrictions at work within the framework of the linguistic code: "Father" is made up of phonemes each of which has been selected and combined with the other phonemes. But each of the phonemes itself is a product of selection and combination. So too are any longer items—morphemes, words, phrases, sentences, each on its own level ... Finally chunks of discourse such as stories, or explanations, are combinations of selected sentences. In all speech, at every level, selection and combination are fundamental and ubiquitous." "Roman Jakobson on Metaphor and Metonymy," *Philosophy and Literature* 8.1 (1984): 90.

24. Wolfgang Iser "The Reading Process: A Phenomenological Approach," *Twentieth Century Literary Theory. An Introductory Anthology*. V. Lambropoulos and D. Miller, eds. (Albany: SUNY Press, 1987) 381.

25. Le Huenen and Perron discuss this "opening" of the narrative image in different terms when they write that "... the word is neither the thing nor its stand-in, but an index that points and that causes to point, a signal that releases, as in those cases of paramnesia, an impression of déjà-vu, which revives an imprint woven into memory by knowledge and experience. To represent is to always resort to the antecedence of a trace, to invoke a reference; that is, through the intermediary of the sign, to establish a topological translation affecting the space of reading." "Reflections on Balzacian Models of Representation" 712.

26. An example of such a difficult entry into the realm of the signified is provided by Artaud when he writes:

> ... et nul s'en empara
> des singes,
> la guenon fut pulée au milieu
> par la grand-mise du zob en dieu
> quand dernière grand'messe eut lieu
>
> MERDE.
>
> raibend
> oi na mintrend
> ointrend
> neintrend
> o pennitra ...

Antonin Artaud, *Œuvres Complètes* (Paris: Gallimard, 1978) 14: 195.

JAMES R. McGUIRE

The Feminine Conspiracy in Balzac's
La Cousine Bette

There is something suspicious about the deaths of Lisbeth Fischer and
Valérie Marneffe. Bette dies outside of the narrative, parenthetically, of a
"phtisie pulmonaire," yet she is the title character; the scene of Valérie's
death is rife with melodrama and moral symbolism. The awkward,
expeditious elimination of these two principal female figures leads one to
question the actual nature of their transgressive role in *La Cousine Bette*.
Clearly, the theme of deviancy, linked historically to the rise of an acquisitive
bourgeoisie and the erosion of traditional social values based on heredity, is
central to Balzac's narrative. Few critics, however, have emphasized the
textual evidence suggesting that such deviancy takes the form of a lesbianism
that seeks to supplant the increasingly weakening patriarchal social
structures, namely the Family and the Church. Bette and Valérie conspire, in
effect, to legitimize their marginal sexual identification by vengefully taking
control of all the men around them. The text exhibits a marked absence of
vigorous, licit, heterosexual relationships; the only man who exudes any
virulence is the Brazilian, Montès, and his function as such is critical to the
possibility of a preserved patriarchy. The other men in the novel are
characterized as either doddering philanderers (Hulot), ostentatious
bourgeois (Crevel), infantilized and feminized objects of feminine desire
(Steinbock), or exceedingly uninteresting (Victorin). From the perspective of

From *Nineteenth-Century French Studies* 20, nos. 3 & 4. ©1992 by *Nineteenth-Century French
Studies*.

the somewhat contrived expurgation of two dangerous women, the ironic and hasty recuperation of the "legitimate" values of the Family and the Church at the end of the novel merits some attention.

Balzac's wordplay with the name "Bette" and the word "bête" is clearly intentional. Repeatedly the title character, nicknamed "la Chèvre" by Baron Hulot, is the object of animalization. Her description is, moreover, diametrically opposed to that of her more socially anchored cousin Adeline who is painted in angelic tones; she is a "déesse" (*La Cousine Bette*. Paris: Gallimard "Folio," 1972, 58). The deification of the young Hulot couple is set against the beastliness of "la Bette." Adeline, one of those "caractères sublimes," is likened to Venus and "notre mère Eve" (52), while the young Baron Hulot is "en homme, une réplique d'Adeline en femme" (53). This passage is clearly evocative of the biblical first family of Genesis; yet, curiously, here the male seems to be fashioned after the female. Man's difference springs from his original likeness with the woman, not vice-versa. This first suggestion of the inversion of sexual roles linked to the survivability of the Family will surface as a principal motivation of the narrative. Indeed, the Baron, "from the beginning," is as godly as his wife, but the suggestion of which sex might be capable of "failing" or "falling" is subtly implied: "pour Adeline, le baron fut, dès l'origine, une espèce de Dieu qui ne pouvait faillir" (54). This sacrosanct rendering of the Family dominated by the Father unites later with the sober presence of another patriarchal social force, the Church.

The divine Hulots are thus staged to clash with the sullen portrait of Lisbeth Fischer who "était loin d'être belle comme sa cousine … Paysanne des Vosges, dans toute l'extension du mot, maigre, brune, les cheveux d'un noir luisant, les soucils épais et reunis par un bouquet, les bras longs et forts, les pieds épais, quelques verrues dans sa face longue et *simiesque*, tel est le portrait de cette vierge" (59). This is not the only simian description of Bette. Later Balzac states: "Parfois elle ressemblait aux singes habillés en femme" (65); and later, Valérie addresses her as "ma tigresse" (233). Bette is not merely one "bête," but beastliness itself; she is a composite monster, at once goat, ape, and tiger. Although Bette's marginality is due in part to her provinciality, her low social rank and her homeliness, her status as a "monstrosity" derives for the most part from her "abnormal" sexuality, her celibacy. For Balzac, the virgin is invested with a singular reserve of nearly superhuman, unpredictable forces: "La virginité, comme toutes les monstrosités, a des richesses spéciales, des grandeurs absorbantes. La vie, dont les forces sont économisées, a pris chez l'individu vierge une qualité de résistance et de durée incalculable. Le cerveau s'est enrichi dans l'ensemble de ses facultés réservées" (138). The sexual monstrosity of virginity emerges from the shadows of the underworld; the action of "les gens chastes" is motivated by "une force diabolique ou la magie noire de la Volonté" (138). Patriarchal sexual norms are thus, from the first pages of the novel, pitted against the maleficent forces of sexual abnormality.

Bette's marginal social status as a monstrous virgin seems her lot. Hulot's efforts to "civilize" her by arranging acceptable candidates for marriage and by procuring her a position as a haberdasher's apprentice are wasted. Despite learning to read and write and becoming "une assez gentille, ùne assez adroite et première demoiselle" (60), Bette's jealousy of her cousin Adeline causes her to regress to her original social position— "elle redevint simple ouvrière" (60). Unable to ignore the imposing beauty and comfortable social position of Adeline, Bette is overcome by that burning jealousy that "formait la base de [son] caractère plein d'excentricités" (59). Bette is in fact far from the center of sociosexual norms. She inhabits the dismal fringe of Parisian society.

Set apart from a world where patriarchal structures demand strict gender identification, Bette seems to thrive on her difference, her resistance. She is at home in the "barbarie" of a "quartier en démolition," in one of those houses "envelopées de l'ombre éternelle … noircies … par le souffle du Nord" (80–1). Her marginality is willfully sustained— "elle aimait son chez soi" (65). It is significantly in this infernal quarter that Bette will first encounter Valérie Marneffe. Bette embraces and nurtures her eccentricity, consciously opposing herself to the sacred Hulots. She is no longer one of them, she has intentionally demarcated the boundary of her difference: "Cette fille perdit alors toute idée de lutte et de comparaison avec sa cousine" (61). The seed of revolt has been sown, for "l'envie resta cachée dans le fond de son cœur, comme un germe de peste" (61).

Reinforcing thus her status as a feminine anomaly, Bette becomes the antithesis of the woman "comme il faut." She will not agree to marriage, even if "maintes fois le baron avait résolu le difficile problème de la marier" (61). Cognizant of her difference, Bette will not allow men to penetrate her unsocial circle, to dominate her. She is unable to regard herself as an object of male desire; she wants to be a dominator of men: "[elle] eût aimé à protéger un homme faible" (62). Indeed, Bette possesses attributes which are more masculine than feminine and, in an effort to de-feminize her appearance, she defaces the finery given to her by Adeline. She is too much a man to take on the traditional role of the passive, servile wife. As a masculinized woman, Bette desires a feminized man. Her virginal monstrosity is only accentuated by the fact that she "possédait … des qualités d'homme" (68). For many characters in the novel, there is an irresolvable vacillation between their actual and their functional gender. For example, Bette, as an actual female, functions as a male and desires another actual male, Steinbock, himself functioning for a time as female. In turn, Steinbock will function as a male in relation to Hortense, but once again as a female for Valérie. Bette's functional gender is also seen to slip from male to female as her desire shifts from Steinbock to Valérie. This slippage prohibits a comfortable gender identification and inaugurates the sexual confusion to come.

Wenceslas Steinbock, of course, becomes Cousin Bette's "homme faible," at least temporarily. Bette is fifteen years his elder, however, and her love for him is more parental than sexual. She tells Wenceslas, "Eh bien! je vous prends pour mon enfant" (95); but he becomes in effect her "esclave" (102). Bette dominates Wenceslas because he feels indebted to her for having prevented his suicide and taking him under her wing. Because she is homely, she would doubtfully have been loved by him as a "woman." Her control of him is only through a parental tyranny; Bette, the manly, sexless virgin becomes the "entreteneuse" of Wenceslas, who here is characterized at once as a woman-child and as Bette's "homme faible." Just as Bette is both motherly and masculine in her relationship with Steinbock, so is he a feminine man. Balzac acknowledges this peculiar blurring of sexual roles: "on aurait pensé que la nature s'était trompée en leur donnant leurs sexes" (89). This gender whirligig serves to inform the dynamics of the entire narrative, and it is the unfixed functioning of sexual roles which threatens to destablize the moral constancy of patriarchy. Bette, for example, undertakes to subvert traditional sexual conventions by forming this "unnatural" bond with Wenceslas. The relationship defies the sanctity of the patriarchal model in that the identity of the male has become ambiguous. In fact, Bette and Wenceslas have come to represent the very opposite of traditional expectations of man and woman. Thus Balzac consciously qualifies their relationship with atypical adjectives: "le mariage de cette énergie femelle et de cette faiblesse masculine, espèce de contresens" (92). This "contresens" (which can be read as "contrary/wrong meaning" or "contrary/wrong direction") marks the union of Bette and Wenceslas as sexually aberrant and forebodes the subsequent disorder.

As Bette's protégé, Steinbock is initiated into her marginal universe and is himself, to some extent, animalized. Bette brags to the inquisitive Hortense that the name "Steinbock" means in German "animal des rochers" (70), as though such a quality should make him compatible with her. She strives to neutralize their differences, to see him as she is seen by others. The young Pole is more reticent, however, to consummate "cette alliance bizarre" (90), to submit to the "tyrannie d'une mère" (90). Bette fails, ultimately, to realize a union founded on the disregard of sexual conventions which demand gender stability between a male and a female. Wenceslas loves "real women"; Bette accuses him, "Vous aimez les femmes ..." (90), as though she were not one herself. In short, Bette is too manly for him, and he is too much a part of the socio-sexual mainstream. He will not commit to this inversion of the norm. Bette is forced consequently to withdraw completely from this attempted semblance of normalcy, semblance because Steinbock is, at least by appearance, of the opposite sex.

Steinbock's marriage to Hortense Hulot marks Bette's definitive break with conventional feminine sexuality. Here begins the "transformation de la Bette" (138). This transformation involves more the sexual clarification of the object of Bette's desire than her own gender identity. Embracing completely now her monstrous self, she transfers her "energie femelle" from Steinbock to Valérie Marneffe. There is no longer any need to feign the necessity of forming a licit heterosexual relationship. Bette's vengeance takes the form of a conscious plot to undermine the patriarchal, heterosexual social order in favor of love between women. Unable to belong to the world of the Father, Lisbeth sets out to create a counter-universe founded on a dominant femininity. Bette's pursuit to legitimize a feminine love can easily be read as a mere "compensatory" lesbianism, which threatens the demise of the Family so dear to Balzac, and which, therefore must be eradicated. Yet, as we will see, this menacing homosexuality represented by Bette and Valérie seems nearly to succeed in spite of itself.

Homosexual relations between Lisbeth and Valérie are far from explicit in the text. Yet, several passages demand that this aspect of their friendship be reckoned with. In the first phase of this homosexual bond, the two women enter into a secret pact against the Hulot family. Valérie's objective is clearly social elevation. It is Bette who is obsessed with ruining the Hulots, wreaking her vengeance for having lost Steinbock, and founding a "licit" homosexuality. Both take as their common enemy and the means to their end, the moneyed men around them. As their scheme progresses, the emotional bond between them strengthens and Valérie becomes "une jeune femme qui, pour elle [Bette], avait des semblants d'amitié, qui lui disait tout, en la consultant, flattant et paraissant vouloir se laisser conduire par elle, devint donc en peu de temps plus chère à l'excentrique Cousine Bette que tous ses parents" (127). For Bette, familial values, the values of heterosexuality represented by the Hulots (and especially by the righteous Adeline), are subsumed by her relationship with Valérie. Even Valérie, whose

stunning beauty does not exclude her from "normal" social circles and a licit
sexual life, scorns familial responsibility; one can recall the description of her
bedroom in that bleak quarter of the Louvre "où l'enfant abandonné à lui-
même, laissait traîner ses joujoux partout" (85). Not only is Valérie an
apparently ineffective mother, she confides to Bette that she much prefers
her company to that of her husband:

> —Mon Dieu, comme vous disposez de moi! ... dit alors madame
> Marneffe. Et mon mari?
> —Cette guenille?
> —Le fait est qu'auprès de vous c'est cela ... répondit-elle en riant.
> (129)

To consummate their bond, the two women move into the same house to
form, in the words of Bette, their own "ménage": "Dès lors, mon petit ange,
ma véritable vie, mon vrai ménage sera rue Vaneau" (129). The suggestion of
homosexuality between Bette and Valérie finds even stronger support in this
provocative dialogue between the two women, alone in Valérie's bedroom:

> —Es-tu belle, ce matin! dit Lisbeth en venant prendre Valérie par
> la taille et la baisant au front. Je jouis de tous tes plaisirs, de ta
> fortune, de ta toilette ... Je n'ai vécu que depuis le jour où nous
> nous sommes faites sœurs...
> —Attends! ma tigresse, dit Valérie.... (233)

First, the sexual tone of the verb "jouir" colors the passage and suggests that
Bette takes pleasure from Valérie as she does with her many male lovers.
Bette derives pleasure vicariously from the money Valérie acquires because
of her physical beauty. Valérie's body becomes, at least symbolically, the locus
of Bette's only erotic pleasure. Bette's embracing gesture and kiss, as well as
Valérie's use of the word "tigresse," accentuate the sexual undercurrent of the
passage. Furthermore, the word "sœur" serves to mark both as functionally
female. Pierre Barbéris, in a note on this passage in the Gallimard "Folio"
edition, cautiously proposes that the evidence here of at least a latent
homosexuality supports the notion of a feminine conspiracy:

> Valérie est sensuelle et débauchée. Bette est vierge. Mais Bette
> jouit par personne interposée. De plus Bette et Valérie
> s'entendent pour exclure et juger les hommes. Elles vivent toutes
> deux dans un univers particulier, fait d'intérêts communs mais

aussi d'une sorte de complicité féminine. Balzac a-t-il voulu suggérer l'existence entre Bette et Valérie sinon de relations homosexuelles concrètes au moins de tentations? (493)

Whether merely "tentations" or true homosexuality, Balzac is clearly staging the illicit nature of Bette and Valérie's relationship as the primary threat to patriarchal society. Whatever the case may be, the two women conspire, Bette as the monstrous virgin whose "dissimulation est impénétrable" (in the sexual sense?), and Valérie as a prostitute whose relations with Hulot and Crevel are a mere ploy to acquire wealth and social status. One will argue that Valérie's love for Steinbock and for Montès is sincere. Indeed it is. She confesses to Bette that she loves Wenceslas "à en maigrir" (190), and to Crevel: "Je crois bien que je l'aime, mon petit Wenceslas! ... je l'aime au grand jour comme si c'était mon enfant!" (411). Just as in Bette's case, however, Steinbock functions as female and childlike. He is also for Valérie an "homme faible," a coddled, infantile artist. In effect, Balzac says of Polish men in general that they "se parent comme des femmes" (252). Valérie's love for Steinbock is more homosexual, given his overall feminine characterization. His inability to be an effective husband for Hortense supports his function as a female figure and serves to affirm Bette and Valérie's proclivity for the feminine sex.

As for Valérie's love for Montès, his case is also exceptional. Montès functions as a catalytic character in the novel. His presence ultimately serves (along with that of Victorin as we will see) to effect the necessary dismantling of the feminine conspiracy. His relationship with Valérie is justified mostly because of his vast fortune. She fully intends to exploit him as she does Hulot and Crevel. It is symbolically important that Montès, unlike the other men of the novel, exhibits a certain virility and that Valérie is attracted to him as a man since he will be the agent of her death and the ultimate unravelling of the conspiracy. Montès reconciles in a way the reconstitution of a male order and the inevitable installation of wealth, not name, as the determining factor of social status. It is in this role that Valérie is able to "love" Montès; she never loves for love's sake. She admits herself that her liaison with Montès is pure "fantaisie" (233). Indeed, she even unemotionally considers abandoning Montès observing, "Montès est Brésilien, il n'arrivera jamais à rien" (232). Bette reminds her, however, of the times they live in: "Nous sommes, dit Lisbeth, dans un temps de chemins de fer, où les étrangers finissent en France par occuper de grandes positions" (232). Clearly, her primary aim is not to establish a heterosexual relationship with Montès but rather to revel in the possibility of an exotic wealth and a higher position in a burgeoning bourgeois social structure.

The episode in which Valérie persuades Wenceslas to execute the sculpture of Samson and Delilah is an allegory for the sexually subversive mission of the two conspirators. The sculpture posits not only a dominant femininity, but precisely the designs of Valérie and Bette, to wrest power from male order in a moment of vulnerability. Samson's emasculation as he lies sleeping signifies the cutting off of traditional masculine power—represented by a symbolically phallic extension of the male body, hair or money—by the woman. Valérie explains to Steinbock:

> Il s'agit d'exprimer la puissance de la femme. Samson n'est rien là. C'est le cadavre de la force. Dalila, c'est la passion qui ruine tout … voilà comment je comprends la composition. Samson s'est réveillé sans cheveux … elle a dû aimer Samson devenu petit garçon … Ce groupe … [sera] la femme expliquée. (256–7)

Delilah's passion empowers her as it nullifies the force of the male. This passion is clearly that for another woman, that is, the emasculated (castrated), childlike Samson. Valérie demands that she be the model for this monument to the founding of a new femininity that emerges beside the corpse of male domination.

How is this sexual rebellion put into action in the narrative? How can homosexual love between women be legitimized in a society structured after the Family and the Church, a society literally generated out of heterosexual love? It is by controlling the substance that is, in the careless hands of Balzac's male characters, a measure of virility, or the lack thereof: money. Money, in fact, comes to represent the vulnerability of masculinity as it becomes more and more a force controlled by women. Bette and Valérie set out to usurp the nascent social power of money traditionally reserved for men. Like a life source, money flows rapidly to the side of the woman. It is thus that Valérie and Bette sap Hulot's power and force him to abandon his family. They also succeed in disintegrating the Marneffe family and plot the fall of Crevel and the ultimate, interested union with Montès. This brutal attack on the Father is reinforced as Valérie's promiscuity puts into question the paternity of the child she is carrying. This situation forebodes the death knell of the Father since the cornerstone of any patriarchy is certainty of identifying the legitimate father.

The two conspirators seem on the verge of accomplishing the dissolution of the Family's hegemony. Bette's thirst for vengeance is being satisfied, both against the constant Adeline, the religious incarnation of pure and legitimate family values, and against Hortense, who took Steinbock from her to form another "ménage légitime" (233). Yet, even though Bette and Valérie nearly succeed in annihilating the Hulot family their feminine universe must remain an anomaly, at least according to a narrative that must somehow recuperate the Balzacian Family. Theirs is an order based on immorality, illegitimacy, and sexual sterility. Such female perversions must be expunged, or, as is the case with the symbolic Atala, "civilized" and reinstituted into the patriarchal system.

The restoration of the Family is brought about, ironically, by Victorin, son of the absent father Hulot and thus his logical replacement, and, as we have already seen, Montès. Although not a virulent figure like Montès, as a lawyer and a representative of the Law, Victorin is at least master of his money. It is he who saves the Hulots and re-establishes them on rue Plumet. He replaces the original father and in so doing puts an end to the feminine plot with a little plotting of his own. Regaining control of the family fortune, Victorin is victorious also through the power of well-managed money. Fifty thousand francs to madame Nourrison finishes once and for all the cunning of the female accomplices and punishes them in the process. Money is back in the hands of man; masculinity can now be "rightfully" restored.

Adeline, the saint of family values, aids in this recuperation through her constancy as an example of a femininity that recognizes its "proper" place in the patriarchy. Her devotion, in the baron's absence, is transferred from the Family to that other prototypical patriarchal institution that enters near the end of the narrative in the stead of the familial Father, that is to say the Church. The role of the Church is central to both the official re-valorization of the Family and the obligatory termination of the feminine conspiracy. The dénouement is predictable, yet it is markedly telescoped. The female antagonists are too precipitously disposed of. The narrative has nearly become a juggernaut of outlaw femininity. Balzac resorts hastily to contrivance and melodrama to meet the demands of his patriarchally motivated text. Valérie's death, of which Montès (virility) and Victorin Hulot (money) are the agents, is caused by her ingestion of an exotic viral brew. But, as though this narrative stratagem were not enough, Balzac infuses the scene with a heavy-handed symbolism that is difficult to swallow. Valérie's body, the instrument of her sexual rebellion, rots with infection. As her beauty is transformed into pain she is suddenly brought to concede to the "rightful" patriarchal authority and she voices to the attending vicar her desire to repent, to be saved from fiery perdition. This rather abrupt capitulation to the Church tests the limits of verisimilitude; however, it serves to identify

Valérie and Bette's plot as "wrong," as a transgression of the Law and enables Balzac to regain control of the plot, to eliminate the female threat, and to recuperate the Family, all in just a few pages.

Lisbeth is left in the lurch by Valérie. As she enters the scene of Valérie's death, she is horrified, repulsed by the presence of the Church: "[elle] resta pétrifiée … en voyant un vicaire de Saint-Thomas-d'Aquin au chevet de son ami, et une sœur de la charité la soignant" (446). The sober and imposing image of religion is used to drive home the reality of the defeat of aggressive femininity and homosexuality. Heterosexuality, the basis of patriarchy représented here by the Church, inevitably prevails: "le sentiment le plus violent que l'on connaisse, l'amitié d'une femme pour une femme, n'eut pas l'héroïque constance de l'Eglise. Lisbeth, suffoquée par les miasmes délétères, quitta la chambre" (448). The violence caused to society by love between women is put aright; Valérie becomes another "âme à sauver" (447), while, with supreme irony, Bette's "phtisie pulmonaire" is brought about spontaneously by the sight of this heroic constancy of the Church.

The absence of a death scene for Cousin Bette is therefore highly significant and, in light of such melodramatic closure, conforms to the logic of the narrative. Bette must merely disappear. Rejecting conversion like her friend and "déjà bien malheureuse du bonheur qui luisait sur la famille" (466), she dies, appropriately and literally, in the margins. Steadfast in her difference, she cannot occupy much space at the end of a story that, by its formula, seeks to demonstrate the infallibility of the Family. Thus Bette's passing is merely reported, she dies out of narrative sight. The spotlight is filled by the happy "retour du père prodigue" (464); the narrative closes, naturally, with the celebration of a blissfully regained patriarchy: "On arriva naturellement à une sécurité complète. Les enfants et la baronne portaient aux nues le père de famille …" (467). Homosexuality is perfunctorily eclipsed by the heterosexual family unit reinstituted by the Church and the power of money in the hands of dependable men. Only heterosexuality, that is the love sanctioned by Nature and heredity, can be self-regenerating and is thus the only tolerable expression of love and the only safeguard of patriarchy. The sterility of lesbianism and its threat to virility as the foundation of social power necessitates this natural, final, fatherly security. The incursion of an exclusive femininity is, at least temporarily, stalled by renewed hope in a virile, procreative order. The vulnerability of the Family, however, remains interestingly visible as the novel trails off with the black humor of Hulot's marriage to Agathe the cook and the death of the angelic Adeline.

MARTIN KANES

Structures: Organizing a Fictional Universe

Le Père Goriot begins with an enigma. The sign identifying Mme Vauquer's boardinghouse reads "Private Lodgings for Both Sexes and Others." "Others"? Though the radical massacre of language was one of Mme Vauquer's regular habits, radical opinions were not. Could she possibly have been asserting, even in her overblown style, that she welcomed homosexuals? Or did she imagine that such a bizarre announcement indicated a stylish establishment? Perhaps it was a private joke. No explanation is offered.

To be fair, we are well warned that there will be plenty of questions and much mystery. We will be like visitors to Les Catacombes, the narrator tells us. All is dark, and will become darker as we proceed, even though, as he also tells us, "all is true" (50; 8).

Mystery or not, the novel asserts itself from the very start as an effort, against all odds, to make Parisian life intelligible to outsiders. This is part of what Balzac meant when he later insisted that he was society's secretary, whose duty it was to explain and preserve certain facts about the Paris of post-Napoleonic France. At the same time, his literary purpose was to tell a tale about the human heart that is broader than anything that can be said about that particular time and place.

It is astonishing to realize that in the first decades of the nineteenth century Honoré de Balzac was already engaged in a version of a modern

From *Père Goriot: Anatomy of a Troubled World*. ©1993 by Twayne Publishers.

anthropological procedure called "thick description"—a process of extremely detailed depiction that theoretically permits the understanding of a culture "from within." By common consent he was highly successful at it; Frederick Engels was only the first of many historians and social anthropologists to say that they learned more about French history and society from Balzac than from their professional colleagues. Thick description of Paris, however, is not the main point of *Le Père Goriot*. It is one technique among many, and it is applied principally to Mme Vauquer's boardinghouse. This suggests that the "Paris" of the novel is not the city at large; it is really this one building, its occupants and their lives. *That* is the world we are invited to enter.

Balzac's famous descriptions tend to be clustered at the beginnings of his novels, carefully setting the characters into their milieu and establishing themes and motivations. Once this is done, the action moves swiftly. The reader understands events as situations unfolding in real life. It comes as no surprise, then, that whereas the opening can occupy as much as the first third of a novel and span several years, the action that follows may last only a few days. The opening of *Le Père Goriot* typically concerns "the general situation in the boarding house at the end of November, 1819" (76; 37) and occupies about one-tenth of the text. But there is a great deal more to Balzac's openings than mere depiction of milieu and characters. "Thick description" implies the discovery and analysis of human presence among the objects of the material world. This novel is less about the world people make for themselves than about what they do in it. The simplest objects—Mme Vauquer's chipped tableware, Goriot's silverware—are never merely themselves. They are symbols of greed or generosity, weakness or strength, good sense or obsession.

It would be unreasonable to expect Balzac's descriptions to be entirely consistent. We must come to terms with the fact that frequently they contain contradictions and antitheses, that paradoxes abound, and that some things are deliberately left vague. While this can be disconcerting, it forces the reader to *construct* the fictional world rather than merely *observe* it. Is Mme Vauquer's garden a verdant bower (as she sees it) or a collection of spindly plants struggling to survive (as others see it)? Is the murder of young Taillefer a simple business transaction (as Vautrin sees it) or a horrendous crime (as others see it)? Is Goriot a saint or a monomaniac? One of the points of this quasi-anthropological investigation is that it places the reader in the position of the anthropologist, obliged to make judgments and interpretations.

The reader of Balzac must therefore read "closely," to use current terminology, picking up the paradoxes among the consistencies, the contradictions among the confirmations. The rewards are many. Discrepancies lead to questions and to curiosity about people and things, in much the same way as the mysteries of life draw us forward. Here as with so many other nineteenth-century novels, a "good read" cannot be a fast one.

Balzac quite naturally assumed that his novels would be read in this deliberate way. In serial form they were broken up into sections (called "articles") appropriate to newspaper publication and, within each article, into further short chapters. *Le Père Goriot* first appeared in four such articles in the *Revue de Paris* for 14 and 28 December 1834 and for 25 January and 11 February 1835. After the first Werdet editions in book form, the chapter divisions of each article were eliminated. At first glance this seems perverse. Chapter breaks relieve the reader's eye; their titles act as signposts along the narrative way. But for Balzac books were different from newspapers. He now wanted the reader to sink into the world of the novel as into a sea, literally to be lost in pages of solid print.

The ocean of Balzacian prose is not, however, shapeless. *Le Père Goriot* plainly respects the linearity of the reading experience by resolving itself into a series of narrative blocks, each defined by a marker phrase, a dramatic event, or a dominant image. The articles of the serial publication in the *Revue de Paris* were organized into seven blocks, with the following titles:

1. *Une Pension bourgeoise* (A Middle Class Boarding House)
2. *Les Deux Visites* (The Two Visits)
3. *L'Entrée dans le monde* (An Entry into the World)
4. [Untitled—a continuation of the preceding]
5. *Trompe-la-mort* (Cheat-Death)
6. *Les Deux Filles* (The Two Daughters)
7. *La Mort du père* (The Father's Death)

In the second book edition (called "third" because of the serial publication), these were reduced to the following:

1. *Une Pension bourgeoise* (now including what had been *Les Deux Visites*)
2. *L'Entrée dans le monde*
3. *Trompe-la-mort*
4. *La Mort du père* (including the material of *Les Deux Filles*)

Both patterns move from an introduction, through the simultaneous actions of the Rastignac and Goriot plots, toward the dramatic day of Vautrin's arrest and the resolution of the Goriot story. The first pattern corresponded poorly to the practical necessities of serial publication in four installments, as is shown by the "untitled" fourth section. The second pattern simplified the first by consolidating the story of Goriot and his daughters, thus reflecting Balzac's concern for dramatic concision. But the chapter headings also illustrate the problem of the novel's unity. The section entitled *Trompe-la-mort*, which culminates with the arrest of Vautrin, effectively ends a major strand in the novel. The resolution of the Goriot story thereby risks appearing as something of an anticlimax and makes us wonder, retrospectively, which story is really the kernel of the novel. In any case, all these sectional divisions disappeared as of the Charpentier edition of 1839, along with the prefaces.

Part of the problem was that Balzac was constantly struggling to make the complicated events of his story fit into a reasonable chronology—not something in which he always succeeded. If one divides the chronology according to its natural articulations, it turns out to be the following:

BLOCK 1: Description of the Vauquer house; two days in the life of the boardinghouse; Rastignac's first social calls.

INTERLUDE 1: A vaguely defined period of several weeks, ending with Rastignac's receipt of money from his family.

BLOCK 2: First days of Rastignac's campaign; beginning of the seduction of Delphine and attendance at the Carigliano ball.

INTERLUDE 2: A very long, very indefinite passage of time; Rastignac's love scene with Victorine; announcement of the plan to kill young Taillefer.

BLOCK 3: Approximately seven days from Michonneau's interview with Gondureau to the betrayal of Vautrin and finally to Goriot's death and funeral.

Viewed this way, the narrative blocks of *Le Père Goriot* resemble a conventional dramatic arrangement of three precisely defined chronological "acts" separated by two chronologically vague intermissions. There are a major and a minor plot and a traditional grand scene about two-thirds of the way through. Although each block revolves around a principal action, each is literally stuffed with events—so much so that there was hardly time for everything. Mistakes were bound to occur, and did. Rastignac, for example, leaves for his first visit to Mme de Restaud at 3:00 P.M., arrives at 2:30, and then is said to have visited her in the morning. Moreover, Balzac's attempts to establish consistent links between *Le Père Goriot* and other novels also produced errors. In other novels, for example, the Bianchon of *Le Père Goriot* is called "a famous doctor" when in fact he is still a medical student. Nevertheless, these anomalies are visible only to the reader who either reads with an eagle eye or brings to this reading a detailed knowledge of other parts of the *Comédie humaine*. For the average reader what counts are the *narrative centers* of the three blocks, the major event or events around which each is organized:

> Block 1: Mme Vauquer's boardinghouse. This is the neutral territory on which the major characters gather for those encounters that are the very heart of this novel; from here they emerge to pursue their various paths.

> Block 2: Rastignac's disputation with Vautrin. This is the moral center of the novel and occurs approximately at its material center. After Vautrin delivers his long and bitter speech on the immorality of post-Napoleonic France, Rastignac meditates on his situation and Goriot expounds on his own set of values.

> Block 3: 1. The day of drama. All the threads, except for Goriot's, come together here. Young Taillefer is killed, Vautrin is arrested, and Eugène is caught between Delphine and Victorine.

> Block 3: 2. Mme de Beauséant's ball. This archetypal social occasion marks the climax of Mme de Beauséant's life, and indirectly of Goriot's and Rastignac's. Eugene's "education" culminates at the conclusion of the ball.

The three blocks with their thematic centers lend themselves to interpretation according to a number of familiar patterns, the most important of which are the melodrama, the murder mystery, the education novel, and the historical novel. It is the essence of Balzac's skill that *Le Père Goriot* can be seen as any and all of these.

Le Père Goriot, first of all, is a melodrama. It has melodrama's typical characteristics: it proceeds at a headlong pace; it opposes events and individuals in radical ways; it presents us with violent moral opposites; it highlights brutal words and acts; it is peopled by pure villains and pure victims; above all, its narrative surface covers, by implication, a dark and troubling underworld.

Melodramatic as it is, *Le Père Goriot* is also a kind of murder story, although there is relatively little mystery about the murders and the one genuine assassination takes place offstage. Murder stories are all about violence done to accepted notions of the sanctity of life and the reestablishment of the proper order of things. But Balzac was only half-committed to the formula. His story does not follow the traditional murder story path from clue to fact; here the "sign" of the crime is coexistent with the crime itself. Neither Vautrin's red hair nor the brand on his shoulder, for example, is the clue that leads to his exposure as a criminal; these are simply the indicators that symbolize and confirm his criminality.

With respect to homicide, then, there are surprisingly few mysteries here, since it is clear very early on what is being planned, why, and by whom. And so if *Le Père Goriot* is in part the story of two murders, it is not a murder *mystery*.

But there are other mysteries, above all mysteries of identity. Almost all the characters are baffling in one way or another. Early on we learn quite a bit about Rastignac, who in turn finds Goriot worthy of "investigation." But the others seem to emerge from a dense fog, play their role in the story, and disappear again—some to turn up in subsequent stories, some never to be heard of again.

This is most clearly seen in Vautrin, who knows everything about everyone but who is a riddle himself. Why does a mysterious stranger ask Christophe about this odd resident with dyed sideburns (80; 43)? Why does Vautrin come and go at night, and bribe Christophe not to mention that fact? Why does he tease and joke to deflect inquiries about himself? Why does he fuel puzzlement by telling Victorine that he will "see you are both very happy" (134; 104)? He boasts about his inaccessibility ("You'd very much like to know who I am.... You're too inquisitive, little man" [135; 104]), and we are told that somewhere in his life there is a "carefully shrouded mystery" (62; 20). But we have to wait a long time to discover what that mystery is, although Vautrin nearly reveals it in a slip of the tongue: "You can take Trompe (damnation!) Vautrin's word for it" (135; 104).

Eventually we will learn that Vautrin is, in the words of a critic, the "Napoleon of crime." But such knowledge as we can glean requires us to follow trails in other novels of the *Comédie humaine*. His motivations must wait for other novels, and even then the story of his life will raise as many questions as it answers. Meanwhile the Vautrin of *Le Père Goriot* is clearly the most obvious of the pirates who navigate the social ocean, and whose names are Maxime de Trailles, Henri de Marsay, and—in due time—Eugène de Rastignac.

The mysteries of *Le Père Goriot* are never merely mysteries, told for the pleasure of their unraveling. Vautrin corresponds to a certain popular romantic type and is in fact deeply rooted in the sinister heroes of Balzac's own early Gothic novels, such as *The Birague Heir, The Priest of the Ardennes, Argow the Pirate,* and *The Corrupter.* Vautrin is attractive in a demonic way, for he expounds an accurate, one might almost say irresistible, estimate of the world and himself. Buried in the mystery of Vautrin is a source of ethical messages that demand to be dealt with. No more than Rastignac can the reader avoid them.

Mystery also surrounds old Goriot, but it is mystery of a different sort. Why does he receive visits from unidentified elegant women? Why does he gradually but steadily reduce his standard of living (69; 30)? Why does he twist his silver dinnerware into bars (78; 40)? What is he doing at the home of Anastasie de Restaud (95; 61)? Rastignac confides to Bianchon that Goriot's past is too mysterious not to warrant being examined. But in fact no character within the story frame discovers much of anything about the old man, because he is nothing apart from his love for his daughters. No dramatic events mark his life in the boardinghouse; he leads an almost animal-like existence as he gradually subsides into death. His life is a veritable blank, and if all were revealed there would probably be nothing much of interest to observe.

Vautrin and Goriot are but the most prominent of several such enigmatic characters. Anyone attempting to peer into their past encounters only a great void. Who is Mme Vauquer, "born de Conflans," as we are told several times with much sarcasm but without further explanation? What is hidden in her vague matrimonial past? Again, what unmentionable secrets are buried in the past of Mlle Michonneau, who can barely contain an "air of understanding" when Vautrin mentions "men of special tastes" (88; 50)? What is she doing engaged in a conversation with a very suspicious-looking person in the Jardin des Plantes (188; 163)?

The individual with whom Mlle Michonneau and M. Poiret confer is himself a mystery. He had already struck Bianchon as a shady character disguised as a bourgeois (165; 136). Very quickly the narrator appears to adopt Bianchon's intuitive assessment, calling the mysterious gentleman a "fake bourgeois" (189). In the midst of this scene the narrator suddenly refers to the interlocutor as "the detective" (189; 165), then as "the unidentified man" (192). Appellations alternate between "Gondureau" and "the detective" until he is finally identified as "the well-known police chief" (193; 168). All of this is indirect and even a bit confusing. As with Vautrin, we must go to other episodes of the *Comédie humaine* to learn more about this strange man.

The classic mystery story requires that puzzles be solved neatly, all together at the end. That is by no means the case here. Some of the most important answers are supplied halfway through, when we learn that Mlle Michonneau and M. Poiret are police informers and that Vautrin is none other than the criminal Jacques Collin, nicknamed "Trompe-la-mort" ("Cheat-death"). These revelations resolve a certain number of dramatic movements in the novel, but the fact that they come midway suggests that unlike most mystery stories, this tale's real interest lies elsewhere.

For the important question here is not *what* people have done, but *why* they have done it. The search for an answer to that question is what propels the action of the novel and draws the reader ever onward. It is a matter of discovery and of education. And most specifically, the education of Eugène de Rastignac.

Indeed, an alternate way of viewing *Le Père Goriot* is as an education novel, a well-used pattern in prose fiction. Typically, a young and inexperienced hero goes through a number of trials and difficult experiences, at the end of which he emerges as an older, wiser person. There is no indication that Balzac ever read Goethe's *Wilhelm Meister*, the standard example of the type. But we know that he had read Dante, whose *Divine Comedy* can also be interpreted in this way. *Le Père Goriot* has been seen as a descendant of Dante's work, in that it presents a young man being led toward self-knowledge by an older man. The analogy seems only partly applicable, however, since there are two mentors here rather than one as in Dante's work, and since at least one of them wishes to lead Rastignac toward evil rather than virtue.

As with the mystery story, Balzac plays games with the usual pattern of the education novel. Rastignac arrives in Paris as a naive, provincial youth, filled with good intentions. Scion of an impoverished aristocratic family, he plans to study law and enter government service. He is one of those "most highly gifted young men" (74; 35) of whom Balzac was so fond, and has come to the capital to serve his apprenticeship. He is pained by the contrast between the luxury of Paris and the poverty of his family, and he wishes to succeed only by merit. He has a certain openness and purity, as his name Eugène indicates, although it twice escapes the narrator that he has become conceited (169, 182; 141, 156). He learns about "the strata that compose human society" (74; 35) and that happiness is indexed by the level one occupies. He also learns from Mme de Beauséant that society is governed by strategically placed women. Nevertheless, he blunders about a good deal with much hesitation and perplexed soul-searching. He is quick and intelligent but also vague and waffling. He is both revolted and tempted by Vautrin's offer; he is dismayed by his own attraction to Delphine de Nucingen but nonetheless submits to it. Finally, after making some serious errors he learns the Parisian social game and begins to play it with great skill and enterprise.

He also indulges in a certain degree of pathos. His response to his family's financial sacrifice is pure sentimental self-justification. At Mme de Beauséant's house he hears of the perfidy of Goriot's daughters with "tears [in his eyes]" (113; 79), but it does not escape him—nor would Vautrin let it escape him—that he is conducting himself toward his own family very much as Goriot's daughters treat him.

This amalgam of insight and weakness is the very essence of Eugene's character. We see the mixture explicitly when Delphine de Nucingen asks him to play roulette for her (170–71; 143). On the one hand, he is moved by her predicament and wishes to help her; on the other, he is unable to resist a feeling of joy at the possibility it affords him of getting a hold over her. His response is half altruism, half exploitation. It is an exciting combination of emotions, and in reflecting it the narration suddenly shifts from the past tense into a breathless present: "Eugène *takes* her purse ... *runs* to house number 7.... [H]e *goes* in.... [H]e *asks* for the roulette table.... [H]e *asks* how to bet" (171; 143). The narrative remains in the present tense until the end of the gambling scene, whereupon it returns to a historical past: "Delphine gave him a frantic hug" (172; 144). Eugène has won money for the woman and the woman for himself. The complexity of his "education" and the power of the contradictory forces pulling at him could hardly be clearer.

But having "won" Delphine, will Eugène really want such a woman? Consider her position: Delphine is faced with moral decisions on the eve of Mme de Beauséant's ball. The invitation to the ball represents the culmination of her social ambitions, but her father is lying near death in his garret. She cannot be in both places at once. She assures Eugène that she will stay with her dying father but glosses over the fact that she will go only *after* the ball (262; 243). Eugene understands this and clearly recognizes the truth about Delphine, but he also discovers that he lacks the courage and strength to reject her. Instead, he engages in willful self-deception and "murderous rationalization."

This, then, is a mock education novel. Eugène does not rise to some broader and more mature view of himself; he does not deepen his understanding of his own motives. He does learn to be sharp in observation, quick in action, and ruthless in judgment—which are quite different things.

His only education is in the methodology of social conquest and in the techniques necessary to quiet his conscience.

The historical context sketched out in chapter 1 provides the framework for whatever mysteries and whatever education can be found in *Le Père Goriot*. But history is not merely a framework; the work makes a serious claim to being a historical novel as such. One might say that Balzac's ambition was to be the Sir Walter Scott of his own times. Like Scott, Balzac was extremely meticulous in his description. He paid great attention to such things as streets, neighborhoods, and even clothing and food. But Scott created a highly romanticized past; Balzac could not prettify unpleasant facts that were patently visible to his readers. He was interested in describing and preserving the fabric of everyday life in post-Napoleonic French society primarily for people who were living that very life. And for most people, the life was not a very pleasant one. This history of the present, so to speak, brought Balzac before a well-known romantic puzzle: how could one make great art out of a disagreeable topic that readers would recognize as real?

In *Le Père Goriot* Balzac offers no political or historical analysis in the present meanings of those terms. But if "analysis" means the honest and direct description of society as it was, then *Le Père Goriot* is truly an analytical work. In it Balzac identified what he considered to be the two most powerful forces in contemporary Parisian life: the search for money and the search for pleasure. That, for him, was the fundamental historical reality of the times. History, in a word, became psychology.

Neither his youthful liberalism nor the monarchism he had come to embrace seemed viable to Balzac in 1834, and so neither could provide the basis of a critique of society. Yet he had to have some vantage point from which his analysis could be conducted. His device was to contrast those characters who embody the values of the times with others who represent some standard of ethics: on the one hand, Vautrin and Rastignac; on the other, Bianchon, Victorine Taillefer, and—just offstage—the Rastignac family on their country property.

Bianchon stands as an example of the manoeuvering room available to a virtuous individual in a laissez-faire society. He devotes himself to his profession, he judges others in terms of their conduct rather than of their wealth, he is thoughtful, he is kind. He is in no way obliged to become involved in Goriot's life, and yet he ends by becoming one of the old man's main supports. Victorine Taillefer is the epitome of unrequited filial love. Balzac allows her not the faintest shadow, not the faintest hint of reproach. She loves her heartless father and her unworthy brother. She is pure virtue and thereby underscores the perfidy in Eugène's wavering.

The obviously idealized and romanticized Rastignac family appears in one section of the novel only, and there only via letters. But its virtues are implied every time Rastignac's goodness of heart is mentioned. Life in Paris is measured against Rastignac's memories of his tender sisters, his doting mother, and his self-sacrificing aunt. His youth is evoked only indirectly, but it is the unspoken criterion against which the infamy of Paris is measured at every step of the way.

These contrasts permit Balzac to judge the everyday history lived by individuals. On this accounting Parisian society finally condemns itself not so much by its overt cynicism as by its willingness to conceal its darker side. It is almost as if Balzac had merely to present "the facts"—and the problem of the artistic appeal of evil was resolved. As history becomes psychology, wickedness becomes interesting.

This can be clearly seen in the story of Mme de Beauséant. The corollary to the principle that wealthy women were the key to power was the principle that the loss of a lover was also a loss of status. Abandoned by her lover—in this case, a strictly platonic one—Mme de Beauséant feels that she must withdraw from society and retire to the country. Balzac makes clear his respect for this last representative of the quasi-royal house of Burgundy. He represents her departure without the slightest irony as a noble act of renunciation worthy of a goddess of the *Iliad*. Her final downfall is marked by her most glittering ball. In Balzac's words, "Everyone in the fashionable world had flocked so eagerly to see this great lady in the hour of her downfall that the reception rooms ... were already packed by the time Delphine and Eugène appeared" (263; 245). All through this scene Mme de Beauséant is represented as rising above her disaster, as a woman "superior" to the situation in which she finds herself. Who can fail to ask why, if she is so noble, she should care about this superficial and unforgiving world, in which she herself can discern neither goodness nor candor?

It is not until the ball is over that there is a hint of an answer. Taking leave of his wife, M. de Beauséant remarks, "It's a mistake, my dear, to go and shut yourself away at your age. Do stay with us" (267; 248). His remark suggests that her withdrawal is not required by any overall sense of right and wrong, or even by the criteria of society. It suggests, rather, that she has internalized the code of the faubourg Saint-Germain to the point where she becomes its most severe administrator. It is perfectly obvious that Mme de Beauséant is complicit in her own undoing.

None of this is entirely satisfactory. Many choices would have been open to her: she could have lived a reclusive life right in the noble faubourg itself; she could have taken another lover as, much later in her rural seclusion, she eventually does. Her obstinate desire to leave Paris, and to do so with a spectacular final ball, shows the extent to which the troubled values of this ostentatious world have in fact become her own. By leaving the faubourg Saint-Germain physically, Mme de Beauséant remains within it morally. Lived history has never insinuated itself more subtly into a novel.

In this way *Le Père Goriot* is both history and fiction. Certain characters, such as Vautrin and Rastignac, force the issue of ethics into a much larger context and will have to be considered in a broader framework. For now, however, it can be said that if *Le Père Goriot* is a historical novel it is in making us feel with intimacy and vividness what it was like to live in post-Napoleonic Paris. As always, Balzac's main point was the nature of human experience.

BEATRICE GUENTHER

The Crisis of Narrative Doubling:
Balzac's La Comédie humaine

I. Death as Exile

The anxiety of finding himself without a place in the world does not seem to threaten the author of *La Comédie humaine*. Balzac's immense creation, firmly situated in nineteenth-century Paris, is almost overrun with images of himself. Through the disparate figures of Z. Marcas, Balthasar Claës, Albert Savarus, Louis Lambert, or Séraphîtüs/Séraphîta, Balzac can explore his own hidden capacities as politician, scientist, lawyer, madly exalted philosopher, and even that of angel. The roles of dandy, sculptor, musician, painter, or simply that of stand-up comedian are enacted, respectively, by the more familiar Rastignac (as well as by Lucien de Rubempré and Raphaël), Sarrasine, Gambara, Frenhofer, and, finally, Bixiou of *Les Employés*. Each of these characters resembles Balzac in some way, and each shares a common fate—that of an (often mad) genius destroyed by society or consumed by his own desires.

An account of Balzac as a writer filled with energy and vision, easily and masterfully projecting himself, Vautrin-like, upon his new world, forging it, as it were, in his own image, conveniently ignores the sheer labor of the artist struggling to define his subject. Moreover, to assume that Balzacian narratives represent or even enact "desires" implies a clear relation of

From *Nineteenth Century French Studies*, vol. 22, nos. 1 and 2. © 1993 by Nineteenth Century French Studies.

continuity between Balzac and his doubles. And yet, in *Les Proscrits* (1831)—the only text in which the author of *The Divine Comedy* appears—we have a clear example of how disruptively complex is the relation between the "double" and the "writing self." At a first glance, Dante's creativity can be interpreted as an exalted copy of Balzac's own, in that he draws words from silence and ideas from the night.[1] Here the concept of Oedipal rivalry helps to illuminate the ironic reversal that apparently reduces Dante to a figment of Balzac's imagination.

But there is another "double" in this text, even if he is less recognizable and less central. This is "Honorino," the sole male character in the entire *Comédie humaine* to bear a variant of Balzac's own name. Honorino does not even belong to the fictional world of *Les Proscrits*; he is a character in Dante's vision, used to warn against the perils of suicide. The hierarchy of paternal creativity, which transformed Dante into a latecomer and imitator, has here once again been inverted; now it is Honoré/Honorino who becomes, in effect, an image created by the poetic text.

Honorino does resemble Honoré; both are able to "lose" themselves in other characters. Honorino's self-sacrifice is extreme—he commits suicide in order to share the destiny of his love—whereas Honoré as narrator loses himself only figuratively. In *Facino Cane* (1836), for instance, we learn that a storyteller must obliterate himself to enter fully into the lives of others [4: 257-8], to find stories to narrate.[2] The cost of becoming another is personal annihilation.

The state that follows Honorino's suicide intensifies the parallels between double and writer. Although the character is exiled and alone, still his experience in hell resonates with figures and images often identified with Balzac's own poetic fantasy [7: 238]. Honorino's exile—echoing Dante's exile in Paris—is characterized by bleak isolation, and yet, it is also marked by the free, multi-directional movement of the banished soul. This ambivalent image also affects our evaluation of his suicide. If the swooping movements of the damned soul can be associated metaphorically with poetic imagination, then it follows that the necessary precondition of writing is an (at least symbolic) self-obliteration. The playful undermining of Balzac's authorial mastery in *Les Proscrits* masks the more serious threat of (self) annihilation implicated in the process of poetic creation.

In *Les Proscrits*—through the analogy produced by the names—we have two contradictory statements: on the one hand, a voluntary suspension of the writer's identity leads to the frame of mind necessary to literary creation. On the other hand, once achieved, this state of metaphorical death is equated with exile, with extremely negative values producing an impression of deep-seated ambivalence toward the (represented) experience of literary production.

Les Proscrits is only one vivid example of the conjunction of writing and death—a conjunction that takes place, we should note, not within Balzac's confessional writings but within the framework of a fictional account. (Later, we shall look at Balzac's letters). Our preliminary question remains: to what extent does scrutiny of the representation of death better illuminate an *oeuvre* more often interpreted in the light of structures of "desire"?[3]

We could begin by considering how "desire" is used to explain the scope of Balzac's text, the "insatiable" quality of his literary genius (Picon 158). Gaëtan Picon, for instance, uses literary and personal documents to identify a dynamics of desire both in Balzac's fictional characters and in the writer himself.

Of greater importance to our argument, however, is the claim that Balzac writes to achieve immortality. Picon cites Balzac's letter of 1822 to his mistress, Mme de Berny, as indicative of that desire: "Inaperçu sur la terre, et c'est un de mes plus grands chagrins, j'aurai vécu comme des millions d'ignorés qui sont passés comme s'ils n'avaient jamais été...." (Balzac, *Correspondence* 1: 194). One would expect a great emotional investment in texts that are meant to secure the immortality of their author. But Picon's story of Balzac's masterful projection of the self is marked by a strange phenomenon.

> Cette œuvre à laquelle il a voué sa vie, comme il l'a peu aimée, peu relue! Mais s'il lui préfère l'amour et la gloire, n'est-ce point parce que l'œuvre est une réalité moins indéfinissable, s'incarnant en des objets tangibles, vers lesquels on peut se retourner, alors que l'amour et la gloire sont des limites vers lesquelles on avance toujours sans pouvoir les saisir. (Picon 138)[4]

This passage makes it clear that the text cannot simply be interpreted as a projection of the self; it is separate from the writer. Or, if we prefer the family metaphor: Balzac's texts are cast-off, disowned children rather than the guarantors of his god-like creation, necessary to validate his paternal, Creator's role.

Picon's depiction of Balzac's relation to his doubles is equally ambivalent. Although it is meant to serve as another example of the continuity between the writer and his text, his description could easily be perceived as an expression of Balzac's violent attempt to disengage himself from those doubles.

Mais les vaincus qui lui ressemblent? Ceux qui, justement,
mènent son combat? En eux, il ne contemple pas, apitoyé et
serein, des défaites étrangères; il exorcise la hantise de sa propre
défaite, il interroge passionément, assumé par d'autres lui-même,
un échec qu'il évitera peut-être puisqu'il le crée, le prévoit, et
surtout le délègue à ces représentants fraternels.... (Picon 93).

Reading Picon against the grain, we could argue that the violence directed
by Balzac against his "doubles" proves that his writing is not meant to extend
the self infinitely but rather to shatter its productions, tending to mask and
even perhaps to destroy the self at the source. Here Balzac's disassociation
from his doubles is reminiscent of Rousseau's confessed account of the effect
of writing upon him:

C'est une de mes singularités de ma mémoire qui méritent d'être
dites. Quand elle me sert, ce n'est qu'autant que je me suis reposé
sur elle: sitôt que j'en confie le dépôt au papier, elle m'abandonne;
et dès qu'une fois j'ai écrit une chose, je ne m'en souviens plus du
tout. (Rousseau 1: 350).

In this account, writing does not affirm the self but supplants it; it leads to a
loss—the death of memory—within the writing self. Rousseau's case may
appear more extreme than Balzac's, but it allows us to reflect on how central
the consciousness of loss is to the project of writing. This consciousness
informs *La Comédie humaine*.

One of the most troubling representations of death occurs not in Balzac's
fictions but in his letters. By studying the trajectory of Balzac's letters
preceding the day of his death, May 21, 1850, we can follow Balzac
struggling—in the face of his impending death—to articulate his anxiety. In
1847 Balzac writes to Mme Hanska:

... je suis sans âme ni coeur; tout est mort ... je mourrai épuisé de
travail et d'anxiété, je le sens ... Ecoute: non seulement le coeur
et l'âme sont attaqués; mais je te le dis bien bas, je perds la
mémoire des substantifs, et je suis prodigieusement alarmé.
(Balzac, *Lettres à Mme Hanska* 3: 615)

It is crucial to be aware of the way in which Balzac's own representations attempt to master the threat of death. Unlike Montaigne, for whom death chiefly threatens the integrity of the body, Balzac's account profiles the "mind" (or "head") as the controlling center, as the place where he suffers "loss" and aphasia. In Balzac's personal experience "death" is signaled by the "emptiness of self" and the "loss of a center."

The passage reminds us that none among the abundant accounts of death in Balzac's fiction contains any suggestion of a playful attitude. The drive to finding narrative solutions that might overcome the primacy of death is a very serious anxiety, one that implies especially that the narrating self is itself at risk.

But Balzac's personal anxiety is not reflected in his narrative accounts with a comparable intensity. Those characters portraying artists are not themselves stricken with death. They find their art and their productivity threatened, but this is not depicted, strangely enough, by a rhetoric of loss. Here it is precisely the artist's (excessive) controlled, theoretical analysis that leads to his failure or madness. The pattern extends from 1831 until 1846, spanning, in effect, Balzac's most creative years. Whether the artist is figured as a primary or secondary character, he seems to fall into one of two categories. Either he literally defaces his own work because of his hyper-lucid reflections upon art, or the careful, preparatory analysis leads him to defer his "execution" endlessly, so that he ultimately condemns himself to speechlessness or sterility.

Claude Vignon in *Béatrix* (1839) is a fairly straightforward example of this. Clearly, he possesses an almost divine ability to penetrate and understand the world around him. But this power turns against him, since it also forces him to see all those obstacles that might hamper his creation. The result is a loss of artistic power; he is finally reduced to fleeing his mastery: "Indifférent aux plus petites comme aux plus grandes choses, il est obligé, par le poids même de sa tête, de tomber dans la débauche pour abdiquer pendant quelques instants le fatal pouvoir de son omnipotente analyse" (2: 41).

Vignon's metaphorical self-dissolution is a weak version of the rather flamboyant self-destruction of Frenhofer in *Le Chef-d'oeuvre inconnu* (1831). Frenhofer's destiny is also marked by a curious antithesis, in that his artwork is destroyed by his intense redefinition of the medium. Initially obsessed with evading the deathly immobility of the painterly copy, he calls up the need to redefine the object of *mimesis*. According to him, nuances of color (as opposed to the sketch or line) must attempt to reproduce the *invisible* world. His artistic vision rejects as secondary the opaque, material world: "Nous avons à saisir l'esprit, l'âme, la physionomie des choses et des êtres" (6: 579).

The light liveliness of the artwork is guaranteed by stressing the *causality* rather than the effects of phenomena in the world (and these terms are disturbingly close to Balzac's own when he writes to Mme Hanska in October 1834 that he hopes to "paint the causes of sentiments and ideas" in his *Etudes philosophiques*).[5] The culmination of Frenhofer's painterly vision is an opaque wall ("muraille de peinture" [6: 586]), one that calls attention primarily to the mimetic "instruments," to the syntax or self-reflexivity of painting, rather than to the mimetic object itself. This artistic narcissism ends with the painter's suicide. It also ends with the willful burning of all his paintings, for Frenhofer can no longer separate self-referential, chaotic paintings from his earlier masterpieces that continued to follow the discipline of (a more material) *mimesis*.

Frenhofer's complete self-destruction has already been hinted at earlier in the narrative. Porbus, a more traditional fellow-painter, explains to Poussin, the young initiate:

> Il a profondément médité sur les couleurs, sur la vérité absolue de la ligne; mais, à force de recherches, *il est arrivé à douter de l'objet même de ses recherches*. Dans ses moments de désespoir, il prétend que le dessin n'existe pas et qu'on ne peut rendre avec des traits que des figures géométriques; ... le dessin donne un squelette, la couleur est la vie, mais la vie sans le squelette est une chose plus incomplète que le squelette sans la vie. (6: 583, my emphasis)

In the fictional world of the *Comédie humaine* it is the masterful gaze attempting to define art theoretically—Porbus speaks of the quarrel between "le raisonnement" and "les brosses"—that ends up destroying the creation, creativity, and even the creator.

If Vignon and Frenhofer represent artists who destroy their works and creativity through excessive (retrospective) analysis, the characters of Wenceslas in *La Cousine Bette* (1846) and of the eponymous hero in *Gambara* (1837) represent examples of artists, who are unable to suspend their desire for control. They thereby become incapable of producing great or intelligible masterpieces; indeed, they are unable to produce anything at all. Wenceslas—a Polish émigré sculptor—is a character not struck down by physical annihilation, although he is afflicted with figurative death, with sterility. He is described as a "charming eunuch" (5: 83), able only to "conceive" and dream about sculptural projects, but unable to summon up the energy necessary to "execute" his visions. His lucid analysis paralyzes rather than consumes him.

It is at this juncture that Balzac defines the terms of what is to be the antidote to creative paralysis. The artist must be willing to bracket out his consciousness; he must submit voluntarily to the (temporary) death of his intellect and will power:

> Que les ignorants le sachent! Si l'artiste ne se précipite pas dans son œuvre, comme Curtius dans le gouffre, comme le soldat dans la redoute, sans réfléchir; et si, dans ce cratère, il ne travaille pas comme le mineur enfoui sous un éboulement: s'il contemple enfin les difficultés au lieu de les vaincre une à une, à l'exemple de ces amoureux des féeries, qui, pour obtenir leurs princesses, combattaient des enchantements renaissants, l'œuvre reste inachevée, elle périt au fond de l'atelier où la production devient impossible, et l'artiste assiste au suicide de son talent. (5: 81)

If the artist fails to suspend control, he will find his self displaced. He can only be present at the suicide of his talent; he finds himself shifted to the marginal role of spectator, much as Wenceslas is relegated to a secondary narrative position.

Although the emotional response to the experience of death diverges widely depending on context—Balzac's letters or his fictions—the associations that present themselves in conjunction with the word "death" seem to turn on the issue of control and mastery. What is the effect on (fictional) artists and their projects of a strategy that seeks to undermine itself, that turns on the need to suspend narrative mastery?

In *La Cousine Bette* the artist's readiness to endure the threat of being destroyed becomes the very precondition for creating a work of art. It might seem more logical to posit death simply as the limit of what can be represented in fiction. But, for the narrator of *La Cousine Bette*, "death" comes to mean the artist's refusal to employ a sovereign, masterful strategy for producing a text. He must hurl himself into a void in order to create. The anxiety of death has thus been re-directed; the narrator has transformed the limit of mortality into a threshold, thereby marking the writer's ultimate triumph over his own "self-displacement." Through the narrator's description, the risk of death has become, in effect, an essential stage in the process of artistic creation.

II. The Crisis of Doubling: A Study of Honorine

A brief return to *Les Proscrits* allows us to perceive that for Balzac the fluctuating position of the double vis-à-vis its creator highlights the author's attempt to displace himself, to move beyond the vision where a written text can be considered a projection and affirmation of the writing self. In *Les Proscrits* the doubling of the double introduces a crisis into the assumption that each narrative simply mirrors and extends the powerful author named "Balzac." *Les Proscrits* leaves unanswered, however, the question what is at stake in this crisis of doubling.

The text that confronts this question most radically, that is, the adequacy of doubling, is Balzac's short *récit Honorine* (1842).[6] The title alone signals that the relation between the writing self and its double will be explored. This text contains, namely, the only two other characters of *La Comédie humaine* bearing variants of "Honoré's" name. Here, however, the hypothesis that the author is mirroring himself in the text becomes shaky; both of the "doubles," Honorine and Onorina Pedrotti, are female.

We might first question why the characters in *Honorine*, unlike Honorino in *Les Proscrits*, are masked as female doubles. The pretext motivating the second narrator's story about Honorine is made explicit in the narrative frame introducing her story:

> En parlant littérature, on parla de l'éternel fonds de boutique de
> la république des lettres: la faute de la femme! Et l'on se trouva
> bientôt en présence des deux opinions: qui, de la femme ou de
> l'homme, avait tort dans la faute de la femme? [1: 562]

Implicit in this question is the very real problem of whether Woman is a controlled, controllable image of Man. Is her "faute" (or erring) to be understood as the attempt to determine her own autonomy—narrate her own story, as it were—or can she be subsumed into Man's fantasy only as something forever reacting to his initial mistreatment of her? Is Woman to be understood as Man's double, even when she tries to break free of his masterful gaze?

The structure of *Honorine* can be understood as the conflict between two "writer's" plots—that of Honorine and that of Octave, her cuckolded, but loving, husband. The figure of the secondary narrator, Maurice, is caught between the two plots, first in his attempt to coordinate the two narratives, and, second, in his self-imprisoning obsession to explain the enigmatic, resisting Honorine. He refuses to accept that his own narrative—that attempts to explain all after the fact—must remain inadequate to his subject matter.

Honorine's plot is more difficult to follow, initially, and it only gradually helps to undermine the self-abnegating, idealistic vision of Octave as paternal and supportive husband. Her plot is based on withdrawal, on the refusal to participate in the community, and on the attempt to banish Society from her enclosed, self-sustaining "citadel." Honorine's greenhouse, which is ultimately shattered by the invading gaze of Octave through his various proxies, among them Maurice, seems to symbolize her attempt to resist the plots of faithful wife and obedient mother that Society would have her enact. The "citadel" marks her resistance to being appropriated as a "double" into a masculine plot.

The project Honorine selects to support herself within her "separate" world is one that attempts to break free from narcissistic self-representation. In other words, her own "creations" are not presented as necessarily mirroring or extending her producing self [1: 577]. Neither does she wish her signature to be stamped on her art—her artificial flowers—(especially since she hopes to elude her husband's control).

The manufacture of flowers extends Honorine's hope that such "non-referential" creativity will not contribute to "fixing" or "enthralling" the creating self. Yet, the pull of perceiving a continuity between the self and its artistic creations is one not even Honorine can resist. And once the flowers are seen to mirror the self, that mirroring soon fixes the artist; it soon becomes the trope used to explain the enigmatic nature of Honorine, their creator. Honorine actually becomes, in the words of her husband: "… cette fleur [qui] se dessèche solitaire et cachée" [1: 574]. In Honorine's case, the flower—which was meant to protect her autonomy—is fixed upon by Octave and Maurice both to trace her and to summarize her being. Her creation becomes the means to define the elusive self that Honorine might be,[7] and this identification prepares Honorine's re-integration into Octave's more familiar plot of domesticity, ultimately leading to her death by this appropriation. Indeed, the violence inflicted upon Honorine does not stop with her death, since Maurice will attempt to redefine her, by giving her a narrative contour through his account of her "illogical" behavior.

If the attempt to remain detached from the textual product does not protect Honorine from being determined by it, it seems that the plot of *Honorine* is signalling to us both the necessity and the ultimate impossibility of a strategy of creative disjunction. The producing self will be made vulnerable through its creations, as is repeatedly shown in Balzac's other short narratives. His short texts tend to contain elaborate frames highlighting the narrator's role and the effect of his story on himself. Indeed, the frame, which predominates in the *récits*, re-enforces the impression that the narrator's autonomy is called into question by his own activity of narrating stories. That loss of autonomy goes beyond assuming the traits and thoughts of his fictional characters. The pattern in texts as disparate as *Sarrasine*, "Un drame au bord de la mer," *Louis Lambert*, and *Albert Savarus*, for instance, creates the impression that by telling a tale the speaker ends up reduplicating the textual experience.

In *Sarrasine*, as Roland Barthes points out, the narrator is affected by a symbolic castration. In "Un drame au bord de la mer" Louis writes about a family's destroyed future, only to find his own energy and future endangered, whereas in *Louis Lambert*, the narrator experiences a fragmentation of his style that mirrors his friend's form of madness that he is supposedly documenting objectively. And in *Albert Savarus*, the storyteller, who too transparently narrates his own story, literally becomes the protagonist of his reader's manipulations.

Perhaps the most dramatic example of a fatal narrative "reduplication" takes place in *Honorine*, since, here, the crisis of doubling marks the plot doubly; it is not only Honorine who is tracked and destroyed through the productions that identify her. The narrator himself experiences a form of dispossession that may leave him alive, though hardly unscathed by the end of his tale. It is this dispossession that explains, in part, why Maurice equates the need to appropriate Honorine's image through his narration with violence; he deliberately disregards Honorine's injunction to "keep her secrets as the tomb will keep her," [1:, 589] even drawing a parallel between his narrative project and the act of dissecting a "real" corpse.

By turning to the complex narrative frame of the text we can begin to understand the reasons behind Maurice's violence. The structure of *Honorine* is itself marked by a radical fragmentation. Here, at least seven different voices interconnect, each potentially displacing the other six: an anonymous narrator, who conjures up a cluster of Balzacian characters abroad, is supplanted by Maurice who orientates their aimless conversation regarding the status of an adulterous woman. Next, in Maurice's account of his childhood, we hear the voice of his first adoptive father who, in turn, will provide him with a second "father," Octave. Octave's own story sends Maurice into Honorine's world, where the account is now invaded by Honorine's voice, as Maurice communicates the content of their conversations. Maurice then draws on Octave's letters to Honorine (of which he has been the bearer) and on Honorine's letters to himself, after she has been reunited with Octave. The *récit* ends with conflicting interpretations provided by the narrative audience that had initially motivated the question determining the relation of Man to his (Biblical) double. At this point it has become impossible to distinguish storyteller from narrated subject. In other words, the direction of doubling can no longer be determined. The control of the narrator becomes dubious.

Through this list we immediately see that the "Byronesque" Maurice, who seemed poetically enigmatic, apparently has difficulty controlling his own text. His voice is constantly invaded by his "subject" or his story. Indeed, one way to understand this complex narrative structure is to consider that Maurice's project of "organizing" the subject is obsessive because it is at the same time an ordering of his own life through the story. The attempt to uncover and to articulate or master the invisible, enigmatic core—the attempt to break into the tomb—determines the trajectory of the storyteller's life. This imprisonment of the narrator by his story finds its most extreme figuring in the character of Maurice's wife, Onorina Pedrotti—obviously a double of Honorine—and who represents the displaced object of Maurice's desire to possess Honorine herself.

Paradoxically, then, Honorine may seem to have the last word. Through Maurice's obsession and despite Honorine's own appropriation by Octave and her death, she appears to be the more successful writer. It is she, after all, who shapes Maurice's destiny. Maurice's violence toward her, paralleling his violence toward Octave, can also be read, then, as the double's violence toward one of its would-be creators.

The narrative fragmentation of *Honorine* helps to illuminate the unstable process of doubling. In this *récit* the desire to control leaves no one in control; there is no nearly masterful nor controlling narrator in this text. Neither Octave nor Honorine is able to survive. Both of their attempts— either to determine another's role or one's own—are unsuccessful. Even the surviving narrator, Maurice, does not represent a controlling narrator, since he remains captivated by Honorine's and Octave's story. He is himself a double of both deposed narrators.

The study of "doubles" in *Honorine* brings to light that the fragmented text does seem haunted by the spectre of parricide (which takes the form of Maurice's violence or betrayal of the two parental figures in the text). The *récit* does, then, support—by "punishing" the "son," Maurice—more traditional readings of Balzac as a "conservative" rather than as "revolutionary" writer (Prendergast 117, Beizer 176). Nonetheless, the instability of the relation between double and paternal or maternal "narrator" created by the excessive narrative fragmentation in *Honorine* makes it plain that both "creator" and "textual product" seem on the brink of annihilating one another. The text (as flower or story), which might invade and engulf the different narrators, is itself threatened by the narrator's "surgical" violence upon the subject matter.

Rather than simply considering that the nineteenth-century novel is haunted by the spectre of the decapitated, deposed king, we should turn to the other troubling figure in nineteenth-century French history, who also contributes to the literary dilemma surrounding the question of authority. This other figure, whose own role in the "family romance" is difficult to identify, is Napoleon.[8]

Napoleon's creative vision—the shaping of a new national identity of France as Empire rather than as Kingdom—is also destroyed by the resistance (and autonomy) that stems from his "fragmented" creation. Let us note, however, that the political commentary in *La Comédie humaine* is ambivalent. In *Le Cabinet des antiques* [1833–36], Napoleon's role is presented as that of the youthful, would-be creator. Balzac anxiously unmasks the splintering of Napoleon's new creation produced by the opposition of the old aristocracy. In *La Vendetta* [1830], however, Napoleon begins to resemble a more established paternal figure. Here Balzac criticizes the "Emperor's" vision, primarily on the grounds that Napoleon has failed to determine his own originality and "atemporality." In the latter text Balzac points to Napoleon's continued and crippling adherence to the old Corsican tradition of the feud. It is this permissive adherence to tradition that allows the "throttling" of young energy needed to supplant the old order.

This disturbing ambivalence surrounding Napoleon—of the creation turning against the creator, and the creator betraying the originality of his creation—allows us to reconsider the struggle at stake in Balzac's project of representing "original" narrators. Through the example of Napoleon, we can note that the construction of a national myth and, indirectly, of any original narrative must be understood as the piecing together of the often self-contradictory and even invasive narrative voices. Paradoxically, these also ultimately undermine a narrator's mastery, finally calling into question the autonomy of the creator.

The figure of the created double in Balzac's *récits* helps to supplement the model of desire usually used to decipher Balzac's narratives. In *Honorine*, as well as in other short texts like *Les Proscrits*, it is the experience of the narrator's anxiety—of being displaced by his story—that ultimately drives the Balzacian text forward.

NOTES

1. Honoré de Balzac, *Les Proscrits*, *La Comédie humaine*, 7 vols (Paris: Aux Editions du Seuil, 1966) 7: 281. All subsequent references are drawn from this edition and will be in corporated in the text.

2. In the opening pages of *Facino Cane* [4: 257-8] the narrator explains his ability to "empathize" completely with individuals on the street. This ability explains the confidence of the protagonist, Facino Cane, and his willingness to communicate with the narrator. Whether the narrator has complete mastery or abdicates his own control is left ambivalent, as is the conclusion itself, since we never do learn whether Facino's narrative is true fabricated, or simply mad.

3. By using "death" rather than "desire" as the touchstone of my study, I tend to analyze the text as a response to anxiety, as an attempted response to the invisible and unnameable rather than as the playful experimentation with fantasy and desire. Thus, Leo Bersani's discussion of "desire" in the literary text might at first glance seem diametrically opposed to my analysis of death. But there do seem to exist points of intersection, especially if one considers Bersani's critique of the phenomenon of desire within the context of Balzac's narratives. "Desire" is here described as a disruptive, even destructive force: "The fear of desire in Balzac can be discussed as a fear of psychological fragmentation. Desire dynamites the Balzacian view of character—the "essentialist" psychology which allows Balzac to present characters in terms of a fixed, intelligible, and organizing passion. It threatens, in short, those coherent portraits of personality which are an important part of Balzacian expositions, and which characters' subsequent behavior will mainly illustrate and confirm. Can desires be contained by the ordering strategies of a descriptive narrative? If they cannot, narrative itself risks being fragmented into the mere juxtaposition of images of energy like those which assail Raphaël in the antique shop.... The Balzacian narrator is, precisely, the godlike presence who imposes a kind of providential order on his own fictional histories. And the rigid structure of a Balzac narrative is both menaced and energized by desires which may destroy characters, but which the narrative manages to contain at least formally" (Bersani 73).

Bersani uses Balzac's *La Comédie humaine* as a foil to Proust's narratives. Both share a terror of desire, but Proust's Marcel "lacks" a completely definable or continuous character and is thus able to experiment more fully with partial, fragmentary selves—with (potential?) self-dissolution (Bersani 86-7). In Balzac's case it is certainly true that the character's "portrait" (also Balzac's fascination with the world of thought or mental states) help to define the individual. Nonetheless, the complexity of Balzac's narrative situations, as well as his own critique of the storyteller's mastery, seems to be underplayed through the contrast with Proust's *A la recherche du temps perdu*.

4. We should keep in mind at this point that Balzac never disassociated himself completely from his work. His numerous corrections, of his proofs are legendary. See Peter Brooks and Christopher Prendergast in their respective studies of melodrama.

5. Pierre Citron makes mention of this letter in his own preface to the *Etudes philosophiques*: "Une lettre d'octobre 1834 à Mme Hanska précise que les *Etudes de moeurs* peindraient les sentiments et la vie, les *Etudes philosophiques* 'pourquoi les sentiments, pourquoi la vie.' Dans les premières, les 'individualités typisées.' Dans les secondes, 'les types individualisés.' Mais le sens de l'œuvre ne nous apparaît pas exactement avec le recul, celui qu'y mettait Balzac" (6: 413)

6. Pierre Citron explains the historical context of Honorine in his preface to the *récit* in the Seuil edition: "Cette longue nouvelle, qui eut peut-être comme premier titre prévu *la Séparation*, fut écrite en trois jours, à la fin de décembre 1842, selon une confidence de Balzac à Mme Hanska; sans doute le romancier ne voulait-il parler que de la première rédaction: il la revit et la corrigea en février 1843, et la fit paraître dans la *Presse* du 17 au 29 mars 1843, puis, en volume, en 1844. L'œuvre prit place en 1845 dans *la Comédie humaine*, au tome IV des *Scènes de la vie privée*" (1: 559).

7. Franc Schuerewegen, one of the two critics to write about Honorine, also notes the importance of the "flower" in this *récit*: "Le raffinement de l'écriture dans *Honorine*, à l'avis de Gide une des nouvelles-'des mieux écrites' de la *Comédie humaine*, se fait sentir avec une intensité particulière autour du thème des fleurs. Honorine est métaphoriquement et métonymiquement liée aux fleurs, dans un symbolisme à première vue homogène mais dont la co hérence se dissout à la relecture" (194).
Schuerewegen notes the overdetermination of the floral motif and sees in it primarily a hidden allusion to the troubled relation between Honorine and Octave. "Ainsi, les fleurs dissumulant une signification essentielle, il importe de lire Honorine avec tout le "génie du sous-entendu" (525) que célèbre son incipit. L'opération herméneutique sollicitée par le texte est double: il incombe au lecteur d'effacer d'abord la thématique obturatrice pour remplir ensuite lui-même l'abîme en-dessous" (196).

8. Marthe Robert also discusses the importance of Napoleon to Balzac's own creative enterprise, although she focusses primarily on Napoleon as symbol of success and power: "…il fortifie le romancier virtuel

dans l'idée que tout est possible; que l'Histoire ellemême s'incarne devant le mythe de toute-puissance infantile ..." (238). Her reading remains a powerful one, in that she notes Balzac's resemblance to the usurping "Bâtard" through his rewriting the world in order to subject it to his desires. But she fails to take into account the destructive violence wreaked upon the authorial narrators in such varied texts as *Honorine*, *Louis Lambert*, *Facino Cane*, *L'auberge rouge*, *Le Colonel Chabert*, and *Sarrasine*, to name but a few. This pattern seems to suggest a certain ambivalence toward the "Demiurgic" powers of the "Bâtard" figure.

Works Cited

Balzac, Honoré de. *La Comédie humaine*. Paris: Aux Editions du Seuil, 1966. 7 vols.

―――. *Correspondence (1809-Juin 1832)*. Ed. Roger Pierrot. Paris: Editions Garnier Frères, 1969.

―――. Lettres à Mme Hanska. Ed. Roger Pierrot Paris: Les Bibliophiles de l'Originale, 1969.

Beizer, Janet. "Madmen and Visions, Sages and Codes: Illusions perdues, Splendeurs et misères des courtisanes" in *Family Plots: Balzac's Narrative Generations*. New Haven: Yale University Press, 1986.

Bersani, Leo. "Realism and the Fear of Desire" in his *A Future for* Astyanax. *Character and Desire in Literature*. New York: Columbia University Press, 1984.

Brooks, Peter. *The Melodramatic Imagination: Balzac, Henry James, Melodrama and the Mode of Excess*. New Haven and London: Yale UP, 1976.

Picon, Gaëton. *Balzac*. Paris: Seuil, 1956.

Predergast, Christopher. *Balzac: Fiction and Melodrama*. London: Edward Arnold, 1978.

―――. "Balzac: Narrative Contracts" in his *The Order of Mimesis. Balzac, Stendhal, Nerval, Flaubert*. New York: Cambridge University Press, 1986.

Robert, Marthe. "La Recherche de l'absolu," in *Roman des origines et origines du roman*. Paris: Grasset, 1972. 237-291.

Rousseau, Jean-Jacques. *Œuvres complètes*. Bibliothèque de la Pleiade. Paris: Gallimard, 1959.

Schuerewegen, Franc. "Pour effleurer le sexe. A propos d'*Honorine* de Balzac" in *Studia Neophilologica* (1983): 193-197.

CHRISTINE RAFFINI

Balzac's Allegories of Energy
in La Comédie humaine

> Le vieillard se tenait debout, immobile,
> inébranlable comme une étoile au milieu d'un
> nuage de lumière. Ses yeux verts, pleins de je
> ne sais quelle malice calme, semblaient éclairer
> le monde moral comme sa lampe illuminait ce
> cabinet mystérieux.
>
> Balzac, *La Peau de chagrin*

"We cannot speak," C.S. Lewis observes, "perhaps we can hardly
think, of an 'inner conflict' without a metaphor; and every metaphor is an
allegory in little. And as the conflict becomes more and more important, it is
inevitable that these metaphors should expand and coalesce, and finally turn
into the fully-fledged allegorical poem."[1] Indeed, allegory may seem as
universal as conflict itself, and allegorical poems flourish well beyond the
Middle Ages, although often in surprisingly altered forms. If allegory can be
defined in a general way as the personification of abstract concepts, we might
add that it does not disappear; even as late as the nineteenth century it can
be seen to find a new and vital expression in the vast poem, which Honorè
de Balzac—with Dante obviously in mind—named *La Comédie humaine*. Like
Dante, many medieval poets are predisposed toward experience "... of

From *Analecta Husserliana XLII*. ©1994 by Kluwer Academic Publishers.

personified beings of a supersensual nature …"[2] and Balzac as well, through his interest in esoteric lore, often inclines naturally toward allegorical modes of expression. Moreover, in late antiquity and in the Middle Ages, allegory served to bring "… poetry close to philosophy …"—a rapprochement which Balzac also achieves in his philosophical novels.[3]

In medieval allegory, Love, Wrath, Clemency—indeed, almost any abstraction might be personified; in Balzac's world instead we discover, as I now hope to show, only two opposing forces which combine and recombine in a surprising number of variations. These expressions can be good or evil, positive or negative according to the context in which they are found, and thus they are in many respects reminiscent of medieval psychomachia. However, unlike medieval allegories which tend to consist of one-dimensional and easily identifiable embodiments of virtues and vices, Balzac's personifications are first of all complex characters, replete with habits, desires, aversions and ambitions. In writing off these characters as inflexibly and rigidly constructed on a particular central passion, many critics have failed to take this complexity into account. In the following pages, I will attempt to show that many of the protagonists of *La Comédie humaine*, despite their great diversity and complexity, consistently personify on the one hand forces of conservation, preservation, retention and expansion and, on the other, opposing forces of release, self-sacrifice, prodigality and dispersion.

In contradistinction to traditional allegory, these forces are personified to the extent that they essentially determine, motivate and galvanize the characters in question. For example, greed, a negative aspect of the force of conservation, governs and determines every aspect of the thinking and behavior of a secondary character such as Madame Vauquer. Clearly, this abstraction is the overriding force in her 'existence.' In that she is inconceivable without it, does not in fact think a thought or utter a word that is not motivated by it, she can be said to personify it. In a somewhat more complex fashion Balzac's major characters also develop, evolving and fulfilling their destinies as virtual personifications of either forces of conservation or of the opposing forces of dispersion.

In certain instances, these antithetic forces combine harmoniously in one individual. Where, for example, friendship, loyalty and love are involved, characters preserve their existence and define themselves by giving and even sacrificing themselves. Thus Henriette de Mortsauf, the heroine of *Le Lys dans la vallée*, knows that the infinite care and attention she bestows on her two sickly children is tantamount to giving birth to them every day: "I will blow life into them," she promises herself. "I will give birth to them every day."[4] Through this perpetually renewed effort she literally keeps them alive, sustaining as well her own strength and voluptuous beauty. When Félix de Vandenesse, however, causes her to fall in love, the symbiotic balance that preserves her and her children is irreparably disturbed. Guilt, frustrated desire and jealousy finally vitiate the life-giving transfer of energy, causing her to fall ill, waste away and die, as her doctor explains, of hunger: "Rich, young, beautiful, and dying emaciated, aged by hunger, for she will die of hunger! For forty days, her stomach, as if it were closed, has rejected all nourishment in whatever form it is presented."[5] Likewise, Henriette, in the name of virtue, has rejected Félix's advances while refusing to relinquish the thought of him. When he arrives at last at her side, he finds her hideously changed, for she has become an outward manifestation of the hunger that comsumes her:

> She was no longer my luscious Henriette, nor was she the sublime and saintly Madame de Mortsauf, but instead Bossuet's nameless thing which struggled against the void, and which hunger and thwarted desire had pushed into the egotistical combat of life against death.... Her colorless lips spread across her hungry teeth, attempting one of those forced smiles in which we also hide the irony of vengeance, the expectation of pleasure, the drunkenness of the soul and the fury of disappointment.[6]

Madame de Mortsauf, who lives and dies for virtue as well as for love, indeed exemplifies self-sacrifice. Old Goriot, however, who, to the very end, draws his vitality and the whole meaning of his life from dwelling on the thought of his absent daughters, embodies perhaps more completely than she the force of self-sacrifice. His parental love amounts to veneration:

> So then! When I became a father, I understood God. He is everywhere, completely so, since creation came out of him. Sir, I'm like that with my daughters. Only I love my daughters more than God loves the world, because the world is not as beautiful as God and because my daughters are more beautiful than I.[7]

Unlike Henriette de Mortsauf, who was able to give her children love and attention, and ultimately to justify herself to Félix, old Goriot, because of his daughters' selfish disdain, can only worship them from afar as he doles out his worldly goods to them and their husbands. When the supply is at last exhausted, he also is consumed and dies.

Parental love is a recurrent theme in this novel: the same life-giving tendency also motivates the noble and refined Vicomtesse de Beauséant as well as the criminal, Vautrin, both of whom act as mentors and teachers to the young Eugène de Rastignac. When she explains the sordid nature of Parisian society to the young man, her disinterested advice is as exact and compelling as Vautrin's: if one is not the executioner, she warns, one will become the victim. Both, the Vicomtesse and the exconvict, despite their differing motives, speak to Rastignac with the same probity and passionate intensity. Although Vautrin's intentions are to exploit and seduce Rastignac, there is no duplicity in his apparent means. In connection with Lucien de Rubempré he will, instead, resort to duplicity, but in the end, a forthright expression of paternal devotion characterizes his relationship with the young man. Upon learning of Lucien's suicide, he is dumbfounded:

> This blow for me is much worse than death, but you can't know what I'm saying.... You're a father, if you are one, only in one sense; ... I am a mother. too! ... I ... I am crazy ... I feel it.[8]

Lucien is indeed Vautrin's creation. Like all the sincere pedagogues, devoted friends and faithful servants in *La Comédie humaine*, Vautrin, the outlaw, the corrupter and tempter of youth, also embodies the energy of self-sacrifice as well as that of self-renewal and preservation.

Lisbeth Fischer, the hard and cunning protagonist of *La Cousine Bette*, instead only simulates self-sacrifice. While methodically eroding the foundation of her relatives' lives, she, in their eyes, remains a charitable figure—part of the family. Driven by her thirst for revenge, she orchestrates their ruin while cleverly preserving her own reputation. She works patiently yet swiftly in order to demolish:

> ... this family which every day grew odious to her, for one hates more and more, just as one loves more every day, when one loves. Love and hatred are feelings which feed themselves; but, of the two, hatred lasts the longest. Love is confined by limited forces, receiving its powers from life and prodigality; hatred resembles death, greed, and is in a sense an active abstraction, above beings and things.[9]

Bette is indeed the embodiment of hatred, and although in a sense blinded by it, she nonetheless succeeds in skillfully directing it to her own ends. Her machinations are despicable, but highly plausible. A critic notes that "A full decade before Freud was even born, Balzac has endowed this poor relative from the provinces with a psychological depth that anticipates all analytical studies that were yet to come. He speculates with her character on the lasting effects of early trauma and the crippling force of unresolved emotions."[10] Balzac specifically attributes her resourcefulness to her primitive nature, alluding as well as to her virginity. "When chaste people need their bodies or their souls, having recourse either to action or to thought, they then find steel in their muscles or science infused in their intelligence, a diabolical force or the black magic of willpower."[11] As Bette preserves her virginity, she preserves to her death the secret of her jealous loathing.

Like Bette, like Vautrin, all those who cultivate patience and who renounce immediate gratification are those who attain their sought-after goals. Grandet, for example, possesses extraordinary patience. This rapacious and vigilant miser, from whom nothing escapes, who lives in order to weigh, brood, and retain not only gold, but gestures, words, even syllables, always measures at every step the breadth of his grasp and power, so that each investment, no matter how seemingly inconsequential, might bear fruit. Even in death he is not destroyed: his obdurate discipline, his powers of concentration and his fortune are perpetuated in his daughter, Eugénie, who, although her father's nemesis, is endowed with his stubbornness and his will. Unlike her father, however, Eugénie is by nature a loving, giving being: "faite pour aimer." Ultimately forsaken, unable to fulfill her natural destiny, she accepts the monotonous patterns of existence established by her father, without, however, being untrue to herself or uncharitable toward others. At forty, she is exceedingly rich, but, still obedient to her father's wishes, lights a fire in her room only on those days when he would have allowed it.

> The house at Saumur, the house without sunlight, without heat, incessantly in shadows, melancholy, is a mirror image of her life. She carefully accumulates her revenue, and perhaps would seem parsimonious if she didn't belie gossip through the noble use of her fortune.... The hand of this woman bandages the secret wounds of every family. Eugénie walks to heaven accompanied by a cortège of good deeds. The greatness of her soul lessens the narrowness of her upbringing and the customs of her early life.[12]

Thus like her father, Eugénie exemplifies the force of conservation, but tempered by her purity and goodness, it is manifest as a redeeming strength.

In *La Comédie humaine* the force of conservation when carried to extremes can be far more destructive than any impulse toward dissipation. The latter, for example, in the case of Baron Hulot, enslaves the senses and the will, but the former has the power to annihilate even the spiritual dimension of being, and it is precisely these circumstances which form the conflict in *Louis Lambert*. From childhood, Lambert, the misunderstood genius, is gifted with total recall. He understands everything:

> A man of ideas, he had to slake the thirst of his brain which sought to assimilate all ideas. Whence his readings, and, as a result of his readings, his reflections which gave him the power to reduce things to their simplest expression, to absorb them into himself to study them there in their essence.... In order to exist didn't he have to toss fodder incessantly into the abyss he had opened in himself?[13]

Even the metaphor suggests the vast reserves of energy needed to sustain this character's life. Indeed, Lambert does not study—he devours knowledge and ideas, incorporating them and preserving them in himself, and through him Balzac explores his own notions of the materiality of thought and will, drawing on notions gleaned from reading Lavater, Mesmer and Swedenborg. There are, according to Lambert, three levels or spheres of being: the lowest is assigned to instinct and feeling, the second to reason and abstract thought, and the highest to sight and ethereal vision. Lambert, however, despite his genius, creates nothing, produces nothing save a single book, "Le Traité sur la volonté," which is lost before anyone can read it. In the beginning he attempts to explain it, but, finally, having understood and felt everything—having attained omniscience—he has nothing left to say, and, incapable of communicating what he knows, he is cut off from the world. He is not, however, invulnerable to love: "As soon as he noticed Mademoiselle de Villenoix, he sensed the angel within her form. The rich faculties of his soul, his inclination toward ecstasy, everything in him was then resolved by a limitless love...."[14] But the power of love, rather than reconnecting him to life, threatens to annihilate the vast stronghold of his inner self. To avoid physical involvement, he escapes at the last moment into insanity, becoming the most unsettling and perplexing example of the force of conservation in the work of Balzac. Seeing him after the crisis, the anonymous narrator describes him as "... a debris snatched from the grave, a kind of conquest made by life over death."[15] Mademoiselle de Villenoix instead affirms that he is in heaven, gifted with ethereal vision, yet still conscious of the world, although perceiving it in a form that is incomprehensible to mortals.

Raphaël de Valentin's fate in *La Peau de chagrin* both complements and opposes that of Louis Lambert. Both protagonists are the victims of occult forces, and, significantly, both compose treatises on willpower. Both are in love with women named Pauline, but there the resemblances seem to end. Whereas Lambert's struggle illustrates the ravages of conservation, Raphaël de Valentin's emphasizes those of waste. From the outset, Raphaël is presented as a fallen creature, his name further heightening both the allegorical and ironic overtones of the story. The life of this lost "angel without rays" unfolds under the aegis of dissipation: having gambled away everything in a single night of debauchery, he resolves to commit suicide. While waiting for nightfall, he wander into an antique shop, and there amid the accumulated debris of "twenty worlds" he finally notices a piece of shagreen, no larger than a fox skin, but unusual in that it casts an inexplicable glow in the darkness of the shop.

As the new owner of this magic talisman, Raphaël soon discovers that under its spell, each uttered wish saps his energy and shortens his life, degree by measurable degree. Ironically, he who once lavishly squandered himself in the pursuit of pleasure, and then in despair sought only to put an end to his life, is finally forced to conserve at all costs a colorless and desireless existence. His servant Jonathas has been instructed to anticipate Raphaël's every need:

> I must give him his dressing gown, always made up in the same fashion and of the same material. I am obliged to replace it when it wears out, just to spare him the trouble of asking for a new one....The menu for the whole year is made up in advance, day by day. Monsieur le marquis has nothing to wish for. He has strawberries when there are strawberries, and the first mackerel to arrive in Paris, he eats it.[16]

This painfully contrived mode of existence contrasts with the positive self-preservation which first characterizes both the cold and haughty Foedora and the mysterious keeper of the antique shop. The latter attributes his remarkable longevity directly to the powers of seeing and knowing. Likewise, Vautrin and all those in *La Comédie humaine* who succeed as a result of a single-minded drive toward conservation, value seeing, watching and knowing. As Vautrin explains: "I have obtained everything because I knew how to disdain everything. My only ambition was to see."[17] Raphaël, on the other hand, as the embodiment of desire, is destined to wear himself out. The old shopkeeper warned him of the danger:

> The soul is composed of terrible poisons as a result of the rapid concentration of its pleasures, through the strength of its ideas.... Wanting burns us up and being able destroy us: but knowing leaves our weak organization in a perpetual state of calm.[18]

As he consumes himself, Raphaël becomes a virtual allegory of the power of these two verbs, *vouloir* and *pouvior*. In this respect, he becomes a paradigm of the young Balzacian protagonists who, spurred by ambition and goaded by desire, risk everything. If, however, they, like Rastignac or especially like Vandenesse, learn to think coolly and to observe and listen patiently, their success is assured.

Lucien Chardon de Rubempré despite his aspirations, stands apart from the other protagonists. Like Rastignac and Vandenesse, he is young, ambitious, good-looking and of provincial origin, yet he lacks their perseverance. He tends toward profligacy, yet without being driven by the will to pleasure that characterizes Raphaël. Although he clearly belongs in the rank of the squanderers, his case is more complex. He evinces the simplicity and the undisguised selfishness of a child. His bitterest disappointments can be assuaged by the merest distraction: a meal in a restaurant, for example, has the power to soothe his wounded vanity. Among the handsome, young Balzacian protagonists, Lucien alone proclaims himself to be a poet, yet, entirely lacking the tenacity and concentration to express his artistic vision, he instead flutters from attraction to attraction, continually shifting his alliances and scattering his energy. Thus divided, leading several lives at once, he seems both less and more than a single entity. In prison, he must at last confront the reality of his shameful failure, compounded, it seems, by his multiple selves:

> ... suffering from all his overturned hopes, hurt in all his social pretentions, crushed in his annihilated pride, in all the selves presented by the ambitious one, the lover, the fortunate one, the dandy, the Parisian, the poet, the voluptuous one and the privileged one. Everything in him had broken in this Icarian fall.[19]

Balzac often chooses to stop short of omniscience in rendering this character, and thus the reader sees primarily an exterior, a physical presence of extraordinary beauty given to involuntary smiles, clever quips and abundant tears. In prison, we are privy to Vautrin's monologue, but to the end, Lucien remains an impenetrable mask. When at last he prepares to kill himself, his divided nature is once again accentuated:

> Lucien saw the palace in its original beauty.... He accepted this sublime view as a poetic adieu from civilized creation. While making calculations for his death, he wondered how this marvel could exist unknown in Paris. There were two Luciens, Lucien, the poet, taking a walk in the Middle Ages, under the arcades and towers of Saint Louis, and a Lucien preparing to commit suicide.[20]

Because of the young man's nature, Vautrin is able to live through him; Lucien becomes in fact Trompe-la-Mort's alter ego:

> His powerful faculties, absorbed in Lucien, functioned only for Lucien; he took delight in his progress, in his loves, in his ambition. For him Lucien was his visible soul. Trompela-Mort would dine at the Grandlieu's, slip into the boudoirs of great ladies, love Esther by proxy. In a word, he saw in Lucien a Jacques Collin who was handsome, young, noble, on his way to becoming an ambassador. Trompe-la-Mort had realized the German superstition of the DOUBLE through the phenomenon of moral paternity.[21]

Indeed, Lucien is everyone's *doppelgänger*: a long sought-after reflection, a mirror, a soulmate, a kind of nexus of powerful transfers of energy.

Careless squanderer, wastrel, ingrate, he exploits others just as easily as he falls prey to each temptation that comes his way, afterwards weeping hot tears of repentance. Curiously enough, deprivation, humiliation, and failure do not lessen him; up to the end, he remains invincible, thus appearing to defy the Balzacian system where endurance is determined by the amount of inner strength and willpower a character possesses. As we have seen, Lucien has neither one. He is, in fact, a kind of mirage, which may explain the tendency of other characters to seek to live through him. Not only Vautrin, but Lucien's friends, lovers and family invest all their hope, strength and even their fortunes in him. When he first leaves home, his family continues to support him: "... Eve, Madame Chardon and David had offered to the poet, each of them separately, the purest of their blood."[22] As Daniel D'Arthez, the high-minded friend whom Lucien has betrayed, explains in a letter to Eve:

> Rest assured, Lucien will never go as far as crime—he wouldn't have the strength, but he would accept a crime that had already been committed. He would share the profits without having shared the dangers, which seems horrible to everyone, even to criminals.... Lucien is a harp whose cords grow taut or slack in response to atmospheric variations. He might write a beautiful book in a phase of anger or in one of happiness and not be sensitive to its success—after having nonetheless desired it.... He is a brilliant assemblage of fine qualities embroidered on a canvas that is too flimsy; age carries off the flowers, and one day only the fabric remains, and if it is of bad quality, one sees only a tattered rag.[23]

Lucien, then, perhaps more than any other character, embodies the force of dissipation in that the vitality and substance he squanders are never his own, but are drawn from those around him, and whereas they, with the exception of Vautrin, are diminished, he continues to thrive, untouched by life. Even in death, he seems to lack substance; in prison, friends are shocked to discover: "... Lucien hanging as if his clothes had been placed on a porte-manteau...."[24] An insatiable void during his lifetime, even after his death, Lucien continues to sap the strength and hope of those who knew him. Camisot, the judge, assesses his ruined career, noting that the dead have power over the living: "Lucien carries our hopes into his coffin."[25]

Thus Lucien de Rubempré, in projecting the most negative aspects of the force of dissipation, strikingly illustrates another aspect of Balzac's use of the allegories of energy. He is exceptional in that his energy derives almost exclusively from others. His wastefulness consists primarily of an inability to make proper use of his advantages, and thus his personification of self-depletion differs from that of Raphaël de Valentin.

Each of the characters examined here offers in fact a different perspective on the effects of opposing forces which, as we have seen, may manifest themselves singly or in combination. When forces of release and self-sacrifice are positively personified, they are almost always found in conjunction with tendencies toward conservation. Madame de Mortsauf, for example, exemplifies both selfless dedication and repressive abstinence, whereas destiny holds Eugénie Grandet's giving nature in check. Vautrin's dedication, instead, is tempered by tireless vigilance and self-discipline. The latter's resourceful self-preservation contrasts both with Lucien's destructiveness and with Louis Lambert's deadly form of conservation.

If space allowed, it would be possible to continue almost indefinitely this inventory of Balzac's allegorical personifications: Foedora, Arabella, Nucingen, Madame d'Espard, and Nanon exemplify different aspects of conservation, and stand in opposition to such characters as Pauline, Coralie, Esther, David Séchard and Hulot.

Balzac's allegories are rooted in conflict and perpetuated, as we have seen, through dynamic transfers of energy. Energetic single-mindedness, and in some instances, outright monomania enables many of his characters to achieve allegorical status in *La Comédie humaine*. In reference to his own use of allegory, the German dramatist Hugo von Hofmannsthal has alluded to "... a certain timeless European mythology: names, concepts, figures, with which a higher meaning is bound up, personified forces of the moral or mythical order."[26] Balzac, in fact, constantly draws on this mythological patrimony while at the same time renewing it and increasing it. His realism is thus often ominously or majestically overshadowed by a mythic level of thought, causing his allegorical entities to ring truer and echo longer than they otherwise might.

NOTES

1. C. S. Lewis, *The Allegory of Love* (rpt. Oxford: Oxford University Press, 1970), p. 60.

2. Ernst Robert Curtius, *European Literature and the Latin Middle Ages*, trans. Willard R. Trask (rpt. New York: Harper Torchbooks, 1963), p. 205.

3. *Ibid.*, p. 207.

4. Honoré de Balzac, *Le Lys dans la vallée* (Paris: Gallimard, Le Livre de Poche, 1970), p. 96. All translations from the *Comédie humaine* are mine.

5. *Ibid.*, p. 310.

6. *Ibid.*, p. 321.

7. Balzac, *Le Père Goriot* (Paris: Garnier-Flammarion, 1966), pp. 130–31.

8. Balzac, *Splendeurs et misères des courtisanes* (Paris: Classiques Garnier, 1953), p. 511.

9. Balzac, *La Cousine Bette* (Paris: Garnier, 1968), pp. 153–54.

10. Diana Festa-McCormick, *Honoré de Balzac* (Boston: Twayne, 1979), p. 112.

11. *La Cousine Bette, op. cit.*, p. 103.

12. Balzac, *Eugénie Grandet* (Paris: Garnier Frères, 1965), p. 256.

13. Balzac, *Louis Lambert* (Paris: Gallimard, Le Livre de Poche, 1968), p. 104.

14. *Ibid.*, p. 128.

15. *Ibid.*, p. 163.

16. Balzac, *La Peau de chagrin* (Paris: Gallimard, Le Livre de Poche, 1966), pp. 233–34.

17. *Splendeurs et misères des courtisanes, op. cit.*, p. 498.

18. *La Peau de chagrin, op. cit.*, pp. 55–56.

19. *Splendeurs, op. cit.*, p. 380.

20. *Ibid.*, p. 479.

21. *Ibid.*, p. 506.

22. Balzac, *Illusions perdues* (Paris: Gallimard, Le Livre de Poche), p. 459.

23. *Ibid.*, pp. 472–73.

24. *Splendeurs, op. cit.*, p. 483.

25. *Ibid.*, p. 491.

26. Quoted by Curtius, *op. cit.*, p. 144.

Chronology

1799	Born on May 20 in Tours, France to Anne-Charlotte-Laure Sallambier and Bernard-François Balzac.
1807-13	Boarding student at an Oratorian school at Vendôme. Sent home sick; doesn't return.
1814	Family moves to Paris, where Balzac completes his secondary schooling, boarding at the Lycée Charlemagne.
1816	Works as law clerk in Guyonnet de Merville's office.
1819	Gives up law to become a writer. Writes a neoclassical play, *Cromwell*.
1820	Begins, but does not finish, two novels. At Villeparisis, meets Laure de Berny, 22 years his senior, who becomes his mistress.
1821	Using a pseudonym and occasionally in conjunction with other writers, publishes a series of potboilers.
1825-27	Editor of French classics, then enters the printing and publishing business, resulting in excessive debt.
1829	Father dies. Publishes *Le Dernier Chouan* (translated as *The Chouans*), the first novel to be produced under his own name. Publishes *Physiologie du mariage* (*Physiology of Marriage*).
1830	Publishes *Scènes de la vie privée* (*Scenes of Private Life*), a two-volume collection that later will be expanded. Writes extensively for newpapers; enters society.

1831	Publishes *Romans et contes philosophiques* (*Philosophical Novels and Tales*), initially as a three-volume set. Also publishes first great success, *La Peau de chagrin* (*The Wild Donkey's Skin*).
1832	Publishes *Louis Lambert*. Publishes *Nouveaux contes philosophiques* (*New Philosophical Tales*).
1833	Publishes *Le Médecin de Campagne* (*The Country Doctor*). Receives correspondence from Evelina de Hanska, a wealthy Polish countess. Meets her in September.
1834	Begins publication of the 12-volume *Etudes de moeurs au XIXe siècle* (*Studies of 19th Century Manners*), which continues through 1837. Meets and probably has a child by the Countess Guidoboni-Visconti. His presumed daughter, Maria du Fresnay, is born by an unidentified woman. Allies himself with the Neolegitimist party and writes a series of political pamphlets. Publishes *La Recherche de l'Absolu* (translated as *The Philosopher's Stone*).
1835	Publishes *Le Père Goriot* (translated as *Daddy Goriot* or *Unrequited Affection*). Begins publishing *Etudes philosophiques* (*Philosophic Studies*), 20 volumes, finishing in 1840. Lives in hiding because of his great debt.
1836	Publishes *Le Lys dans la vallée* (*The Lily in the Valley*). Founder and editor for *La Chronique de Paris*, a periodical that dissolves in six months. Birth of Lionel-Richard Guidoboni-Visconti, who may be his son. Mme de Berny dies.
1837	Buys a house near Sèvres, "Les Jardies." *César Birotteau* and *Illusions perdues* (*Lost Illusions*) published.
1838	In Sardinia, reopens a silver mine, which fails. Visits friends in France, then returns to live in "Les Jardies."
1839	Publishes *Béatrix, Scènes de la vie de province* (*Scenes of Provincial Life*), and *Scènes de la vie parisienne* (*Scenes of Parisian Life*). Begins serious playwriting.
1840	Performance of his play *Vautrin*. Starts the magazine *Revue parisienne*, which lasts for three issues. Within it publishes an essay on Stendhal that becomes famous.
1841	Evelina de Hanska's husband dies; Balzac, seriously ill, again hopeful of marrying her.

1842	Starts publishing 16-volume edition of his work called *La Comédie humaine* (*The Human Comedy*), which will continue through 1846. His personal copy containing marginal notes becomes the basis for all future modern editions. Writes his famous "Avant Propos" introduction. Publishes *Albert Savarus* and *Ursule Mirouët*.
1843-46	Travels to St. Petersburg to visit Mme Hanska. During the next three years travels extensively, mostly to be with her, in Germany, Holland, Belgium, Switzerland, and Italy. Health failing; stays with Mme Hanska in Dresden.
1847	Publishes *La Cousine Bette* (*Cousin Betty*) and *Le Cousin Pons* (*Cousin Pons*). Mme Haska comes to Paris but after a few months returns to her home in the Ukraine. Balzac moves into a house in Paris's rue Fortunée.
1848	Volume 17 of *La Comédie humaine* published. Revolution in Paris; Balzac stays with Mme Haska in the Ukraine from September until the spring of 1849.
1849	Returns to Paris; becomes quite sick from cardiac and digestive problems.
1850	Marries Mme Haska on March 14 in the Ukraine. Both return to Paris in May. Balzac dies on August 18. Victor Hugo gives a eulogy that becomes famous.
1855	Volumes 18-20 of *La Comédie humaine* published.

Contributors

HAROLD BLOOM is Sterling Professor of the Humanities at Yale University and Henry W. and Albert A. Berg Professor of English at the New York University Graduate School. He is the author of over 20 books, including *Shelly's Mythmaking* (1959), *The Visionary Company* (1961), *Blake's Apocalypse* (1963), *Yeats* (1970), *A Map of Misreading* (1975), *Kabbalah and Criticism* (1975), *Agon: Toward a Theory of Revisionism* (1982), *The American Religion* (1992), *The Western Canon* (1994), and *Omens of Millennium: The Gnosis of Angels, Dreams, and Resurrection* (1996). *The Anxiety of Influence* (1973) sets forth Professor Bloom's provocative theory of the literary relationships between the great writers and their predecessors. His most recent books include *Shakespeare: The Invention of the Human*, a 1998 National Book Award finalist, and *How to Read and Why*, which was published in 2000. In 1999, Professor Bloom received the prestigious American Academy of Arts and Letters Gold Medal for Criticism.

LAWRENCE R. SCHEHR teaches in the Foreign Language Department at North Carolina State University. He is the author of *Rendering French Realism* and has written, and been a joint editor or author on, a number of other titles.

WILLIAM W. STOWE has been an Assistant Professor of English at Wesleyan University. He is the author of *Going Abroad* and *The Poetics of Murder: Detective Fiction and Literary Theory*.

JANET L. BEIZER teaches French at the University of Virginia. She is the author of *Ventriloquized Bodies: Narratives of Hysteria in Nineteenth-Century France*.

RONALD LE HUENEN is Professor of French at the University of Toronto. PAUL PERRON teaches French at University College in Toronto. They are co-authors of two books on Balzac. Mr. Perron also has written *Semiotics and the Modern Quebec Novel*.

D. A. MILLER has taught English and Comparative Literature at the University of California, Berkeley. He has written *Bringing Out Roland Barthes*, as well as other books.

DAVID F. BELL teaches in the Department of Romance Languages at Duke University. He is the author of *Circumstances: Chance in the Literary Text*.

JANE A. NICHOLSON has taught at the University of Tulsa.

ALEXANDER FISCHLER has taught French and Comparative Literature at the State University of New York at Binghamton. He has translated a book of Pierre Garnier's and has published a number of articles on nineteenth- and twentieth-century French and English literature.

SCOTT McCRACKEN has taught English at Salford University. He is the author of *Pulp: Reading Popular Fiction*.

LESLIE ANNE BOLDT has taught in the Department of French, Italian & Spanish at Brock University in Ontario. She translated into English and wrote the introduction for Georges Bataille's *Inner Experience*.

JAMES R. McGUIRE has taught in the Department of French at Northwestern University. He has translated a book on Argentina by Guillermo A. O'Donnell.

MARTIN KANES has taught French and humanities at the State University of New York at Albany, where he has been Chairman of the Department of French Studies and founder and director of the doctoral program in humanistic studies. He has written books on Balzac and Zola, as well as numerous essays on French and American literature.

BEATRICE GUENTHER teaches in the Department of Modern Languages and Literatures at the College of William & Mary. She is the author of *The Poetics of Death: The Short Prose of Kleist & Balzac.*

CHRISTINE RAFFINI has taught at the University of Miami. She has written two books, most recently one on Renaissance Platonism.

Bibliography

Adamson, Donald. "*Le Père Goriot*: Notes towards a Reassessment." *Symposium* 19 (Summer 1965): 101-14.

Affron, Charles. *Patterns of Failure in* La Comédie Humaine. New Haven: Yale University Press, 1966.

Aynesworth, Donald. "The Making and the Unmaking of History in *Les Chouans*." *Romanic Review* 76, no. 1 (January 1985): 36-54.

Beebe, Maurice. *Ivory Towers and Sacred Founts. The Artist as Hero in Fiction from Goethe to Joyce.* New York: New York University Press, 1964.

Bellos, David. *Balzac Criticism in France. 1850-1900. The Making of a Reputation.* Oxford: Clarendon Press, 1976.

Besser, Gretchen. "Lear and Goriot: A Re-evaluation." *Orbis litterarum* 27 (1972): 28-36.

Blades, Margaret W. "Seagulls in the Mind: Realism in Robbe-Grillet and Balzac." *Cincinnati Romance Review* 14 (1995): 80-87.

Brooks, Peter. "Balzac: Melodrama and Metaphor." *The Hudson Review* 22 (1969): 213-38.

———. *The Melodramatic Imagination.* New Haven: Yale University Press, 1976.

Butor, Michel. "Balzac and Reality." *Critical Essays on Balzac*, edited by Martin Kanes, Boston: G. K. Hall, 1990.

Canfield, Arthur Graves. "*The Reappearing Character in Balzac's* Comédie Humaine." Chapel Hill: University of North Carolina Press, 1961.

Dargan, Edwin Preston, ed. *Studies in Balzac's Realism.* New York: Russell and Russell, 1967.

Diani, Marco. "Balzac's Bureaucracy: The Infinite Destiny of the Unknown Masterpiece." *L'Esprit Createur* 34, no. 1 (Spring 1994): 42-59.

Diengott, Nilli. "Goriot vs. Vautrin: A Problem in the Reconstruction of *Le Père Goriot*'s System of Values." *Nineteenth Century French Studies* 15, nos. 1-2 (Fall-Winter 1986-87): 70-76.

Fanger, Donald. *Dostoevsky and Romantic Realism.* Cambridge, Mass.: Harvard University Press, 1965.

Fernandez, Ramon. *Balzac.* Paris: Stock, 1943.

Festa-McCormick, Diana. "Linguistic Deception in Balzac's 'Princess de Cadignan.'" *Nineteenth Century French Studies* 14, nos. 3-4 (Spring-Summer 1986): 214-24.

Garval, Michael D. "Balzac's *La Comédie humaine*: The Archival Rival." *Nineteenth Century French Studies* 25, nos. 1-2 (Fall 96-Winter 97): 30-40.

Geertz, Clifford. *The Interpretation of Cultures.* New York: Basic Books, 1973.

Giuriceo, Marie. "The Virgi-Dante Relationship." *Studies in Medievalism* 2, no. 2 (1983): 67-79.

Green, Paul. "*La Cousine Bette*: The Tales of the Prodigal Father." *Recovering Literature* 19 (1990): 5-20.

Guenther, Beatrice Martina. *The Poetics of Death: The Short Prose of Kleist and Balzac.* Albany: State University of New York Press, 1996.

Heathcote, Owen. "Balzac's Go-Between: The Case of Honorine." *Nineteenth Century French Studies* 22, nos. 1-2 (Fall 1993-Winter 1994): 61-76.

Hemmings, F. W. J. *Balzac: An Interpretation of "La Comédie humaine."* New York: Random House, 1967.

Kanes, Martin. *Balzac's Comedy of Words.* Princeton: Princeton University Press, 1975.

Levin, Harry. *The Gates of Horn: a Study of Five French Realists.* London: Oxford University Press, 1963.

Lock, Peter W. *Balzac. Le Père Goriot.* London: Edward Arnold, 1967.

Lukacs, Georg. *Studies in European Realism.* New York: Grosset and Dunlap, 1964.

Marcus, K. Melissa. *The Representation of Mesmerism in Honoré de Balzac's* La Comedie humaine. New York: Lang, 1995.

Maurois, André. *Prometheus: The Life of Balzac.* New York: Harper and Row, 1969.

Mortimer, Armine Kotin. "Writing *Modeste Mignon.*" *L'Esprit Createur* 31, no. 3 (Fall 1991): 26-37.

Nykrog, Peter. "On Seeing and Nothingness: Balzac's *Sarrasine.*" *Romanic Review* 83, no. 4 (1992): 437-44.

Pasco, Allan H., with Anthony R. Pugh. "Balzac." *Cabeen Critical Bibliography of French Literature: The Nineteenth Century.* Syracuse: Syracuse University Press, 1992.

——. *Balzacian Montage: Configuring "La Comédie humaine."* Toronto: University of Toronto Press, 1991.

——. "Dying with Love in Balzac's *La Vieille Fille.*" *L'Esprit Createur* 35, no. 4 (Winter 1995): 28-37.

Pireddu, Nicoletta. "Between Fantasque and Fantasmagorique: A Fantastic Reading of Balzac's *La Peau de chagrin.*" *Paroles Gelees* 9 (1991): 33-47.

Prendergast, Christopher. *Balzac: Fiction and Melodrama.* London: Edwin Arnold, 1978.

Pugh, Anthony. *Balzac's Recurring Characters.* Toronto: University of Toronto Press, 1974.

Rogers, Samuel. *Balzac and the Novel.* New York: Octagon Books, 1969.

Sharpley-Whiting, T. Denean. "The Other Woman": Reading a Body of Difference in Balzac's *La Fille aux yeux d'or.*" *Symposium* 51, no. 1 (Spring 1997): 43-50.

Siebers, Tobin. "Balzac and the Literature of Belief." *L'Esprit Createur* 28, no.3 (Fall 1988): 37-48.

Steele, H. Meili. *Realism and the Drama of Reference: Strategies of Representation in Balzac, Flaubert, and James.* University Park: Pennsylvania State University Press, 1988.

Taine, Hyppolite. *Balzac. A Critical Study.* Translated by Lorenzo O'Rourke. New York: Haskell House, 1973.

Testa, Carlo. "The Sins of Utopia: Balzac's *Le Medecin de campagne.*" *Nineteenth Century French Studies* 25, nos. 3-4 (Spring-Summer 1997): 280-92.

Thomas, Gwen. "The Case of the Missing Detective: Balzac's *Une tenebreuse affaire*." *French Studies: A Quarterly Review* 48, no. 3 (July 1994): 285-98.

Wilkinson, Lynn R. "*Le Cousin Pons* and the Invention of Ideology." *Publications of the Modern Language Association of America* 107, no. 2 (March 1992): 274-89.

Young, Michael. "Beginnings, Endings and Textual Identities in Balzac's *Louis Lambert*." *Romanic Review* 77, no. 4 (November 1986): 343-58.

Acknowledgments

"Fool's Gold: the Beginning of Balzac's *Illusions perdues*," by Lawrence R. Schehr. From *Symposium* XXXVI, no. 2 (Summer 1982): 149-165. Reprinted with permission of the Helen Dwight Reid Educational Foundation. Published by Heldref Publications, 1319 Eighteenth St., NW, Washington, DC 20036-1802. Copyright © 1982.

Stowe, William W. *Balzac, James, and the Realistic Novel.* ©1983 by Princeton University Press. Reprinted by permission of Princeton University Press.

"Victor Marchand: The Narrator as Story Seller Balzac's 'El Verdugo,'" by Janet L. Beizer. From *Novel: A Forum on Fiction*, vol. 17, no. 1 (Fall 1983): 44-51. ©1983 by Novel Corp. Reprinted by permission.

"Reflections on Balzacian Models of Representation," by Roland Le Huenen and Paul Perron. From *Poetics Today* 5, no. 4 (1984): 711-728. Copyright, The Porter Institute for Poetics and Semiotics, Tel Aviv University. All rights reserved. Reproduced with permission.

"Balzac's Illusions Lost and Found," by D. A. Miller. From *Yale French Studies* 67 (1984): 164-181. ©1984 by Yale University. Reprinted by permission.

"Epigrams and Ministerial Eloquence: The War of Words in Balzac's *La Peau de chagrin*," by David F. Bell. From *Nineteenth-Century French Studies* 15, no. 3 (1987): 252-264. ©1987 by *Nineteenth-Century French Studies*. Reprinted by permission.

"Discourse, Power, and Necessity: Contextualizing *Le Cousin Pons*," by Jane A. Nicholson. From *Symposium* XLII, no. 1 (Spring 1988): 48-61. Reprinted with permission of the Helen Dwight Reid Educational Foundation. Published by Heldref Publications, 1319 Eighteenth St., NW, Washington, DC 20036-1802. Copyright © 1988.

"Eugénie Grandet's Career as Heavenly Exile," by Alexander Fischler. From *Essays in Literature* XVI, no. 2 (Fall 1989): 271-280. ©1989 by Alexander Fischler. Reprinted by permission.

"*Cousin Bette*: Balzac and the Historiography of Difference," by Scott McCracken. From *Essays and Studies 1991: History and the Novel*, edited by Angus Easson. ©1991 by The English Association. Reprinted by permission.

"The Framed Image: The Chain of Metaphors in Balzac's *Le Père Goriot*," by Leslie Anne Boldt. From *Nineteenth-Century French Studies* 19, no. 4 (Summer 1991): 517-535. ©1991 by *Nineteenth-Century French Studies*. Reprinted by permission.

"The Feminine Conspiracy in Balzac's *La Cousine Bette*," by James McGuire. From *Nineteenth-Century French Studies* 20, nos. 3 & 4 (Spring-Summer 1992): 295-304. ©1992 by *Nineteenth-Century French Studies*. Reprinted by permission.

"Structures. Organizing a Fictional Universe," by Martin Kanes. From *Père Goriot: Anatomy of a Troubled World*:21-34. ©1993 by Twayne Publishers. Reprinted by permission of the Gale Group.

"The Crisis of Narrative Doubling: Balzac's *La Comédie humaine*," by Beatrice Guenther. From *Nineteenth-Century French Studies* 22, nos. 1 & 2 (Fall-Winter 1993-94): 48-60. ©1993 by *Nineteenth-Century French Studies*. Reprinted by permission.

"Balzac's Allegories of Energy in *La Comédie Humaine*," by Christine Raffini. From *Allegory Old and New in Literature, the Fine Arts, Music and Theatre, and Its Continuity in Culture*, edited by Marles Kronegger and Anna-Teresa Tymieniecka. ©1993 by Kluwer Academic Publishers. Reprinted by permission of Kluwer Academic Publishers.

Index